THE GUIDE TO REFLECTIVE PRACTICE IN CONFLICT RESOLUTION

ACR Practitioner's Guide Series
Series Editors

Michael Lang is a mediator with more than thirty years' experience in the areas of family, workplace, organizational, congregational, and public policy disputes. Michael is the founding director of the Master of Arts Program in Conflict Resolution at Antioch University.

Susanne Terry is a pioneer in mediation and conflict education. Susanne created the Mediation Program of Woodbury College, which later moved to Champlain College and became a highly respected graduate degree program.

Books in the ACR Practitioner's Guide Series are *field guides* for the benefit of practitioners actively engaged as third-party intervenors, scholars, educators, trainers, researchers, and participants in conflict resolution processes. Each book is a practical guide that illuminates thought processes that lead to action—the underlying rationale for practice decisions—rather than simply describing "what to do." Grounded in Reflective Practice principles, the books examine the application of theory and research in relation to practice choices and guide the reader/user in a deeper understanding of why we make particular choices in our work.

About the ACR

The Association for Conflict Resolution (ACR) is a professional organization enhancing the practice and public understanding of conflict resolution. An international professional association for mediators, arbitrators, educators, and other conflict resolution practitioners, ACR works in a wide range of settings throughout the United States and around the world. *Our multicultural and multidisciplinary organization offers a broad umbrella under which all forms of dispute resolution practice find a home.* Website: www.acrnet.org; X: @ACRgroup.

THE GUIDE TO REFLECTIVE PRACTICE IN CONFLICT RESOLUTION

SECOND EDITION

MICHAEL LANG

ROWMAN & LITTLEFIELD
Lanham • Boulder • New York • London

Published by Rowman & Littlefield
An imprint of The Rowman & Littlefield Publishing Group, Inc.
4501 Forbes Boulevard, Suite 200, Lanham, Maryland 20706
www.rowman.com

86-90 Paul Street, London EC2A 4NE

Copyright © 2024 by The Rowman & Littlefield Publishing Group, Inc.
First edition © 2019

All rights reserved. No part of this book may be reproduced in any form or by any electronic or mechanical means, including information storage and retrieval systems, without written permission from the publisher, except by a reviewer who may quote passages in a review.

British Library Cataloguing in Publication Information Available

Library of Congress Cataloging-in-Publication Data

Names: Lang, Michael D., 1944- author.
Title: The guide to reflective practice in conflict resolution / Michael Lang.
Description: Second edition. | Lanham : Rowman & Littlefield, [2024] | Series: The ACR practitioner's guide series | "First edition © 2019"--Title page verso. | Includes bibliographical references and index.
Identifiers: LCCN 2024025812 (print) | LCCN 2024025813 (ebook) | ISBN 9781538188941 (cloth) | ISBN 9781538188958 (paperback) | ISBN 9781538188965 (ebook)
Subjects: LCSH: Conflict management. | Interpersonal conflict. | Mediation.
Classification: LCC HD42 .L359 2024 (print) | LCC HD42 (ebook) | DDC 303.6/9--dc23/eng/20240612
LC record available at https://lccn.loc.gov/2024025812
LC ebook record available at https://lccn.loc.gov/2024025813

Anne-Marie Georgia Paizis Lang

Anne-Marie's spiral of joy and beauty came to an end on December 1, 2022. I lost my partner, my Anam Cara, and my editor. Anne-Marie edited every line of the first edition of this book, and she was the muse on my shoulder as I revised, edited, and wrote for this version. I felt her encouragement, knew she was appraising each word and phrase. I could hear her voice, reminding me of her lessons about good writing. I treasured her as an editor—she was fiercely honest and impeccable in polishing my words to allow the ideas to emerge as I had envisioned.

Her favorite poet wrote these lines, which I share with you in celebration of Anne-Marie:

Life is a journey up a spiral staircase; as we grow older we cover the ground we have covered before, only higher up; as we look down the winding stair below us we measure our progress by the number of places where we were but no longer are. The journey is both repetitious and progressive; we go both round and upward.
—*William Butler Yeats*

This flower grows on a vine that Anne-Marie planted in our garden and then spent hours carefully weaving the tendrils into a wall of color.

Contents

Acknowledgments		ix
Chapter 1	Beginning of the Spiral	1
Chapter 2	Reflective Practice: An Introduction	15
Chapter 3	The Attributes of a Reflective Practitioner	41
Chapter 4	Theory: What We Think Shapes What We Do	71
Chapter 5	Research Improves Practice	93
Chapter 6	The Methods of Reflective Practice	111
Chapter 7	Reflective Practice Groups	133
Chapter 8	Reflective Debrief®	151
Chapter 9	Reflective Practice in Training and Education	173
Chapter 10	Spiraling into the Future: Becoming Reflective Practitioners	191
Appendices		
Appendix A	Guides for Reflection	199
Appendix B	Sample of Structured Reflective Instrument Questions	203
Appendix C	Learning Journals	205
Appendix D	Some Guidelines for Reflective Debrief®	207
Appendix E	Case Presentation Instructions for Reflective Debrief®	209
Appendix F	Reflective Practice Group Basics	211
Appendix G	Reflective Debrief®—What Not to Ask or Say/What to Ask or Say	213
Appendix H	Asking Elicitive Questions	217
Appendix I	Guidelines for Your Debriefing	219

Appendix J	Comparison of Roles—Mediator/Debriefer	221
Appendix K	Potential Roles of a Reflective Practice Group Leader/Facilitator	223
Appendix L	Guidelines for Starting a Reflective Practice Group	225
Appendix M	Initial Handout—Reflective Practice Group	231

Bibliography	233
Index	241
About the Author and Contributors	247

Acknowledgments

We do NOT know the past in chronological sequence. It may be convenient to lay it out anesthetized on the table with dates pasted on here and there, but what we know we know by ripples and spirals eddying out from us and from our own time. —Ezra Pound

I am a lucky guy. It's really that simple. In *The Reflective Practitioner*, I discovered a path that for nearly four decades has wound in brilliant spirals, in ever-widening arcs, sweeping me into connections with kind and generous people and leading me to profound learning experiences. To list them all, I would need to begin with the people who in 1985 first motivated and encouraged me and then to the current members of reflective practice groups who are my constant teachers: I would not be writing this book without a four-decade friendship and professional collaboration with Susanne Terry. Longtime friends, like intersecting spirals, we separately found our way into the work of reflective practice and are now partners in the Reflective Practice Institute International. We have shared ideas and experience, frustrations, and achievements. Above all, we have learned together, constantly curious and always honest, in a joyful exploration for new discoveries.

Mark Kerr, acquisitions editor at Rowman & Littlefield, inspired me to write this second edition. Actually, he told me that I needed to collect new material that I suggested publishing as a companion workbook and to incorporate the ideas, worksheets, and guides into a new version of the book. Although he is retired now, I am continually grateful for Mark's encouragement, wisdom, and playfulness.

I am again lucky because Michael Tan, who became my editor, has been a wise, thoughtful guide. I had particular goals with this edition, such as including other voices (there are thirty-two contributors to this volume) and adding photographs of spiral objects, things that he embraced. His support and gentle guidance have been invaluable.

Cinnie Noble read an earlier draft of one chapter, then a nearly polished version of another. I trust her judgment. She was enthusiastic about the book while offering pointed critiques and helpful suggestions. And, most important, Cinnie is a true friend.

One of my oldest and dearest friends, David Webster, used his architectural drawing skills to produce the exceptional drawing of the Spiral of Reflective Debrief® in chapter 8.

I invited four colleagues to contribute special essays for this book. In addition to Susanne Terry, my good friends and brilliant collaborators who responded with characteristic generosity are Ava Abramowitz, Jodie Grant, and Tzofnat Peleg-Baker. Their perspectives and experiences—their voices—add immeasurably to the breadth and quality of this book.

As you read the book, you will encounter the words of the Greek chorus—twenty-seven in all. They are members of reflective practice groups who unhesitatingly offered to contribute to the book. Their names are listed on the contributors page as well as with each of their brief essays. Leading reflective practice groups with these accomplished and remarkable practitioners is a privilege and a treat. We learn together. They inspired me to write this book and through our conversations provided much of the new material in the book.

With these words of heartfelt gratitude as prologue, let's begin the journey.

I Live My Life in Growing Orbits
by Rainer Maria Rilke
(Translated by Robert Bly)

I live my life in growing orbits
which move out over the things of the world.
Perhaps I can never achieve the last,
but that will be my attempt.

I am circling around God, around the ancient tower,
and I have been circling for a thousand years,
and I still don't know if I am a falcon, or a storm,
or a great song.

CHAPTER 1

Beginning of the Spiral

The spiral in a snail's shell is the same mathematically as the spiral in the Milky Way galaxy, and it's also the same mathematically as the spirals in our DNA. It's the same ratio that you'll find in very basic music that transcends cultures all over the world. —Joseph Gordon-Levitt

Here's an interesting question as you begin this book. What do these items have in common: seashells, the Milky Way Galaxy, flower petals, weather patterns, whirlpools, pea vine tendrils, the DNA double helix, and the nautilus shell? The photo above should be an obvious clue to the answer. Each holds the shape and form of a spiral. Beginning at the center (named variously the point or the bulge), the shell expands, sweeping outward in an unceasing series of expanding curves. Now that I've called your attention to spirals, countless examples will come to you. Spirals are ubiquitous in nature—think of the array of pinecone scales, sunflower florets, or the crown of hair on a child's head. Spiral shapes are often sacred elements in religious images, paintings (think of the sky in Van Gogh's *Starry Night*), sculpture and other works of art (Robert Smithson's *Spiral Jetty* in the Great Salt Lake, Utah), and architecture (spiral staircases or the Guggenheim Museum in New York). My first recollection of a spiral is the Slinky, a favorite childhood toy.

The "triple spiral" is a pre-Celtic and Celtic symbol found on a number of Irish Neolithic sites, most notably inside the Newgrange passage tomb in County Meath,

Ireland (built around 3200 BC). The exact symbolic meaning of the triple spiral for the pre-Celtics is unknown, since writing had not been invented yet. However, since the spirals are found in a tomb, it is likely that they possessed a sacred quality. . . . Spirals are also found throughout Pre-Columbian art in Latin America and Central America. (https://bluelabyrinths.com/2015/03/19/why-do-spirals-exist-everywhere-in-nature)

I can imagine you're puzzled, wondering what images of spirals have to do with reflective practice and conflict work. Then you presume there must be a connection, and there is. I'll explain. Whether in nature or in human-created objects, spirals represent growth and evolution. In the examples I mentioned and those you may have recalled, consider how the circles are ever expanding in three dimensions in a series of seemingly limitless arcs. As the number of rings increases, spirals open out, growing larger in diameter. They also develop end to end, each orbit building on previous loops. Look at the photo, and you can clearly see how the shell grew and evolved in both diameter and length.

In its design and its growth and evolution, the spiral is a perfect metaphor for professional development. With each engagement, in nearly every moment, we have a chance to test our skills and knowledge. And if we pay attention, we may also learn. We can learn to be more adept and responsive, we can learn to adapt to novel situations, and we can increase our understanding of and ability to address even routine conflict circumstances. Skilled at working with two disputing parties, we may develop the skills needed to work with small groups. Adept at responding to certain types of disputes, our practices might evolve to include a wider range of conflict situations or to work with more complex problems. If we are on a path toward continued evolution and growth, if we are committed to learning, then the arc of our careers resembles the spiral. If, however, we remain fixed in our approach, relying on favored routines regardless of the circumstances, then our professional development will be hindered, halted at a certain level of ability, and our careers will resemble a loop—fixed, circular, and unvarying.

Most discoveries even today are a combination of serendipity and of searching. Siddhartha Mukherjee

As the stories below illustrate, I was and remain committed to a continued state of evolution and growth. And because of that commitment, when I learned about reflective practice, I understood the potential for myself and others to become more adept, resilient, and effective practitioners because the mindset of reflective practice is that we can grow and evolve, and, like the spiral, we can increase our ability to engage resourcefully and capably. Throughout this book, I will return to the spiral as a metaphor. As you proceed through the book, you will follow the sweeping arcs of a spiral, gaining insights, building knowledge, and increasing awareness of your limitations and your competencies.

All spirals begin with a center, a point, a bulge (a term used in astronomy), an origin. We can't really understand the evolution of the spiral, of our own professional development, unless we return to that moment when it all began. I use the term "origin story" to describe that early moment in our professional development when the first seed of recognition was planted. We all have them. And for each of us, they are an extraordinary moment when we awaken to our potential. To understand my view of reflective practice, my thinking about adult learning, my appreciation for our evolution as practitioners, I want to begin with two origin stories—the beginning of my understanding of and commitment to reflective practice and the process of learning and evolving through experience. The stories have a common starting point; then they spiral in parallel arcs, outward and upward like the image below of an Archimedean spiral. The distinctive light and dark spirals share a common point of origin.

One spiral represents my exploration of reflective practice—reading and learning about the principles and methods, teaching others, and writing. The second and parallel spiral represents the development of the method, Reflective Debrief®.

My common origin story begins in August 1985. I attended the second annual meeting of the Academy of Family Mediators in San Rafael, California. I had been slowly building my family mediation practice over the previous seven years, gaining experience and confidence. In that time, apart from my clients, no one had observed my work, and I had not received supervision or feedback. With a desire to learn whether I was doing mediation "right," I promised myself that I would volunteer as mediator in any demonstration or role-play exercise. I didn't have to wait because an opportunity appeared during the first session on the first morning of the conference. The workshop was titled "Ericksonian Hypnotherapy Approaches to Mediation." Having learned about Milton Erickson's methods in a family therapy training program, I was slightly familiar with his work and eager to hear the presentation. During the first hour of the two-part workshop, the presenters walked us through twenty-five of Erickson's techniques, referring to butcher-block paper taped to the walls of the large meeting room.

After a short break, the session leaders asked for volunteers for a demonstration role-play. Before they had completed their explanation of the demo, I shot up my hand and was selected to act as mediator. Although I couldn't know this until years later, this innocent decision helped shape the arc of my professional work for the next four decades. Two others were drafted to enact a scenario, playing divorcing spouses. My only instructions were to "use Erickson's techniques." The next twenty minutes flashed by. The demonstration ended when the presenters—I had my back to the audience—approached, each placing a hand on one shoulder, and said, "Thank you. That was brilliant." More than feeling elated or relieved, I was just grateful to have made it through this public exhibition without humiliating myself in front of forty strangers.

The story doesn't end there. That evening, reflecting on the experience as I lay sleepless on my bed, I realized that at best I had been a performer—uncritically and mechanically following instructions, reacting in some automatic and intuitive fashion, without knowing the reasons for my choice of words and techniques. I didn't understand the reasoning behind my actions, so how could I do something similar with my clients? My success in the role-play experiment was bittersweet. In addition to compliments from the presenters, others at the conference greeted me with kudos: "Great work. How did you know what to do?" or "I didn't know a lawyer could do something like that." Yet I knew the role-play was a performance, not a demonstration of knowledge and skill.

Because I had no theory to guide my actions, I was adrift. As Leonardo da Vinci reflected, "He who loves practice without theory is like the sailor who boards a ship without a rudder and compass and never knows where he may cast."

Later in the conference, talking with a new acquaintance about my discordant and unsettling reactions to the demonstration, he recommended a book that might help me better understand my dilemma. That book was *The Reflective Practitioner* by Donald Schön. His description didn't immediately draw me to the book, but he insisted I give it a read. Back in Maine, busy with family and practice, I forgot about the book until several months later. And when I finally read the book almost a year later, I experienced a moment of awakening as I realized that this book and the methods and principles of reflective practice were the answer to my dilemma. There was both a rationale for and a proven method for learning from practice experiences. That conference role-play and *The Reflective Practitioner* have had an intense, astonishing, and enduring impact on the course of my professional life.

Another Origin Story

Like the parallel spirals, the companion story integrates what I experienced at the conference with what I was learning as a student in a family therapy training course. Around the same time as the conference, I was a trainee at a family therapy institute. I was seeking new approaches and techniques for working with divorcing couples and other family conflicts. We were instructed that every intervention must be supported by a hypothesis based on theory—a possible explanation for the parties' behavior, thoughts, and feelings. I understood this idea—at least in principle. Intellectually, it made sense. But I was struggling to figure out how to put this principle into practice. I can recall the exact moment when the penny dropped. It was near the end of the second term during a weekly case supervision seminar. I presented the perplexing problem of the playful couple. The couple gave me every reason to believe their divorce mediation would be uncomplicated. They had remained friendly following their separation, cooperated in parenting their three children, and had few disagreements about their finances. So what was the problem—my problem? What proved difficult—ironically—was their warmth and ease with one another.

Assurance, action, and evidence influence each other in an ongoing process. This helix is like a coil, and as it spirals upward it expands and widens. These three elements of faith—assurance, action, and evidence—are not separate and discrete; rather, they are interrelated and continuous and cycle upward. David A. Bednar

We met each week for two hours, and after three mediation sessions, they had identified the core issues, collected key pieces of information, and were well prepared for each session. Yet when the discussion turned to the details for financial settlement, one or the other would launch into a story, often comical, occasionally serious, about an event that had occurred years before. One story would rekindle the memory of another. They were playful, teasing, even flirtatious at times. The pragmatist in me was concerned about "progress" in completing their settlement. In addition, I wondered whether their behavior suggested my lack of skills to redirect their attention. I was puzzled at how deftly they could sidetrack substantive discussions. This is the conversation that followed between me and the practice supervisor (PS):

PS: Were you expecting them to make progress according to a certain time schedule?

Me: I suppose I was—not a schedule as such, but forward progress at all. In other mediations, clients would make some substantive progress during every meeting—like seeing the image in a jigsaw puzzle gradually take shape. And I assumed that reaching a settlement agreement on the terms of their divorce is why couples would choose mediation.

PS: How did these clients explain their reason for choosing mediation?

Me: They were divorcing and wanted to settle issues about coparenting their children and make decisions about their finances. They hoped a neutral guide would help them get through the difficult parts of the negotiations.

PS: So, describe why you are frustrated with the behavior of this couple.

Me: I was frustrated with the pace of decision making—the utter lack of progress on these issues. I tried every technique in my collection of mediator tools. I altered the seating in the room so they were opposite one another rather than side by side. I used newsprint to chart their finances. I cajoled, humored, prodded, and encouraged them to focus on decisions necessary for a settlement. Nothing altered the pattern of their behavior—one step forward . . . then another story.

PS: What do you make of their behavior; what's behind their actions? [It was the kind of question the supervisor asked routinely, inviting us to identify an explanation for clients' behaviors. This time, the impact was electrifying. I had been so fixated on choosing and applying techniques that I hadn't stepped back from the situation to consider why they continued to engage in behavior that was off task.]

Me: I know I've been putting all my effort into trying techniques that have been successful with other couples. I wanted to address the behaviors that I found so distracting and puzzling. But I never stopped to think about why they were acting in this way. Honestly, I don't know what's behind their actions. I don't have a hypothesis.

PS: Perhaps not yet. But try this: think of as many possible explanations as you can. Just list them. Don't worry if they seem odd, far-fetched, or even ridiculous. Once you have a list, we will help you evaluate them.

With the encouragement of my colleagues and the supervisor, I stood for several minutes at the easel, staring at the blank page of newsprint, mentally casting about for answers, then wrote a list of likely explanations. I wasn't confident that any was accurate. Next, the supervisor asked me to evaluate the merits and faults of each until I spotted one hypothesis that seemed to fit: they were behaving in my office as they had in their marriage and were now acting toward one another in their separate lives. I didn't think they were purposefully avoiding conflict; they weren't unwilling to negotiate the terms of their settlement. Ironically, even though they were divorcing, they genuinely liked one another—they just couldn't live together. So in my office, they were following a pattern familiar to them and unknown to me. I was trying to push them into a way of interacting that was driven by my own experience, not based on what they needed. The theory that formed the basis for my hypothesis was that resistance strengthens when confronted and relaxes when engaged.

> Throughout this conversation, my fellow classmates were largely silent, withholding their opinions and advice. In the end, and following the lead of our supervisor, a couple of them asked questions to support my efforts.

When I explained my ideas and the basis for my thinking, the supervisor, with a nod and wry smile, asked,

PS: How will you test this hypothesis? How can you determine whether their social natures are causing the behavior you find difficult to address?

Me: [Standing in front of my classmates, I felt pressure to come up with the right answer.] My first idea is to tell my own playful stories. But I don't think that will be helpful. I need to find a method that acknowledges what's happening and reminds them of the reason they want my help. I am having difficulty thinking creatively. I don't want to keep doing the same thing, though—just trying one technique after another.

PS: I understand your challenge. You want to act confidently, in keeping with your professional role, and you want to carefully and respectfully test this new hypothesis.

Me: Yes, that's my dilemma.

PS: What do you think might happen if, instead of working to change their approach, you accept who they are; don't fight against their being playful and distracted? What would happen if you mirror their sociability?

Me: I have an idea [as the proverbial lightbulb lit]. Perhaps I could relax, but without giving up my professional responsibilities. Maybe I could treat the session informally the way they do rather than having any kind of structure and expectations about progress. Maybe that's how I can join their resistance, feel more relaxed, and stop trying to persuade or coax them to be serious about making decisions.

When I next greeted my clients, I invited them to enjoy the cheese and crackers and a chilled bottle of chardonnay I had set out for us. The husband teasingly asked, "Did you learn this in Mediation 101?" They both laughed, and for the next thirty minutes, we enjoyed the late afternoon treat and talked about music and an exhibit of sculptures at the local art museum. Within the next hour, they shared financial information, discussed options, and finalized the terms for their divorce settlement.

> *I hear and I forget. I see and I remember. I do and I understand.* Confucius

I was not responsible for their 180-degree swing; I didn't "get them" to shift from avoidance to engagement. There was no subtle psychological trick that induced them to take a different path.

Having identified a pattern to their behavior and generated a tentative explanation, my role as a mediator was to know what to do, when, and (most important) *why*. I had developed a hypothesis to explain their behavior based on theories about resistance and engagement and created a relaxed social environment in order to test that hypothesis. Rather than pushing against their apparent resistance as I had done repeatedly in the preceding weeks, I joined their social behavior. By sharing refreshments and conversation, I was inviting them to alter the pattern of their behavior—and they responded. Their obvious affection for one another, which had blocked progress toward a divorce agreement, became the social lubrication enabling them to develop, assess, and agree on settlement proposals.

I developed an intervention strategy grounded in theory and based on a thorough assessment of previous mediation sessions. I accepted the possibility that my approach might not be constructive or helpful. But because I understood *why* I had chosen the strategy, I had a basis for evaluating their reactions, determining whether the intervention was successful, and, if necessary, producing a new hypothesis to explain their amiability and playfulness.

This is how, in that moment during the supervision session, the penny dropped. From reading *The Reflective Practitioner*, I knew—in principle—about the process of learning through experience, using reflection-in-action or reflection-on-action to examine, reflect on, and learn from surprising practice moments. Prior to that conversation with the practice supervisor, I had puzzled over and labored to connect the principles of reflective practice to my work as a mediator. Putting the pieces together had, until that day, been a solitary process. I knew but couldn't identify an essential element connecting reflective practice and mediation work. The experience in the supervision seminar and the subsequent "experiment" with the sociable clients showed me how this can be done:

In joining a reflective practice group, I didn't know exactly what to expect. I saw it as an opportunity to work with other mediators and grow my skill set. But a reflective practice group is so much more than I could have imagined. My reflective practice group has been meeting for over five years, and in that time, I have seen the growth in each of us as participants. Reflective practice groups allow you to learn and grow as a professional, without the judgment often found in other peer groups. Instead, your group helps you develop your own solutions and skills while learning along with you in your experience. It is about asking questions and following the person, seeking guidance in the direction they need to pursue rather than you guiding the conversation. It allows you to develop and hone skills that help with your own clients, other business professionals, as well as in your personal life. The experience has been invaluable, and I continue to learn from it years later. —Kristyn Carmichael

I learned, in practical terms, what it means to apply theory to practice. With the supervisor's guidance, I had a tangible example from my own practice of the process they had been drumming into us: observation leads to hypothesis creation, to experimentation, to observation, and to assessment and further action.

With the supervisor's help, I used reflection-on-action (we'll come to that in the next chapter) to become more effective and competent. From reading Schön, I was familiar with the principle and the basic elements of the process. I understood it in theory. But I struggled with its application to actual practice situations.

This is the most crucial lesson of all. This was my first mentoring experience. The supervisor guided me to identify the source of my uncertainty, to search for possible explanations, and finally to devise a plan that might resolve the confusing situation. She never told me what to do; instead, she asked questions that prompted me to explore the source of my puzzlement and make my own discovery.

> Don't compromise yourself. You're all you've got. Janis Joplin

This was an "aha" moment—my awakening to the potential of an elicitive form of feedback, the practical application of Schön's method of reflection-on-action. From that moment, I applied reflective practice methods regularly. I took the practice supervisor's model and experimented with students in the graduate program at Antioch University and in training courses I presented for the Department of Veterans Affairs. In *The Making of a Mediator* (2000), I created the term "elicitive coaching" (pp. 53–64) for this method of nondirective feedback and mentoring. Subsequently, in collaboration with my colleague and friend Susanne Terry, we adopted a term she used for the same process she had independently developed, Reflective Debrief®.

These experiences are part of my origin story. Thinking about a spiral that would depict my career, the two events, the conference role-play, and my reading of *The Reflective Practitioner* are the center point around which the arcing whirls have grown and evolved. They help explain not only what occurred and where and when but also why the events produced an immediate response and a lasting impact on my work.

And so we begin with the twin spirals: the one that describes the arc of my learning and then teaching and writing about reflective practice and the other that describes the evolving and growing spiral of practice of Reflective Debrief®. From that common point of origin, we will explore the nature, use, and benefits of reflective practice and the development and use of Reflective Debrief®. The chapters in the book unfold like the expanding curves of a spiral, each adding to and integrating with the preceding curves, with the goal of inspiring you to experience the evolution and growth in your professional practice through the adoption and use of reflective practice.

In the monthly reflective practice session with my mediator friends, we talk about complicated problems that have occurred in a mediation. Anyone can bring a problem they want to think through, and they understand that no one will fix the problem for them. Instead, the rest of us only ask questions. And not even cleverly constructed leading questions, where they know what your solution should be. I'm good at those.

We ask genuine curious questions that enable the person who brought the problem to think it through. It is amazing how often deep insight occurs, that not only benefits the person but is nourishing for the whole group. I would go so far as to say it is often beautiful to be a part of.

Recently, the group facilitator, who introduced us to the practice, said when he has a problem, he will apply the same principles to himself. He will ask himself curious questions, to open himself up to hidden insight.

So next time someone brings a problem to you, try asking questions that enable them to reflect on their own problem. If the experts in conflict resolution do this, it's probably a good approach! —Leon Bamforth

We are creatures of time—past, present, and future. The spiral embodies these dimensions, and in the whirls, we see the physical manifestation of the spiral's expansion. Beginning with the center point (or bulge, as astronomers refer to the center of a spiral galaxy), the sweeping and ever-expanding coil represents the growth and evolution of our professional development.

The White Rabbit put on his spectacles.
"Where shall I begin, please your Majesty?" he asked.
"Begin at the beginning," the King said gravely, "and go on till you come to
   the end: then stop." —Lewis Carroll, *Alice's Adventures in Wonderland*

Past-Present-Future

Obeying the King's admonition, let's begin at the beginning—the importance of understanding the origins of our careers. It's a truism that navigating where we want to go is dependent on first understanding where we are and then examining how we arrived at this place. Let me use a common situation to illustrate my point.

> The human mind always makes progress, but it is a progress in spirals.
> Madame de Stael

At the outset of our work with clients—as mental health professionals, attorneys, or third-party intervenors—we ask them to describe the origin of the issue, problem, or conflict they want to address. What occurred, when, how, who was involved, and why? Imagine attempting to assist parties if they never disclosed or discussed the origins of the problem. We would be stymied without understanding their relationship (e.g., family, business, neighborhood, or workplace), the events immediately preceding the dispute, what occurred and when, how that event or events led to a dispute, why they failed to find their own solutions, or how they came to choose you and your professional services. Having that information provides a foundation for a useful discussion and potential solutions. The origin stories of the dispute (each party will have one) help explain the present circumstances and point them (and us) toward the future.

Being aware of your origin story, the point of beginning, you can identify what occurred that was pivotal. What caused you to pay attention to what occurred? For example, many who experienced an electrifying moment such as I had at the conference would accept the presenters' compliments and their colleagues' admiration, and that would be the end of it. They might recall this exhilarating moment but would not credit the experience with altering the course of their careers. Each of us has a unique set of moments that form our origin story.

We will return in chapter 4 to the origin story as an element of each person's constellation of theories—the set of values, beliefs, and assumptions that shape our understanding of and response to our clients' situations.

Growth and Evolution

The primary theme of this book is professional evolution and growth, becoming excellent in our practices. I chose the spiral to represent the movement from beginner to experienced practitioner, from the novice who doesn't know what she doesn't know to the accomplished and skillful practitioner who intuitively responds to novel practice challenges. The ceaseless outward and upward movement of the spiral that represents professional development is fueled by learning from our experiences, strengthening our knowledge, and honing our skills. As we proceed along that spiral path of growth and evolution, we make use of our practice experiences as opportunities for learning. Additionally, we may seek out advanced training courses, conference workshops and seminars, and professional journals and books. In a continuing process of professional development, we may also join reflective practice groups or engage in self-directed learning. For those who fail to learn, the path of their professional life is static, like a stationary ring, fixed in its dimensions—never shifting or growing. They practice much the same way after years of experience—repeating the same behaviors and strategies they may have initially learned, content with their methods, and concerned with growth or change. However, for those of us committed to ongoing learning, the arc of our spiral is dynamic, endlessly moving forward, building on, and integrating lessons from our practices. Like a spiral, we grow and evolve.

Evolution and growth, the path of our professional development, occur in two inseparable and parallel aspects. First, if we choose to evolve and grow, we are becoming more resourceful, efficient, and competent in the application of our knowledge and skills. Second, along that path, we are also becoming more aware of how we want to think and act as professionals. You will learn more about the attributes of a reflective practitioner and the essential relation between our behaviors—the actions we take and our mindset—and the principles and beliefs we have about ourselves and our work. We pay considerable attention to the first, aspiring to excellence in our craft. We acquire more and more tools, strategies, and techniques in our effort to become skillful. Less considered and less examined is our mindset—our attitudes, our beliefs, the way we see ourselves as professionals, and the way we think about our role:

> *Participating in a reflective practice group has allowed me to grow professionally. Listening to the experiences of other mediators has taught me new techniques and language that are relevant to my practice—even when those mediators handle different subject matter and practice in other jurisdictions.*
>
> *Having a resource when I struggle with challenges is a godsend. I vividly recall the physical relief after talking through a situation that caused me to reach out to my RPG with an urgent request for help.*
>
> *Reflective practice reinforces mediation skills and vice versa. Each is a reminder to turn off the instinct to be the problem solver and let the colleague or clients arrive at their own solutions.*

Expanding my community of mediators beyond my state, region, and country has been a joy. It is fascinating to learn how mediation is done elsewhere and to incorporate new ideas into my work. —Ellen Waldorf

So if our goals are to grow and evolve in both aspects—competence and self-awareness—then what is the best method? To answer that question, I return to my experience at the conference. I wasn't content to savor the approval of the presenters and my colleagues. I wanted to figure out what it would take to reproduce that experience. How would I know what to do, when, and why? How would I know whether my interventions were helpful or off the mark? And how would I respond if my efforts weren't successful? In that role-play, I had done something that was helpful and apparently in line with Erickson's approach. What was that something? What influenced my actions? What did I observe in the words and behavior of my role-play partners that prompted my response? Intuitively, I knew that unless I answered that question, I could not become a capable mediator.

Keep away from people who belittle your ambitions. Small people always do that, but the really great always make you feel that you too can become great. Mark Twain

Reading *The Reflective Practitioner*, I didn't find an answer to these questions; what I discovered was a method for finding the answers. That method is reflective practice—the notion of learning from and through our experiences. Nearly forty years after first reading that book, the story continues with sharing my experiences, challenges, and discoveries in the process of becoming a reflective practitioner. In this book, as with my teaching about reflective practice and leading reflective practice groups, I have a simple goal. I want to help other practitioners become more skillful and competent, make their own discoveries, and achieve excellence in practice. There is no "one-size-fits-all" standard for assessing excellence. There is no single pathway to achieving excellence that is right for all of us. And there is no one model or style of practice that is ideal for all practitioners, in all settings, and for all disputes. Still, I can say with confidence born of experience as a practitioner, educator, and writer that you can achieve excellence—as you define that quality—by becoming a reflective practitioner.

Reflective practice is a light source on the experience of mediation. A wonderful supportive and evolutionary tool for mediators to see deep in the experience and get self-awareness on mediation practice. —Adamandia (Mandie) Maleviti

Why Reflective Practice?

Reflective practice is a method through which we thoughtfully and critically examine our professional experiences, test our assumptions, strengthen our practice skills, and deepen our knowledge. It is a profound and powerful yet deceptively simple process. It requires an intention to learn from our experiences sustained by a consistent commitment to growth and evolution. To encourage that intention and promote your commitment to developing a reflective routine, the elements in this book provide a practical foundation. I have included worksheets and guides, reflective exercises, examples that illustrate the principles and methods, and comments from practitioners describing their experience with reflective practice. In the end, evolution and growth mean increased competence in our practices—the extrinsic benefit doing our best for our clients. It also means increased confidence in our skills and knowledge—the intrinsic benefit of knowing that we are working to the highest level of our ability.

Reflective practitioners transform experience into knowledge. Linda Finlay (2008) describes the process of learning from and through experience as a process of

> examining assumptions of everyday practice. It also tends to involve the individual practitioner in being self-aware and critically evaluating their own responses to practice situations. The point is to recapture practice experiences and mull them over critically in order to gain new understandings and so improve future practice. This is understood as part of the process of life-long learning. (1)

Similarly, Christopher Johns (2010) describes learning through experience as an opportunity for practitioners to examine and challenge the limits of "ritualized patterns of practice."

In this book, I will describe and define reflective practice, providing examples of time-tested, commonsense, and effective reflective practice methods. Using these methods allows practitioners to learn through their experiences and ultimately to become more effective.

Perfection is not attainable, but if we chase perfection we can catch excellence. Vince Lombardi

Three personal characteristics inform each facet of this book as they have influenced all my reflective practice activities. These values are at the core of my constellation of theories that I will present and explain in chapter 4.

I am a practical person. What I write about or teach should ultimately produce tangible and practical results—the "takeaways." Equally, I pay attention to the intrinsic values of professional satisfaction and self-confidence.

I am a practitioner at heart. In my writing and teaching and my leadership of reflective practice groups, my aim is to help conflict practitioners improve their competence and confidence.

I am an idealist. I am aspirational. I believe in the potential for each of us to achieve excellence and professional fulfillment.

With this second edition, my goal is to produce a down-to-earth guide (not exactly a DIY handbook but something similar) for becoming a reflective practitioner. To accomplish that goal, I will do the following:

- Define reflective practice—the basic elements as well as its underlying principles—and illustrate with examples from my own practice and from members of reflective practice groups
- Explain how reflective practice works—how it nurtures professional evolution and growth
- Describe various methods of reflection (in particular, Reflective Debrief®) and provide examples to illustrate the process
- Expand the appendices, including exercises, worksheets, instructions, and guides, to encourage your engagement with individual and group reflection

As further expression of my commitment to continued curiosity and ongoing learning in this second edition, I have revised and expanded the section on reflective practice groups, integrating what I leaned in the past six years from leading hundreds of reflective practice group sessions. In a subsequent chapter, I will also explain the evolution of my thoughts about the structure and flow of Reflective Debrief® and, as a result, revisions to the model I offered previously. Further, I identified a tenth attribute of a reflective practitioner—humility—and, influenced by the spiral metaphor of continued evolution and growth, I revised my thinking about and explanation of the constellation of theories.

Reflective practice, as a model for seeking artistry in our practices, has become more widely known and embraced by practitioners, scholars, teachers, and trainers. I use another metaphor to explain this extraordinary development. Vines that are planted, pruned, watered, and meticulously tended to will eventually yield a bountiful harvest. For more than two decades, I have been given the opportunity to be the vineyard's caretaker. But I have not been a solitary figure wandering among the rows of vines. Many others have been writing about and teaching the value of reflective practice for conflict practitioners, and they have experimented with the use of reflective practice in a variety of learning settings. Four of these notable and gifted colleagues agreed to contribute to this book, describing their experiences and pointing to the benefits of reflective practice. Susanne Terry explains the rationale for and her application of reflective practice principles and practices in training conflict practitioners. Ava Abramowitz describes the activities she uses in her law school course on negotiation and mediation to prepare students for becoming reflective practitioners. Jodie Grant provides an example of and explanation for the use of reflective practice methods in her practice as a mediation supervisor. Tzofnat Peleg-Baker, in an essay describing the research and theory that underpins the guide she created, the Structured Reflective Instrument®, urges practitioners to engage in reflection that is structured, systematic, shared, and safe. Finally, I wanted to include the voices of practitioners who have participated in reflective practice, a sort of Greek chorus of voices, describing the practical influence of reflective practice on their work, the first of which are included in this chapter. As the late-night infomercials promise, there's more.

> I encourage all of you to seek out teachers and mentors that challenge you to think for yourself and guide you to find your own voice. Renee Olstead

I have been speaking about and teaching the principles and methods of reflective practice for more than twenty-five years. I have witnessed "aha" moments as practitioners engage in self-reflection that produces insights that lead them to improve the quality of their work. I know you can too:

> I have been working on reflective practice for years. By participating in regular reflective practice groups, I have deepened and improved the skills and techniques I use in mediation. Preparation, connecting empathetically, staying curious, and not offering suggestions became more than intellectual ideas; they became part of my persona.
>
> For example, high-conflict parents are ordered back to mediation because they fail to reach a mediated agreement. I take time to prepare myself, and when the parents arrive, I am prepared to respectfully see them as people with a unique situation and unique needs.
>
> I met with each party privately for a shorter time than usual. Surprisingly, these high-conflict parents requested a joint session (which I rarely do), but, because of reflective practice, I understood they knew best. They had a respectful discussion about what they cared most about. Their children. I had taken the time to deeply and respectfully listen. They were at their best, focusing on their children. I was at my best by empathetically assisting the parents' efforts to negotiate and solve their own problems, providing them with a unique opportunity and supportive atmosphere to create a long-lasting solution for their children. —David Hubbard

During presentations, I am often asked about the objectives, methods, and benefits of reflective practice.

- What am I supposed to reflect on? What do I look for?

  We reflect on unexpected behavior or comments in our practices when something occurs that is perplexing and for which our practice routines do not provide a ready response. I refer to them in this book as critical moments, when "the results are better or worse than expected" (Velayutham and Perera 1993, 291).

- Isn't this simply a kind of navel-gazing? If not, how is it different?

  There is a difference between idle musing and the intentional process of reflection. As reflective practitioners, our deliberations are purposeful—seeking insights and new knowledge. "Reflective practice is more than a self-awareness process in which we pause and think back after something has happened" (Zalipour 2015, 1).

- Will I have to change my style and method of practice?

  Becoming a reflective practitioner does not require you to adopt a different model or style of practice or to learn new practice strategies or techniques. Members of reflective practice groups I lead will variously label themselves as facilitative, transformative, directive, narrative, and hybrid. Reflective practice isn't a form of practice; it is a means of becoming the most competent and confident within your style or model.

- I already think about my cases. I talk with fellow practitioners all the time and occasionally ask for advice. Isn't this a type of reflection?

  Thinking about practice moments or reviewing those moments with colleagues has undeniable value. However, without the intention to learn from experience, you are unlikely to achieve "purposeful learning—derived not from books or experts, but from our work and our lives" (Amulya 2011, 1). More on this in chapter 2.

- How does it work? What would I need to do?

  Integrate the attributes of a reflective practitioner into your day-to-day work. Then use the basic methods of reflective practice. Make time. Become familiar with the reflective process. It is not arduous. Adopting the mindset and methods will be awkward at first, but they will grow to be intuitive. Try these methods until they become a normal part of your practice routine.

- What does it take to become a reflective practitioner? What do I need to learn?

  Reflective practice is as much a mindset as a process. You must be curious, pay attention, and be willing to learn. "The key to reflection is learning how to take perspective on one's own actions and experience—in other words, to examine that experience rather than just living it" (Amulya 2011, 1).

- I don't have time to sit and muse about my work.

  We tend to make time for activities when we recognize the benefit of doing so. Once you start, you will realize that becoming a reflective practitioner is neither burdensome nor time consuming. In addition, you will quickly experience the practical benefits.

- Will becoming a reflective practitioner make me a better practitioner?

  I'm still learning.
  Michelangelo at age 87

  In a word, yes. You will become more adept, more resourceful, and more effective—and more confident. Discussing reflective practice in sports coaching, Laura Farres (2004) observes that "reflective practice is different than trial-and-error practice. Trial and error simply involves doing something and when it fails, doing something else until something works. The approach is random and unpredictable. . . . In reflective experimentation, the idea is to build upon existing knowledge by drawing from experiences and learning to make educated selections based on the relevant information. This approach is more predictable and thoughtful and promotes a more effective learning environment" (3).

Becoming a reflective practitioner is a well-recognized and proven process for improving the quality of professional practice. Isn't that our goal as practitioners; isn't that why we bother? In the words of Duke Ellington, "It don't mean a thing if it ain't got that swing." We may not always be able to measure "that swing" or say exactly what it means. But we certainly know it when we see it or hear it. We know it exists, even if we don't have criteria for describing the "swing" in our practices.

Nevertheless, there are qualities, characteristics, and mindsets common to those who strive for excellence in practice; they are the attributes of a reflective practitioner.

> Excellence is not a skill, it is an attitude. —Ralph Marston

For reflective practitioners, competence involves a dynamic and ongoing process of learning through experience. It is the ever-expanding spiral of professional evolution and growth. Competence is not a destination. It is not a static condition. A celebrated musician describes competence as mastery and says, "It is not a fixed point in our professional lives. Because once we reach a certain point—even mastery—we realize there is still so much more to learn." Reflective practitioners learn from their experiences to increase their knowledge, strengthen their skills, and enhance their ability to choose the most appropriate and relevant intervention.

A reflective practitioner has the following:

1. The mindset of a confident, fearless, and ceaseless learner
2. A fierce commitment to learning through experience
3. A relentless determination to refine practice skills and expand knowledge

These three elements are the fuel for the outward and upward expansion of the spiral of professional development. They are integrated into the experience of the reflective practitioner, mutually reinforcing one another. These three elements function like musicians in a jazz combo; each has a distinct voice, but it is the combination of the voices that produces an extraordinary sound.

Let us not waste our time in idle discourse! Let us do something while we have the chance! It is not every day that we are needed. Samuel Beckett, Waiting for Godot

To explain what it means and demonstrate its practical value, this book describes each element of reflective practice and illustrates each with actual examples. Like a jazz combo, these distinct elements, like melodies and rhythms, hopefully produce a coherent and integrated presentation about reflective practice.

CHAPTER 2

Reflective Practice
An Introduction

The biggest surprise on the soulful journey to authenticity, whether as a philosophy or a spiritual path, is that the path is a spiral. We go up, but we go in circles. Each time around, the view gets a little bit wider. —Sara Ban Breathnach

Uncoiling in a continual process of growth and evolution, the spiral makes another turn, building on itself. In this chapter and building on the previous, I will further define reflective practice, explain its purpose, identify its essential principles, provide examples of its application, and demonstrate its relevance and value for professional development.

Schön (1983) explains that "reflective practice is "a dialogue of thinking and doing through which I become more skilful." We learn by means of the interaction between critical self-reflection and our professional activities. We don't merely reflect on our experience as if we were gazing in a mirror or merely replaying events as if watching a movie version of the engagement. We are not objective observers of those events; we are contributors to them. We are participants with an active role—influencing and being influenced by what occurs. Therefore, if we want to become more skillful, we need to engage actively, critically, and purposefully in a determined effort to learn from our experiences. Elizabeth Anne Kinsella (2001), referencing Schön (1983), notes that "reflection often begins when a routine response produces a surprise, an unexpected outcome, pleasant or unpleasant. The surprise gets our attention. When intuitive, spontaneous performance yields expected results, then we tend not to think about it; however, when it leads to surprise, we may begin a process of reflection" (108). Those unexpected and puzzling moments are the sources for our learning.

I want to use another story to illustrate how this process of reflection unfolds and how it leads to increased skills and knowledge. The events happened during a short-hop flight from Atlanta to Sarasota and involves a dialogue of thinking and doing. The actors were a young girl and her father. I was an observer, privileged to watch the uncoiling spiral of learning as the child played an ordinary game familiar to most of us.

Children learn as they play. Most importantly, in play children learn how to learn. O. Fred Donaldson

It was the last flight of the evening, departing at 9:30. I was tired after several days away from home and eager to return. Having slowly made my way down the narrow aisle, I arrived at my assigned seat and nodded and smiled at my traveling companions, a child of about eight in the middle and her father at the window. I busied myself with the usual preflight preparations, placed my e-reader in the seat back pocket, settled into my chair, and thought about being home.

As the plane left the gate, I noticed the child was playing games on the seat-back entertainment system. Sitting on her knees, control device held in both hands, she was keenly focused on the neon green and blue digital images that danced on the screen. Her movements drew my attention. She bounced on her seat as she pressed buttons and watched the electronic characters move about on the small screen. She was completely absorbed by the game, not even distracted by the shuddering as the plane lifted off. Her father put aside his magazine and looked over, nodding at times, smiling, and occasionally moving in time with her.

She was playing tic-tac-toe, a common childhood game we've all played, occasionally well, and more often to a draw. It's a game I taught my children and enjoyed playing with them.

On the screen, she was the bright turquoise pelican, her opponent a neon-green fish. Most games ended in a tie. Neither she nor the fish was able to consistently defeat the other.

I tried to keep my eyes and my mind on my book, but the girl's excited movements held my attention. Normally, I would not have eavesdropped on their conversation. Normally, I would have been thinking about my wife and being home. Yet her unselfconscious concentration on the screen and the sounds of her delight or disappointment were captivating. Appearing to read, I was instead intently watching her out of the corner of my eye.

After a few minutes, I overheard her complain, "Dad, this game is no fun. The games all end the same. No one wins. I want to play a different game." Her father quietly encouraged her to try a few more times. He shifted in his seat and turning toward her said, "Let's just see what happens." Then, after trying another seven or eight games, she won. She and her dad high-fived. He asked her, "How did you do that?" She shrugged and replied, "I don't know." Then he asked, "Did you do anything differently?" She looked at the screen, thought for a moment, and said, "I started by putting an X in the middle, then put the next one in the corner, and played another one in the other corner. It kind of looks like a V." Her father encouraged her to try again using the same strategy.

She won a second time, then a third, then a fourth. By this time, I was shamelessly absorbed and no longer pretended to be reading. I was watching her choices almost as intently as her father. At one moment, he noticed my gaze fixed on his daughter, nodded, and smiled.

The fifth game ended in a tie. She looked to her father, asking him to explain why she hadn't continued to win. Instead of offering his own interpretation, he asked her, "Why do you think that happened?" She was quiet for a few seconds, then bounced in her seat and said with a smile and a voice just a little too loud, "The computer figured out what I was doing!" Her dad smiled and asked, "So, what do you do now?" Another silence, followed by a hesitant and uncertain response: "I'll try different corners." So she did, and in the next few minutes, she won several games.

The story is undeniably charming. You may identify with the child's delight at discovering strategies, born out of frustration with a game where the default outcome is most often a draw. You may identify with the father (as I did) wanting his child to experience delight, wanting her to succeed. What grabbed my attention—in addition to the child's pure delight—is that the dad resisted the loving parental urge to ease his daughter's frustration and disappointment by instructing her or offering advice. Instead, he encouraged her to think for herself, to find her own winning strategy. When a succession of victories was interrupted by another tie, he prompted her to reflect on and reconsider her strategy. Sitting beside the child, observing her process of creating and testing ways to play the game, I envisioned her spiral of learning. Yes, she was learning new strategies. Even more important, she was learning to think for herself, to evaluate a puzzling situation and test a likely solution.

Some will smile at this endearing example of childhood curiosity and learning, but then you might understandably question its relevance to a book on reflective practice in conflict resolution. How do the actions of an eight-year-old playing a child's game and her father's actions relate to the sophisticated work of a seasoned professional? In this and the following chapters, you will come to see how, using her successes and frustrations to generate and then test a strategy for winning the game, this child's guileless effort illustrates perfectly the reflective practice principle of learning through experience. You will also learn methods for incorporating this commonsense and proven learning process of reflective practice into your professional work. Later in the book, you will see this story's relevance to the evolution and growth of professional development. You will understand how the interplay between father and daughter perfectly illustrates the process of Reflective Debrief® and the goal of helping practitioners become more skillful. Ultimately, that's what really matters to me and is central to reflective practice—our growth and development as competent and effective practitioners. In this, we hope to emulate a child's curiosity and desire to learn. In the next chapter, we will return to the essential quality of childlike wonder—curiosity—as a fundamental attribute of a reflective practitioner.

I thought about that girl and her father, about her interaction with the game, how the father nurtured her curiosity, how he resisted the parental urge to offer explanations, and how he asked simple questions to encourage self-discovery. What I was privileged to witness has stayed with me. In this seemingly ordinary father–daughter exchange was a profound lesson. For days, I kept thinking about the pelican and fish, the child's excitement when she "won," and her frustration when the game ended in a draw. And in my mind, I repeatedly heard the father's gentle encouragement to think for herself:

Attending an alternative dispute resolution conference, my boss insisted I join a reflective practice group. Initially hesitant, I believed I already possessed the necessary skills. However, I reluctantly attended and engaged in a private session with Susanne Terry to address a persistent challenge in a juvenile dependency case. She asked curious questions that helped me recognize the assumptions and theories I was working with. Through this reflective practice, I gained clarity on my assumptions and professional theories. Most significantly, reflective practice illuminated the intersection between my personal and professional life, and I was able to untangle my unresolved traumas from those of my clients. This separation enhanced my advocacy, allowing me to be motivated by personal experiences while empowering clients to become their own heroes. Witnessing their pain became a shared journey, fostering deeper connections and more effective outcomes. Reflective practice has not only sharpened my professional skills but also provided invaluable personal growth. —Hansa Patel

In their parenting column in the June 4, 2018, edition of the *Sarasota Herald Tribune*, Jenni Stahlmann and Jody Hagaman describe a child's hunger to explore and learn:

> In order for kids to find deep interests and ultimately develop those interests into passion, they . . . need to be willing to live more like hunter/gatherers, searching the depths of their hearts, trying new things, analyzing the worth of each experience and then searching deeper and wider.

Two important lessons for conflict resolution practitioners emerge from the tic-tac-toe story. First, experienced professionals risk routinely repeating a pattern of actions; they become reliant on and routinely use techniques that have been successful in similar situations. Novices tend to model their actions on methods and strategies they observed and learned during their first training courses without evaluation or reflection. As a result, for both experienced and beginning practitioners, repeating the same actions over and over and anticipating the same result may be effective—sometimes.

Many a man may look respectable, and yet be able to hide at will behind a spiral staircase. P. G. Wodehouse

We aim for and then celebrate our successes. However, our achievements may have an unintended and paradoxical consequence. Success may—in fact, frequently does—inhibit our curiosity about the reasons for those wonderful outcomes. We seldom ask ourselves, "Why did that strategy or intervention lead to positive results?" Unless we are curious, we are unlikely ever to understand why our actions, at those particular moments, in that setting, and with those individuals, were helpful. Without that knowledge, we aren't able to learn from that experience. As a result, we won't know whether to make use of the same method in similar situations. Or, if we apply the method, we can't possibly know why it may have succeeded or fallen short of the mark. This is the lesson from my conference role-play experience. I was surprisingly and delightfully successful, but why? Not understanding why my actions produced a positive result, I could not successfully repeat them. I wouldn't know when to act or how to assess whether my actions were helpful.

Moreover, what do we do when favored strategies aren't effective? Do we redouble our efforts? Or might we assume our efforts were fruitless because the parties were resistant, uncooperative, or unwilling to respond to our actions? Do we dismiss the adverse reaction, shrug our shoulders, and chalk it up to the idea that sometimes participants can't agree? Or, like the young girl, do we stop and wonder why we were unsuccessful and then consider whether there is another path, an alternate strategy that might be more productive and successful?

> When we develop a pattern of behaviour that works in certain situations, we will tend to repeat it until it becomes automatic. We can't describe the processes involved because we are not aware of what is going on. It is only when something goes wrong or something unexpected happens that we may stop and think about what we did and what we could or should have done in the situation. (Maughan 1996, 76)

In my experience, few practitioners stop, observe, wonder, and reflect. More often, they minimize or ignore situations when something surprising and unsettling occurs. Yet these are exactly the moments rich with boundless possibilities for learning, for professional growth, and for evolution. To learn from our experience, we must pay attention to moments of surprise, puzzlement, and confusion. Progress along the spiral of professional development begins when we acknowledge our uncertainty and puzzlement:

> A practitioner's reflection can serve as a corrective to over-learning. Through reflection, he can surface and criticize the tacit understandings that have grown up around the repetitive experiences of a specialized practice, and can make new sense of the situations of uncertainty or uniqueness which he may allow himself to experience. (Schön 1983, 61)

When we view past successes as determinant of future outcomes, when we are tethered to prior experience and unable (or unwilling) to discover alternatives, we often find ourselves in a *rut*. When that occurs, our work seems labored, and we may feel complacent, inattentive, dispassionate, and even bored. Professional growth is arrested. Instead of an ever-expanding spiral of learning and evolution, our path becomes an endlessly repeating circle. Imagine the young girl using the same strategy over and over in an increasingly unsatisfying and frustrating effort to secure a "win." That is the experience of being in a rut, going round and round in an unending circle.

We are able to avoid a rut and instead find a *groove* when we view perplexing situations as opportunities to test our knowledge and skills and learn from these experiences. In the groove, the spiral of learning continues:

> The practitioner allows himself to experience surprise, puzzlement, or confusion in a situation which he finds uncertain or unique. He reflects on the phenomenon before him, and on the prior understandings which have been implicit in his behaviour. He carries out an experiment which serves to generate both a new understanding of the phenomenon and a change in the situation. (Schön 1983, 68)

Isn't this exactly what the young girl was doing? She was in the groove—curious, undeterred by failure, reflective, and open to new ideas. Reflective practice is a means for achieving this state—being un-self-conscious enough to see the awkward and surprising moments as opportunities for new learning. As reflective practitioners, we temper ego, self-assurance, and professional certainty to seek fresh perspectives.

Second, consider the father's response to his daughter's frustration as well as the curiosity she displayed when the games were repeatedly "tied." The father did not try to solve the problem for his daughter despite her obvious frustration and the parental impulse to protect his child from failure and distress. He withheld his opinion, leaving a gap for her own reflections. As a result, she thought about her dilemma and discovered a possible solution. He remained deeply engaged with her—and she with him. She trusted him, even as he declined to shield her from momentary discomfort and confusion. He used the experience as an opportunity to teach her an important lesson: answers are often within you. You don't need to rely on Dad (expert) to give you the answer. You can find it if you're willing to stop, think about the situation, identify why you are frustrated, look at ways to solve your problem, and then experiment with a potentially helpful solution. He encouraged his daughter to think for herself. He used questions rather than instructions, prompting her without imposing recommendations that would have replaced her ideas with his and likely resulting in her mimicking his suggested responses. Parenting experts would certainly agree with this father's approach:

> The challenge for parents is to inspire and mentor their kids, encourage them and fan the flames of their interests without doing the work for them. (Stahlmann and Hagaman, *Sarasota Herald Tribune*, June 4, 2018)

We know that the best solutions are ones that our clients discover. But we feel an impetus to respond. For example, some practitioners make use of the "mediator's opinion" when it appears that the participants will be unable to find their own solution. My purpose is not to wade into the turbulent waters of the contentious discussions about the mediator's opinion. I simply want to note that while there may be advantages, this approach carries the same shortcoming as the father offering advice to his daughter. The answer may resolve the immediate dilemma, and the parties may be gratified. But they will have lost the opportunity to experience the exhilaration of self-discovery.

Every child is an artist. The problem is how to remain an artist once we grow up. Pablo Picasso

The tic-tac-toe story illuminates the methods and process of reflective practice—learning from and through experience. It demonstrates the direct and immediate benefit, which is finding an answer to the surprising and puzzling situation, and it points to the lasting value, which is learning how to learn, how to solve dilemmas for oneself.

The reflective process of learning from and through experience begins with paying attention and *noticing* when something surprising and puzzling has occurred. In the story, the cycle of learning began when the girl noticed a pattern that was puzzling to her. This didn't seem right to her. "Dad, this game is no fun." Her awareness of that awkward circumstance led her to express curiosity, wondering why the situation occurred. "Why do people play this game when each time it ends in a tie?" Curiosity prompted a search, a hypothesis—an explanation that would account for the situation, its origins, and possible responses. The father asked, "Why do you think that happened?" She replied, "The computer figured out what I was doing." Testing the hypothesis, the next step involves experimenting to assess whether the explanation is valid and useful. "What do you want to do?" he asked. "I'll put my pelican in the corner." The girl tested her hypothesis, and the experiment was successful until it wasn't. The joy of successive victories eventually gave way to the disappointment and tedium of tied games. Encountering a problem, she observed the results of her actions and the computer's responses, examined possible explanations, and considered new methods. With each experiment, observing shifts in the computer-generated tactics and responding with new strategies, she was learning how to play the game (immediate benefit) and learning how to learn from experience (long-term benefit). The spiral of her growth and evolution was expanding. She was learning to think for herself. Unselfconsciously and without understanding the process, she was developing the capacity to learn from experience. Long after the childhood game ceases to hold her interest, she will continue to benefit from the tic-tac-toe experience.

> Every act of learning requires the willingness to suffer an injury to one's self-esteem. That is why young children, before they are aware of their own self-importance, learn so easily. —Thomas Szasz

No matter one's age, education, or professional experience, we all can be lifelong learners. To illustrate and confirm the universal nature of lifelong learning, I will share stories in later chapters about people in other occupations, including phlebotomist, roofer, dental hygienist, leather maker, and salesclerk. From time to time throughout the book, I will use the spiral metaphor to illustrate my evolution and growth—the learning process—that resulted in the decision to revise the first edition and how I am applying those lessons to the structure and content of this book.

With the tic-tac-toe story as an instructive preface and the symbol of the spiral in mind, here are the goals of this chapter.

- Further defining the purpose and goals of reflective practice by distinguishing it from professional development methods commonly misidentified for reflective practice.
- Building on the tic-tac-toe story to describe the nature, foundation, and methods of reflective practice and explain its application to and practical value for conflict resolution professionals.
- Presenting examples of reflective practice methods—reflection-in-action and reflection-on-action—to shine a light on the process of reflection.
- Explaining the practical value—both immediate and long term—of reflective practice for conflict resolution practitioners.
- Describing the elemental qualities, the mindset, of reflective practice and comparing the attitude and behaviors of an "expert" with the mindset and actions of a reflective practitioner.
- Emphasizing that reflective practice is more than a set of methods and processes; it is a distinct mindset. It is a way of thinking about our professional role and responsibility and about the importance of professional growth and evolution achieved by learning through experience.
- Pointing to the use of reflective practice methods individually, with a mentor or colleague, or in a group setting.

> In a spiral galaxy, the ratio of dark-to-light matter is about a factor of ten. That's probably a good number for the ratio of our ignorance-to-knowledge. We're out of kindergarten, but only in about third grade. Vera Rubin

Reflective Practice and Related Methods

I am gratified that over the years since I first began writing and speaking about reflective practice, a growing and sustained interest in the process of learning from experience has developed. The term "reflective practice" now regularly appears in announcements for workshops, courses, and groups—and not just those I present. Tempering my appreciation, however, is that the term "reflective practice" is being applied to all sorts of learning techniques and methods, few if any are grounded in the principles and methods that I believe are the bedrock of reflective practice. They are similar to reflective practice in one respect—the intention to make sense of surprising and puzzling moments in our professional practices in order to learn and thus improve the quality of their work. I am not suggesting that genuine learning can be achieved only through reflective practice. What I am suggesting is that although these methods may share a name, they are as different as chalk and cheese from the principles and practices of reflective practice first described by Schön (1983, 1987). It is these principles and methods that have been widely accepted and used in the professions of nursing, education, social work, medicine—and even sports coaching. This reflective practice DNA is woven into the process and mindset I have been advocating to conflict practitioners for three decades.

To clarify confusion about meaning, goals, and methods of reflective practice caused by commingling a variety of practices under the general label "reflection," or "reflective practice," I want to distinguish the activities and goals of reflective practice from other professional development methods commonly used to improve the quality of conflict resolution practice. Each of these other methods is also concerned with learning and self-improvement. As I point out crucial distinctions, however, the essential qualities, methods, and goals of reflective practice will become clearer.

To shine a light on these differences and to ground my explanation in the practical aspects of professional work, I will use a practice example offered by a member of a reflective practice group that I lead. For reasons of privacy and confidentiality, I have altered several elements of the story:

> Over several hours of intense and minimally productive conversation between partners who were dissolving the business they had created, one partner was hesitant to accept clearly favorable financial terms. The mediator used a variety of techniques to conclude the mediation with a settlement. In joint meetings and private sessions, the mediator meticulously reviewed the issues, data, and rationale for the proposal; to which the partner responded, "I understand everything." Each time—and there were several—when asked whether it was possible to make a decision, the partner variously indicated the need for more information (but couldn't specify what data was necessary) or would return to an issue previously resolved to the parties' apparent satisfaction. Confused by the partner's behavior and hoping a week's adjournment would allow the reluctant partner to evaluate the proposal (and unable to think of other options), the mediator suggested a postponement.

Following my explanation of the related learning methods, I will describe how reflective practitioners would seek to learn from this puzzling practice example.

Private Deliberation

Savoring success or lamenting a frustrating experience, either alone or in conversation with colleagues, we mentally review *what happened*—the brilliant moves, awkward moments, disappointing outcomes, or annoying clients. We recall the events and the outcome as if watching a video replay. We pause, fast-forward, rewind. As the scenes play out, we applaud our success or bemoan a disappointing or frustrating experience. In moments of private deliberation, we may think to ourselves,

> I'm sure that the other partner just needs time to settle into and become comfortable with the terms of the proposal. Postponing the decision was the right call.

Or we mentally recall difficult moments, finding comfort in our assessment of the troublesome and stubborn behavior of the participants:

> I had to suggest a postponement. What else could I do with this partner? All the data are there. The proposal is generous and responsive to what he demanded. Saying yes should have been a slam dunk.

For reflective practitioners: In private contemplation and reviewing the circumstances of the mediation, the reflective practitioner asks herself,

> "I couldn't think of anything else, so I suggested a week's delay. Why did I think that would work? What led me to the conclusion that the partner just needed time away from the pressure of the mediation? Is it possible there is another explanation for his hesitation?"

Consulting Colleagues

Retelling experiences in conversation with colleagues is a common approach for building camaraderie, seeking affirmation or looking for support. The process is *objective* in nature—we relive the experiences, talk about the case, generally emphasizing the puzzling events or outcomes. As we unspool the narrative, our role in the story may be the highly effective practitioner whose actions produced a brilliant outcome or the unappreciated and beleaguered practitioner dealing with difficult, resistant, and impossible clients. In these conversations, as we seek acceptance or support from our colleagues, we want to be confirmed in our assessment of the situation—an understandable and reasonable human response. Little if any learning generally results, yet the value of sharing these stories is consequential and valuable:

> I had this frustrating session. The parties were on the verge of reaching an agreement when one of them asked for more time to "settle into the proposal." What does that even mean? The terms were almost 100% what this person wanted. I tried persuasion, logical thinking, and when those approaches failed, out of frustration I suggested a week's postponement. Ever had something like that happen?

> Reflective space is an opportunity for discovery through dialogue. For an individual this involves asking questions of oneself to achieve the level of understanding of an issue, often from different perspectives, that opens the door to insights. (Clutterbuck and Hirst 2003, 104)

Seeking Advice or Recommendations

Practitioners experiencing a puzzling practice moment frequently consult a trusted mentor or colleague or a group of colleagues (sometimes in what is called a case consultation group). We want them to suggest alternative approaches to our unsuccessful intervention. Seeking advice is a sensible and common reaction to an unsettling dilemma. What have others tried in the same situation? What can they see from their more objective perspective? These conversations begin with a "the story" followed by a request for techniques and strategies that worked for others:

> The one partner was impossible. I couldn't think of anything else to do, so I kicked the can down the road, hoping the partner would realize that the proposal was a good deal. What else could I do? How would you handle this situation?

Eager to be helpful, the colleagues might respond as follows:

> Colleague 1: This is obviously a negotiation tactic, an attempt to squeeze more out of the other partner. I suggest you meet privately, and politely but firmly address the person's behavior.
> Colleague 2: The last time I had this happen, I refused to take "no" for an answer. I knew they wanted to settle. So, I kept pressing for an answer, pointing out the facts, and emphasizing the benefits of the proposal. It took a while, but the case settled.
> Colleague 3: Of course, you did the right thing. You had no choice.

For reflective practitioners: Learning how others view the situation and would respond may yield fresh perspectives and even reveal a successful strategy. However, in most situations, offers of advice are of limited value because (1) these colleagues weren't in the room and have only limited, secondhand information about their behaviors; (2) like the "trailer" for a film, colleagues know only a sliver of what occurred; (3) they view things from their own perspective; and (4) they aren't you—your choices and actions are guided by your mediation approach and your beliefs. (In chapter 4, I will present the Constellation of Theories.) As my colleague and friend Susanne Terry succinctly noted, "We each have a separate brain":

> Through reflection, he can surface and criticize the tacit understandings that have grown up around the repetitive experiences of a specialized practice and can make new sense of the situations of uncertainty or uniqueness which he may allow himself to experience. (Schön 1983, 61)

Notes or Practice Log

Some practitioners write notes or summary comments or maintain a journal, identifying surprising, unusual, or puzzling incidents. The process of putting thoughts into words on a page or computer screen helps make sense of what occurred, see patterns in theirs or the participants' behavior, and possibly question their assumptions about their approach to the conflict. Jan Frankel Schau's book *View from the Middle of the Road* (2013) is a collection of insightful post-mediation musings. She offers thoughtful examples of written reflections that identify and analyze techniques that were successful or ineffective. Schau shows how self-examination of unique and challenging practice situations leads to insights that resulted in adjustments to her strategies and methods:

> The practice of deliberate self-reflective analysis of at least one case per week became something I looked forward to. Just as weekly prayer or yoga practice offers a chance to breathe deeply and be introspective for a time, writing this book gave me the opportunity to look deeply and more thoughtfully at the approach taken to a particular conflict and the reasons why it worked or didn't work. (Schau 2013, xx)

For reflective practitioners: An imaginary journal entry might include the following observations and questions:

The one partner was impossible. We were so close. The proposal was solid, it could be implemented, and it was objectively fair. I tried logic, persuasion, and pointing out the dire consequences of not reaching a settlement. It was an impossible situation, like pushing an immovable object up a hill. As a last resort, I delayed the mediation by a few days. I assumed it would let everyone step away from the intensity of the moment and logically evaluate the settlement proposal. What if my assumption is incorrect? Is there any way I could have been sure? What if in a week's time, the partner is still hesitant?

Mindfulness

When we are mindful, we seek and consider novel interpretations of common experiences. Among other benefits, this prevents us from acting on autopilot. Mindfulness is both an attitude and a practice. It's a determination to notice what is unexpected, different, or remarkable and a willingness to suspend habitual and reflexive responses:

> A mindful approach to any activity has three characteristics: the continuous creation of new categories; openness to new information; and an implicit awareness of more than one perspective. (Langer 1997, 4)

Applying Langer's characteristics of mindfulness, the mediator might respond to the practice dilemma in this way:

> I haven't encountered this before; a party who is struggling to say yes to a proposal that meets their terms. I assumed that the reservations were based on a misunderstanding of the proposal, its basis, or what would happen if it's not accepted. I unsuccessfully tried logic and persuasion, and that didn't help. Maybe there's another way of looking at the partner's reluctance to say yes. I could ask, perhaps in private, "Could you help me understand your thoughts about the proposal?" If I knew what the partner was thinking, if I had more information, then I could be more helpful. I won't know unless I shift my thinking—stop trying to sort this out on my own and ask the partner how I can be helpful.

We always learn more from failure than from success. . . . Success teaches us nothing.
Henry Marsh

> *For reflective practitioners:* An attribute of a reflective practitioner (I will say more about this in chapter 3) is the mindset of being curious about and attentive to unexpected events and being open to new explanations and interpretations. Paying attention and being receptive to alternate perspectives fosters the reflective process, permitting practitioners to learn from their experiences. Resolving a practice dilemma is central to the reflective process—in this case, realizing the importance of learning why the partner is resistant (the short-term benefit). Reflective practitioners also want to understand why this situation, one that was common enough, it became such a struggle to help the reluctant partner (the lasting benefit). "The moment we start reflecting upon a situation, we naturally begin to raise questions on 'how that happened?,' 'Why it happened that way?,' 'Could it be different?'" (Zalipour 2015, 6).

I have not failed. I've just found 10,000 ways that won't work. Thomas A. Edison

> Tell a man there are three hundred billion stars in the universe, and he'll believe you. Tell him a bench has wet paint on it, and he'll have to touch it to be sure.
> —Anonymous

Mindfulness Meditation

Having roots in Eastern meditation practices, mindfulness meditation allows us to quiet our minds. In doing so, it creates an experience of stillness, calm, and concentration, enabling us to pay attention to the moment, detach from self-judgment, and observe one's own and the parties' physical sensations, thoughts, and emotions with "kindly curiosity." By practicing mindfulness meditation, practitioners are better able to remain calm in the face of discord and ambiguity, act with purpose, pay nonjudgmental attention to the participants' behaviors and interactions, set aside assumptions, and listen with curiosity and compassion (Suzuki 1970; Riskin 2002).

For reflective practitioners: Being calm, remaining attentive, listening with care, accepting ambiguity, and withholding judgment are crucial attitudes for conflict resolution practitioners—and are among the attributes of a reflective practitioner. Realizing this mental state through mindfulness meditation enhances opportunities for self-reflection in the moment (reflection-in-action). A calm and focused mind is a helpful antecedent to reflective practice. "The Reflective Practitioner continually engages in the humble process of revising and reinterpreting her understandings and strategies in accordance with the new situations and experiences that she encounters in her practice" (Buchanan 1994, 1035).

To understand the reflective practitioner's response to the partner's puzzling behavior, let's imagine a Reflective Debrief® conversation using the principles and methods of reflective practice between the practitioner and a "debriefer." (I will further explain "debriefer" in later chapters.)

Mediator: I'm struggling with this stubborn party who is incapable of accepting an offer that meets his goals. I've tried everything I know to help him. I carefully reviewed the proposal, pointing out the benefits to him, even reminding him of the consequences of inaction. He didn't budge.

Debriefer: What do you make of this behavior?

Mediator: I don't know. I asked the parties to take a week to review the proposal, then we'll meet again. I figured that he might be able to think more clearly without time pressure.

Debriefer: Are you assuming that time to think is the answer to his struggle to accept the proposal?

Mediator: Yes, of course. He needs to step away from the mediation and the stress of dealing with his partner.

Debriefer: How do you know this is what he needs?

Mediator: I assume that would help because I tried everything I could think of.

Debriefer: If the explanation for his reluctance is different from what you assumed, would you still recommend a week's delay?

Mediator: Maybe, but not necessarily. If there was another explanation for being stubborn, I would try to come up with a different approach.

Debriefer: How could you learn if there is any other explanation? How could you find out whether the behavior could be caused by something other than the stress of being in mediation?

Mediator: Obviously, I could ask. I don't know why I didn't think of that? I was so busy trying to bring the deal together, I didn't think of that. We had been meeting for six hours, and they had made such great progress. I assumed that a bit more pressure from me might be what was needed. When that didn't work, I thought a delay might be helpful to him.

Debriefer: You said you weren't sure why you didn't think of asking about an alternate explanation. Can you think now why you might not have asked? What was going through your mind?

Mediator: Everyone was tired. Plus, I was so intent on helping them create an agreement, iron out misunderstandings, ensure the agreement was responsive to goals, then

	persuade them that they had found a nearly ideal solution. I just didn't think about anything else.
Debriefer:	Take a minute and think about what you've just said. Is there anything there that helps you?
Mediator:	The deal—a settlement that met their objectives—is central to my work. I was so focused on getting it done, and I was working so hard to help them, it was easy to assume that I could use logic and persuasion to bring the partner to sign the agreement. I didn't consider any other explanation for his hesitation. I was hurrying to finalize the deal and his behavior was holding us back.
Debriefer:	What lessons do you take away from this experience and our conversation?
Mediator:	First, check my assumptions. Second, be aware when I am working harder to achieve a result than the parties. Third, remember that I can encourage and support their efforts, but I'm not responsible for their decisions.

Concluding this section and moving to the definition of reflective practice, I want to use the chart below to point out key distinctions between reflective practice and methods referred to as "reflection." Because their objectives are broadly similar, I combined several methods into a single category that I labeled "reflection." Using the hypothetical mediation of a partnership dissolution, I explained that reflective practice is a distinct learning process, differing from other valued and commonly used methods in both philosophy and procedures. Those differences are reflected in the table below.

Reflective Practice	Reflection
Analytical—Why?	Descriptive—What?
Subjective	Objective
Focus on practice dilemma	Free-flowing and wide-ranging
Structured and systematic	Informal and casual
Use of critical analysis	Focus on events and actions
Learn from experience	Rely on trial and error
Understanding the rationale	Identify what worked and didn't

I merged the several methods of reflective activities into the single category of "reflection" because they share many characteristics. These are largely unstructured processes, informal in nature, covering a wide range of events within a conflict engagement and involving an objective examination of pertinent facts and experiences. There are two principal goals of "reflection": (1) When consulting colleagues, we seek advice and recommendations. (2) In private "reflection," we look for answers to three questions: What did I do well? What didn't go well? What could I have done differently? In reflective activities, the practitioner places herself in the role of an observer, seldom considering their aspirations, motivations, frustrations, and reactions. This objective point of view is distinctly different from the way practitioners look at and describe the actions, motives, needs, emotions, and impulses of the parties. It's as if they are detached from the events, clinically examining the moving elements, like pieces on a chess board, identifying which moves either advanced their position (succeeded) or created problems (failed). The goal of these forms of reflection is to locate the techniques and strategies that succeeded or those that feel short. These are outcome-based methods seeking an answer to the immediate practice dilemma without considering why the puzzling moment occurred. The practitioner is searching for concrete, straightforward responses to the dilemma, such as "You did the right thing," "You should have asked the partner to explain his hesitation," or "You should have pressed him to accept the proposal." So, you might ask, what's wrong with giving that advice?

Here's the problem with seeking solutions to puzzling practice moments without questioning your assumption that the party's hesitancy was the result of being in a pressured situation. If you conclude that you were right to postpone the mediation or if you receive this advice from a colleague, does it necessarily follow that when a client is timid and indecisive, you will suggest an adjournment? Further, what would you conclude if your proposed adjournment is rejected or fails to induce the parties to agree? Will you then infer that an adjournment is not a universal response to a party's hesitance? And if an adjournment succeeds in a subsequent situation, does that positive experience suggest that you have found a strategy you can use repeatedly? In the end, what have you learned from the experience of the reticent party that you can apply in other similar circumstances?

> The road to success is always under construction. Lily Tomlin

Advice, being limited to the set of unique circumstances, does not offer learning that can advance our progress along the spiral of professional evolution and growth. What if I told you it's possible to find an answer to immediate practice dilemmas as well as to develop your knowledge and skills by providing lessons that would improve the quality of your mediation practice? Reflective practice is a method that produces both practical and useful answers to puzzling practice situations while also building our capacity to work more capably and effectively. That's a bold assertion. So how can that happen?

Reflective practice is a purposeful process of critical self-examination having the central objective of learning from and through experience. Like "reflection," it begins with a confounding, curious, and surprising practice situation. The mediator seeks to understand how the situation arose, examining her actions, assumptions, and reactions as well as considering the actions, motivations, and needs of the parties. Differences between reflective practice and "reflection" are apparent in the hypothetical Reflective Debrief®. The mediator places herself within the story, acknowledging that she is influencing and is influenced by the actions of the parties. She wonders why the puzzling moment occurred: "What could explain the partner's reluctance?" "What might be motivating her; what is she responding to from the other partner and from me?" The debriefer structures the Reflective Debrief® in response to the question posed by the mediator, relying almost exclusively on questions to elicit ideas and insights from the mediator. Motivating this approach is the commitment to the principle that self-exploration by a mediator yields self-discovery. By uncovering the answer for herself, the mediator (like the young girl on the plane) arrives at a practical and suitable answer. At the same time, understanding why the dilemma arose increases her ability to identify, assess, and respond to similar practice challenges. Reflective Debrief® promotes learning from and through our experiences—relying on a structured process (use of questions) and guided by the belief that lasting learning occurs when we discover our own answers. For all of us, addressing puzzling and unsettling situations is crucial. However, if we want more than a one-off solution, if we aspire to professional growth and evolution, and if we want to experience the enduring value of learning, then reflective practice is the path to choose:

> *In my experience facilitating resolution of conflicts in spiritual and other organizations, I am most successful in these interactions to the degree that I can see myself through the eyes of the others in the room. This "look through others' eyes" guides me to find ways of speaking that the participants can hear, so the process can move forward effectively. When I encounter blocks and difficulties, inevitable in this work, and seek help from my peers, the most effective help generally comes in the form of questions, not advice. Advice, as one of my teachers said, closes off further exploration of the issue, whereas a question invites me to explore further how I acted on the spot, seeing something of my own self "as others see us" and how that self*

may have affected the participants. This in turn opens new possibilities for the next steps in that process—as well as for future matters. For me, this approach is the essence of Reflective Practice. —Tom Rothschild

Further Defining Reflective Practice

The Reflective Practitioner (1983) was the inspiration for my lasting interest in and study of reflective practice and its application to conflict resolution practitioners. In this and other writings, Schön (1987; Argyris and Schön 1974) presents an argument for developing professional competence by learning from and through experience. He asserts that learning from reflection occurs when

> the practitioner allows himself to experience surprise, puzzlement, or confusion in a situation which he finds uncertain or unique. He reflects on the phenomenon before him, and on the prior understandings which have been implicit in his behavior. He carries out an experiment which serves to generate both a new understanding of the phenomenon and a change in the situation. (Schön 1983, 68)

Learning from and through experience begins with surprise and uncertainty and is attained through purposeful and critical reflection—self-guided or with colleagues. In our imaginary partnership mediation, the mediator, puzzled by the partner's unexpected and frustrating resistance to accept the proposal, suggests a week's postponement. Imagine that when they reconvene, the partner agrees to a settlement. Would the mediator possibly conclude that whenever a party expresses indecision or reluctance, a pause is likely to yield certainty and confidence? And would the mediator then employ the same strategy in other, similar situations—always? Only under certain circumstances? And what are those circumstances? Now imagine that the partner remained reticent. What might the mediator conclude? Without exploring possible explanations for the party's surprising behavior, how is it possible for the mediator to identify a relevant and useful strategy or technique? In addition, what criteria would help the mediator evaluate and learn why an intervention succeeded or was off the mark?

I experienced this confusion and uncertainty following the conference role-play experience. I had used techniques described by the workshop presenters and executed them correctly, skillfully, and with surprisingly exceptional results. What did I learn from the role-play that I could successfully integrate into my mediation practice? Unfortunately, very little. By chance, I applied a technique among the Ericksonian approaches presented that appealed to me, and it worked. If you had interviewed me following the demonstration and asked me to explain the choices I made, I would have looked at you searchingly, shrugged my shoulders, and replied, "I don't know. It just seemed the right thing to do." So did that experience provide tools I could use in my practice? Did I advance along the spiral of professional development? Not at all—except, of course, that by thoroughly confusing and unsettling me, I set out on a path of exploration that led me to reflective practice.

Now, thinking of the mediator who was frustrated by the partner's reticence or considering my inexplicable success, is it possible for each of us to benefit from our puzzlement? How could we translate our experiences into further professional growth and evolution? As Schön proposes, learning begins when we become aware of a situation that appears inconsistent with our implicit and commonly held assumptions of practice. In the heat of an interaction, we may overlook the inconsistency, believing it to be a one-off or unimportant event. Both the mediator and I were aware of the inconsistencies; we realized that something different and unexpected was happening. The partner's behavior was at odds with a reasonable assumption that parties come to mediation because they want to end their dispute. In the role-play, my assumption was that positive responses to my interventions were the parties' signal to continue that approach. Neither of us, however, understood the reason for the parties' behaviors (nor did either of us seek an explanation). The mediator acted as if his assumption was universally applicable. As a result, he attributed the party's hesitancy to confusion or intransigence, never considering that there might be alternate explanations. Similarly, I took the parties' positive responses to my interventions as an indication that I was being helpful and looked no further for an explanation.

One of the objectives of reflective practice is to assess the usefulness of assumptions that guide professional practice. Linda Finlay (2008) observes,

> Some consensus has been achieved amid the profusion of definitions. . . . In general, reflective practice is understood as the process of learning through and from experience towards gaining new insights of self and/or practice. This often involves examining assumptions of everyday practice. It also tends to involve the individual practitioner in being self-aware and critically evaluating their own responses to practice situations. The point is to recapture practice experiences and mull them over critically in order to gain new understandings and so improve future practice. This is understood as part of the process of life-long learning. (1, citations omitted)

Also commenting on the importance of examining assumptions, Arezou Zalipour (2015) explains how reflective practice benefits classroom teachers:

> Critically reflective teaching occurs when teachers "identify and scrutinize the assumptions that undergird" their teaching and the way they work as teachers. The questions that arise here are: How to become aware of such assumptions? Are we aware of our own conceptions of teaching? Reflective practice assists teachers to confront inconsistencies between their thinking and their practice, and promote a conceptual change in teachers' views about teaching. Teachers' pedagogical thinking informs their decision-making and behaviours in teaching situations. (4, citations omitted)

Examining assumptions is a key difference between reflective practice and "reflection" methods. None of the "reflective" approaches involves an exploration of the practitioner's theories or beliefs—the ideas that influence why we do what we do. Assumptions are grounded in beliefs, attitudes, theories, and values that shape our perception of experience and influence our responses. Recall the question that the father asked her young girl: "Why do you think that's happening?" With this simple question, she was encouraged to explore her own strategies (assumptions) as well as a possible explanation for the tie games. In chapter 4, we will look more deeply at the nature of theory and its usefulness and application for practitioners.

I went to a bookstore and asked the saleswoman, "Where's the self-help section?" She said if she told me, it would defeat the purpose. George Carlin

For now, recall the case of the hesitant client and the puzzled mediator. Compare the results when asking for advice from colleagues with the results of a Reflective Debrief®. A colleague's advice may be reasonable and credible; there is even a chance the suggestions might effectively address the mediator's dilemma. Nevertheless, the advice is based on the colleague's unique "assumptions of everyday practice," which in turn are shaped by countless factors, such as their practice experiences, their approach to mediation, and their beliefs about the role and responsibilities of mediator. I have yet to hear a colleague preface offers of advice with, "Let me explain my reason for offering this advice." This is the consequence of acting on another's advice. If we don't understand the rationale for the recommendation, how can we judge for ourselves whether the advice is relevant to the situation and likely to be useful? If we act on this advice and the party remains reticent, we are still in the dark about the reason for his hesitation, and there is no agreement. Even if the advice proves helpful and the reluctant party signs an agreement, what have we gained? The parties may have achieved a successful outcome, but what have we learned that will continue the spiral evolution and growth of our practice?

Recall the imaginary Reflective Debrief® through which the mediator discovered the source of this practice dilemma, namely, two operating assumptions: (1) that people in mediation want to find solutions and (2) that by having essential data and applying objective reasoning, people will make sound decisions. The mediator became aware that relying on these assumptions to interpret the partner's behavior narrowed his choice of strategy and tactic. This insight then leads to the mediator's decision to ask the partner to explain the reasoning behind her unwillingness to accept a seemingly ideal proposal. Through Reflective Debrief®, the mediator is learning the importance of identifying and critically examining his assumptions and their influence on his practice choices. Beyond an immediate result—resolving the thorny practice dilemma—the mediator is developing the capacity to critically reflect on his practice. That process yields additional insights about his practice, insights that generate additional techniques and strategies for addressing surprising practice situations. The spiral of learning continues, expanding in an unending growth and evolution of his practice.

I understand that for many, this notion of lasting learning could seem theoretical, nebulous, and lacking a distinct, real-world value. The quick fix of a colleague's straightforward advice—"Here's what you should do"—is uncomplicated, candid, and simple to implement. Acting on that advice may cleanly and effectively resolve the specific practice dilemma. As far as that goes, it certainly seems practical and effective. Advice and a successful outcome are, however, ephemeral and limited to a single event. It might seem ironic to assert this, but the enduring lessons produced by reflective practice—lessons that involve self-exploration and self-discovery—reliably have greater practical value than the one-off usefulness of a colleague's advice. Why? It's the same reason that the principle of self-determination is central to conflict resolution practice—decisions made by those directly affected, freely, without influence and with adequate information, are likely to be durable, relevant, and appropriate. An added benefit to reflective practice is that with each learning experience, we not only solve a puzzling practice dilemma but are also forming a sort of muscle memory, a set of tools readily and continually available to us. When we understand not just what to do but why, when we understand how our assumptions can both strengthen and inhibit our practice choices, then that learning is available to help us unravel any future puzzling moments. That is how our spiral of professional development continues to grow and evolve. We will talk more about the notion of building muscle memory and its day-to-day, real-world implications.

Another story about children and how they learn illustrates the real-world benefits of reflective practice. Schön (1983) describes an experiment involving children and wooden blocks. Groups of children were asked to balance wooden blocks on a metal bar and then add as many as possible on top of them. The children were presented with two types of blocks. They looked identical, but one set consisted of typical wooden cubes, and the other blocks were weighted at one end. The children became frustrated when the weighted blocks behaved differently. Expecting the blocks to have the same properties, they tried balancing them at their physical center. When that strategy was unsuccessful, they shifted their approach. They placed the blocks according to their center of gravity.

The children initially approached their tasks with two assumptions: (1) wooden blocks are all the same, and (2) to balance them, use the physical center as a guide. When the children used the weighted blocks, the children were initially surprised and then frustrated that they couldn't build towers to the same height. They then became curious, realizing that their original assumptions about the properties of wooden blocks were inconsistent with the weighted blocks. To build a tall tower, they needed to alter their assumptions—their theory. They engaged in critical self-reflection. First, because they had successfully constructed tall towers of blocks, they concluded that the unstable and tottering structures were probably not caused by a lack of skill. They wondered what could possibly explain the wobbly towers. Gradually, as they held them and felt the physical differences in the second set of blocks, the recognition dawned on them: not all blocks are the same. To succeed, they had to relinquish their old assumptions and accept the idea that not all blocks that look the same are the same. With these new assumptions, the children became more adept at building towers as they learned to balance each block by finding its center of gravity.

Decisions in sports coaching are unlike the mediation practice example where reflection occurred retrospectively and unlike the tic-tac-toe game where the young girl could pause and reflect before making her move. Sports coaching involves the dynamic and shifting action of athletic competition requiring automatic, nearly instantaneous responses. Sports coaches must respond to rapidly changing circumstances affecting numerous participants, each having distinct personalities, abilities, shortcomings, motivations, and learning styles. Successful coaches adapt their thinking and action in response to the unpredictable events of competition to help athletes gain new skills and become adept at dealing with evolving performance challenges. Examining how reflective practice can bring about improved sports coaching, Laura Farres (2004) notes,

> Reflection is at the heart of the learning process. It is a necessary component in learning to regulate one's thoughts, feelings, and actions. Reflection links experience and knowledge by providing an opportunity to explore areas of concern in a critical way and to make adjustments based on these reflections. This exploration enhances learning and promotes coaches' abilities to identify and respond to cues within the environment. (10)

Reading this, you may think, "I can understand how reflective practice might be helpful if I have enough time to reflect and then act. But how can it possibly work in the heat of the moment?"

In response, I generally offer two answers. First, when you learned to ride a bicycle, drive a car, play an instrument, or use a tool, you were awkward, tentative, hyperaware of every action, and alert to every self-correcting cue. Your attention was riveted on the essential elements—and on the hoped-for outcome. After experience (and perhaps coaching), consider how differently you perform the same functions. You get a "feel" for the tasks and the process. As a result, you are less self-conscious, less tentative, more assured, and capable of effectively completing a variety of integrated tasks.

Find a way to learn something from every disappointment. Laurie Nadel

Now consider conflict resolution practice. We are also faced with rapidly changing circumstances involving multiple participants, each with their own needs, interests, personalities, and communication styles. Undoubtedly and understandably, your actions at first were hesitant, awkward, clumsy, and labored. Yet with several years' experience, you have become more comfortable in the role, responding effortlessly and decisively, rapidly and continually making and executing a succession of instantaneous reactions and decisions. You don't always have time to pause, reflect, and then act. So how does it happen that we are capable of reacting quickly and reliably? One answer is that we learn a series of behaviors, shaped by our experiences, that we incorporate into schema, basically practice patterns (Peleg-Baker and Lang 2022). Through repeated experience, we develop a routine set of responses so that when a certain behavior occurs, we respond automatically. We develop a sort of muscle memory that allows us to identify, assess, and respond in the blink of an eye. In fact, *Blink* is the title of Malcolm Gladwell's (2005) book in which he explores the phenomena of instantaneous recognition and reaction:

> Perhaps the most common—and the most important—forms of rapid cognition are the judgments we make and the impressions we form of other people. Every waking minute that we are in the presence of someone, we come up with a constant stream of predictions and inferences about what that person is thinking and feeling. . . . This practice of inferring the motivations and intentions of others is classic thin-slicing. It is picking up on subtle, fleeting cues in order to read someone's mind . . . and there is almost no other impulse so basic and so automatic and at which most of the time, we so effortlessly excel. (194–95)

As we will explore further in chapter 6, the process of learning through and from experience generated by reflective practice helps us build, adjust, and improve our practice routines.

Why Should Practitioners Care about Reflective Practice?

Since first reading *The Reflective Practitioner*, I have continually considered whether and how the principles and methods of reflective practice could make a difference in my conflict practice. Even after more than thirty years of study, teaching, and writing about reflective practice, I remain curious and ask myself, Why is reflective practice important? What can practitioners gain from systematic and structures introspection and self-assessment? Is there a risk that the reflective process is simply an end unto itself or, worse, leads to paralysis-in-action?

In the stories I have told in this chapter, each person was surprised by something that did not readily fit the patterns or routines they had come to expect. The young girl assumed that games involve winning and losing and was frustrated when so many ended in a draw. The mediator learned (1) that striking a fair deal may not be the only goal of parties and (2) that reticence may not be evidence of bad faith. Children attempting to stack wooden blocks discovered that not all blocks that look alike are alike. By engaging in a reflective process, each of the participants learned "to confront inconsistencies between their thinking and their practice" (Zalipour 2015).

As practitioners, we become proficient in the use of a set of skills—our tool kit. We learn to identify when each tool can be employed most effectively. We develop practice routines that provide a measure of consistency and confidence. If every professional experience would only follow a predictable path, we could reliably apply those tools successfully. But human behavior is unpredictable. Every situation is unique. Every participant sees the world differently and acts in a distinctive manner. There is a danger that if we follow practice routines unconsciously and instinctively without considering the unpredictable nature of human interactions, we risk neglecting or discounting characteristics and behaviors that are novel or inconsistent with our assumptions.

To be competent in responding to these surprising events in our practices, we must be able to adapt our thinking so that we can use our knowledge and skills in situations that don't match our assumptions. As the children and the mediator learned, it's not possible to bend circumstances to fit our assumptions. Reflective practice provides a means for learning to identify, understand, and adapt to these surprising situations.

The practical value of reflective practice is expressed in the following observation:

> It provides early interventionists with an opportunity to explore a range of responses that they experience in their work, from conceptual difficulties about intervention to emotional reactions to families. Through this exploration, early interventionists have an opportunity for open dialogue and a safe place to express and explore their feelings and those of the children and the families. Through this exploration, it's possible to gain insight and perspective that help shape interactions and interventions with families and children. (Gatti, Watson, and Siegel 2011, 34)

Like these interventionists, conflict resolution practitioners may experience tunnel vision that comes from focusing intently on the emotional and practical needs and concerns of their clients and on the delivery of competent professional services. The concentration required is intense. Decisions must be made quickly and in response to rapidly changing behaviors and circumstances.

Liz Griffiths (2004), writing about the rewards of reflective practice, affirms that the underlying goal is "transforming practice":

> An expert professional should be able to create different possibilities as the result of reflecting on what could be routine practice, an unexpected outcome or even some uncertainty. By drawing such experiences together, a meaningful pattern may emerge as a means of transforming practice. (2)

Griffiths further notes—with reference to Christopher Johns, who has written extensively about the application of reflective practice methods in nursing—that reflection is "a window through which the practitioner can view experiences, working toward the resolution of contradictions between what may be desirable and what is realistic in actual practice" (2).

Is there a downside to engaging in reflective practice? Is there a risk that reflective practice may simply lead to paralysis-in-action? Reflective practice has a distinct and practical objective—learning through and from experience to become more competent. We engage in self-reflection as a means of (1) resolving "inconsistencies" between our operating assumptions and the unpredictable realities of practice (Zalipour 2015) and (2) to "gain insight and perspective that help shape interactions and interventions" (Gatti et al. 2011). Reflective practitioners are committed to using analysis and self-assessment as a tool to gain knowledge and improve their practice skills. Having a well-defined goal is the reflective practitioner's safeguard against the risk of unending contemplation.

> *When your mother asks, "Do you want a piece of advice?" It is a mere formality.*
> *It doesn't matter if you answer yes or no. You're going to get it anyway.*
> Erma Bombeck

Mindset of a Reflective Practitioner

Becoming a reflective practitioner does not require specialized knowledge or techniques. Trained and skilled practitioners, or even those with limited experience, have the tools needed to become reflective practitioners—although these tools need to be reoriented toward different objectives. Reflective practice is not its own style of mediation; it is equally available to practitioners who consider themselves facilitative or directive, work within the transformative framework, or adopt an eclectic approach to their practices. Conflict coaches, mediators, facilitators, ombuds, and other conflict resolution practitioners can benefit equally by adopting the methods of reflective practice. There is a single and essential requirement that characterizes and underpins the approach of reflective practitioners, and that is mindset: how we think about our practice and how we become adept, resilient, and resourceful. The reflective practice mindset has three fundamental qualities:

- Willingness to learn from experience
- Commitment to lifelong learning
- Appreciation of the role of theory in shaping practice choices

As you read the next chapter, you will readily recognize the obvious overlap between these qualities and the attributes of a reflective practitioner:

> *I work as a facilitator, mediator, and coach and continually seek to learn and experiment with new concepts and ideas across my practice. Being part of a reflective practice groups means that I learn from the experience, challenges, and reflection of others, also that I am supported to reflect on my own practice and challenges drawing on the multiple different lenses and questioning of those in our group. I am supported and challenged to never get too comfortable in my practice and to always temper my belief that I have reached a point of self-knowledge and self-awareness. —Dolores Geary*

Willingness to Learn from Experience

We often hear the adage "practice makes perfect." Golfers practice their swing with uncompromising dedication, musicians practice a piece for hours, and dancers rehearse a routine dozens of times before a performance. Shelves of books espouse this maxim. By now, we are familiar with the so-called ten-thousand-hour rule, made widespread by Malcom Gladwell in his book *Outliers*—that to achieve mastery in any endeavor requires at least that amount of practice. That's a lot of time at the practice range for golfers, in the studio for dancers, in the cockpit for pilots, and in the meeting room for mediators. I wonder whether that amount of practice is the key to mastery. Just put in the hours (or years), and you'll master your subject.

The wide circulation and general acceptance of the ten-thousand-hours theory has led to a regrettably simplistic belief about the path to excellence—a myth that unfortunately equates mastery with experience. If you attempt ten thousand free throws, how likely is it that you will become an expert shooter? Michael Jordan debunks the notion that practice alone is sufficient. "You can practice shooting eight hours a day, but if your technique is wrong, then all you become is very good at shooting the wrong way."

Musicians Macklemore and Ryan Lewis wrote the song "Ten Thousand Hours" in 2012: "The greats weren't great because at birth they could paint. The greats were great 'cause they paint a lot."

Without doubt, regular practice is an essential element in achieving excellence in practice. However, the widely circulated and generally accepted notion about ten thousand hours to achieve mastery has led to a mindless and regrettably simplistic belief about the path to excellence. Should we believe that if we practice the cello for ten thousand hours, we will play brilliantly? Not if we follow the example of venerable cellist Pablo Casals, who, when asked why at age ninety he continues to practice, answered, "Because I think I'm making progress."

Conflict resolution practitioners repeatedly conflate experience with competence. As evidence of their supposed expertise, they boast of the number of cases they have handled; some proudly claim (and advertise) they have conducted "thousands" of mediations. Some point to their "success rate," the number of disputes that resulted in an agreement. Has their experience led to greater competence? Perhaps in some instances. My question is, have they done a thousand mediations or one mediation a thousand times?

We all know practitioners who continue to rely on the practice routines they adopted long ago. They may be successful—if measured in settlement rates, referrals, and other indices of recognition. They may have surpassed the ballyhooed figure of ten thousand hours. But are they more accomplished or simply more experienced?

> People believe practice makes perfect, but it doesn't. If you're making a tremendous amount of mistakes, all you're doing is deeply ingraining the same mistakes. —Jillian Michaels

If practice alone does not ensure excellence, what is required? Practice without a commitment to learning will never produce mastery. Doing the same thing over and over may produce a sense of accomplishment and perhaps a high degree of self-regard. Practice, enhanced through critical reflection and a commitment to learning, will advance us along the spiral of professional growth and evolution. Practice, without learning from experience, is incomplete for four reasons:

1. Repetition tends to produce mechanical responses. Duplicating previous actions without self-assessment generally leads to operating on autopilot. The result is a rut—repeatedly using the same tools and techniques without consideration for the unique circumstances of the parties, their dispute, and their objectives.

   When we develop a pattern of behavior that works in certain situations, we will tend to repeat it until it becomes automatic. We can't describe the processes involved because we are not aware of what is going on. It is only when something goes wrong or something unexpected happens that we may stop and think about what we did and what we could or should have done in the situation (Maughan 1996, 76).

2. Without a commitment to learning through experience, there is no opportunity for self-correction and improvement. We do the same thing over and over, disregarding or minimizing differences.

   Mindfulness is a state of conscious awareness in which the individual is implicitly aware of the context and content of information. It is a state of openness to novelty in which the individual actively constructs categories and distinctions. In contrast, mindlessness is a state of mind characterized by an overreliance on categories and distinctions drawn in the past and in which the individual is context dependent and, as such, is oblivious to novel (or simply alternative) aspects of the situation (Langer 1992, 289).

3. A practitioner who equates excellence with experience is likely to minimize or overlook mistakes and thereby ignores opportunities to learn from (and correct) those practice errors.

   The outcomes of reflection may include a new way of doing something, the clarification of an issue, the development of a skill, or the resolution of a problem. A new cognitive map may emerge, or a new set of ideas may be identified. The changes may be

quite small, or they may be large. They could involve the development of perspectives on experience or changes in behavior (Boud, Keogh, and Walker 1985, 34).
4. Practitioners who repeat the same behaviors mindlessly and without reflection are at risk of unproven habits becoming permanently etched into their practice routines.

    The reflective practitioner continually engages the humble process of revising and reinterpreting her understandings and strategies in accordance with the new situations and experiences that she encounters in her practice (Buchanan 1994, 1035).

Commitment to Lifelong Learning

Researching *The Making of a Mediator* (Lang and Taylor 2000), I looked for examples of excellence outside the field of conflict resolution to understand how professionals achieve mastery. I interviewed an industrial engineer employed by a company that produces chemicals for the leather industry. I asked, "Are leather makers who are widely recognized as experts—true geniuses?" He said that, indeed, there were experts and offered this explanation for their exceptional abilities:

> When you see them, in their shops or at professional gatherings, they always have a small piece of leather in their hands. You can watch them rub the leather with their thumb and index finger. Feeling the texture of the leather they can identify the type of hide and the methods and chemicals used to produce the leather. They are curious. They want to learn from what others have produced. They are trying to find the perfect methods and materials to create a superb product.

I asked my dental hygienist—when there were no instruments in my mouth—about the difference between a capable hygienist and one who is exceptional. I wasn't surprised by her initial response: "experience," she said. Two minutes later, she added,

> I am a member of a professional education and support group. We meet; we share ideas and information; we discuss difficult cases. We listen to presentations on new techniques and equipment. I really learn a lot at those meetings. Plus, we have dinner and enjoy being together.

At my recent cleaning appointment, while revising this book, she confirmed that the support group still meets regularly.

In an article in the *Sarasota Herald Tribune* on April 18, 2018, Rebecca Abrahamson, an award-winning teacher, describes the process of achieving excellence in the classroom:

> Teaching is a profession that requires grueling work, persistent self-evaluation, and reflection. I am constantly working to identify my weaknesses and acquire the necessary resources to strengthen them. These are the traits that I continually strive to model for my students, hoping my leadership will foster the same characteristics.

There are many types of professional development programs for conflict resolution practitioners—more so as practitioners and trainers become adept at the use of videoconferencing platforms in the years since COVID-19 forced us into online work. Training courses, seminars, and other educational programs increase our knowledge, enhance and refine existing skills, introduce new techniques, and describe novel and remarkable approaches to common practice problems. Reading journal articles, blogs, and books adds to our body of knowledge. Reflective practitioners are voracious learners committed to learning. They radiate an attitude of curiosity and a desire for self-improvement. Reflective practitioners do not merely acquire knowledge or information—they are intent on synthesizing and integrating what they learn.

Appreciation of the Connection between Theory and Practice

In unseen and subtle yet significant and profound ways, theory shapes our view of the world, influences the meaning we assign to events and behaviors, and influences the choices we make and the actions that follow. We make decisions throughout the day, all of which are, to some degree, affected by our beliefs, values, and principles—our theories. For example, deciding what we eat is motivated by our theories of nutrition and health. We choose educational programs (for ourselves and our children) relying on a set of values and beliefs. We employ strategies and investment theories to make financial decisions. Theory even influences ordinary activities, such as playing tic-tac-toe. Theory tends to operate in the background. Action is in the foreground. We think about the decisions we make and the actions we take. For the most part, we aren't conscious about the beliefs that influence these actions. The same is true for professional decisions. If asked about a practice experience, practitioners are far more likely to describe what occurred than to explain the rationale for their actions. They focus on who, what, where, when, and how; they overlook why—the beliefs that shaped their choices. In my experience, this occurs because practitioners are unaware of the underlying theory that motivated their behavior and are thus unable to draw a line between what they think about a situation and how those thoughts influence their actions. In our article, Tzofnat Peleg-Baker and I (2022) refer to studies of mediators that demonstrated the common phenomenon of saying one thing (in pre-mediation interviews) and behaving differently during the mediation simulation. Argyris and Schön (1974) refer to this as the difference between espoused theory (what we say we do) and theory-in-action (what we actually do).

Conflict resolution practice is guided by and relies on (1) a body of beliefs, theories, and assumptions that influence our understanding of the conflict situation; (2) our assessment of the participants' needs, interests, and motivations; and (3) our interpretation of our job description—our role and responsibility.

> Reflective action is bound up with persistent and careful consideration of practice in the light of knowledge and beliefs, showing attitudes of open-mindedness, responsibility, and whole-heartedness. (Hatton and Smith 1995, 34)

Reflective practitioners purposefully use theory to guide their actions. They are aware of their beliefs and purposefully apply them to practice decisions. In this way, their actions reflect the transformation of what is unseeable (theory) into tangible and practical action. As Goethe observed, "To act is hard. But the hardest thing . . . is to act in accordance with your thinking."

Conclusion

This chapter introduced and defined reflective practice, distinguished this approach from other seemingly similar methods, and explained the tangible and practical value of reflective practice and the immediate and long-term benefits of becoming a reflective practitioner. In the next chapter, I will expand the definition of reflective practice by describing the attributes of a reflective practitioner—the mindset and behaviors, the qualities, of a reflective practitioner.

Exercises

Exercise 2.1: Making Use of Informal Discussions of Practice Incidents

The next time you're at a professional meeting talking with a group of colleagues about interesting or puzzling situations, beverage in one hand while balancing a plate of munchies in the other, try this approach. Ask your colleagues these questions:

> I'm curious. Why was this case so fascinating or frustrating?
> What was happening, and how did that influence your approach?
> Did seeking to understand the reasons behind their practice choices transform the conversation from sharing stories to learning how to be more effective?

Exercise 2.2: Using Questions Rather Than Offering Advice

If a colleague were dealing with a frustrating practice situation, how would you respond? Would you be more likely to offer suggestions, or could you imagine yourself, like the father, using questions to prompt the colleague to discover solutions for herself?

Exercise 2.3: Shifting from Storytelling to Learning

Conversations with colleagues can become more than brainstorming a list of possible intervention strategies or arguing which is better. When a colleague asserts, "That's a situation where I always separate the parties," ask, "What told you that convening private meetings was the best approach?"

Exercise 2.4: Mindfulness Meditation

If you have never tried mindfulness meditation, if you assume that it will be too difficult to master, or if you don't think you could find the time, you may gain some of its benefits by trying this approach.

Prior to a session or during a long break, find a quiet, comfortable place to sit. Allow yourself five minutes. Sit quietly. Imagine yourself in the session at your best—thinking clearly, being perceptive and responsive, and maintaining a sense of calm. This is not an opportunity to plan your strategies for addressing the participants and their dispute. The focus is solely on your mindset and how you manage yourself in the session.

Exercise 2.5: Preparing for Mindfulness

When beginning a new conflict resolution intervention, remind yourself to pay attention to discovering "new things":

> The creation of new categories . . . is a mindful activity. Mindlessness sets in when we rely too rigidly on categories and distinctions created in the past (masculine/feminine, old/young, success/failure). Once distinctions are created, they take on a life of their own. (Langer 1989, 11)

If the participant's behavior seems predictable, can you look for and notice anything unexpected or new? Consider whether you are open to alternative explanations for the conflict and for the participants' behavior.

Exercise 2.6: Try This Brief Experiment

- Recall the last professional development program you attended. If it was a skills-oriented session, was there an opportunity for you to practice and receive feedback? What did you learn that you have been able to apply in your practice—successfully and repeatedly?
- Name the title of the last book you read about matters connected to your practice. When did you read this? What can you recall that was of benefit to you and to your practice?
- How frequently do you read professional journals? What was the topic of the last journal article you read? Why did you choose this article? What did you learn?

What do your answers suggest about your curiosity and desire to learn?

Exercise 2.7: From Novice to Proficiency

Think of the time when you learned to ride a bicycle, play a sport, dance, or play a musical instrument. Can you recall those first gawky, faltering, and error-prone moments? Now think of your experience as a proficient bicyclist, athlete, dancer, or musician. How were you able to transcend the unsettling experiences of the novice and become capable and adept?

Exercise 2.8: Success Story

Recall a successful intervention, not the outcome; think of an unexpected or puzzling situation that you responded to successfully. What can you learn from that incident and your response? Are there lessons from this experience that you could apply in other situations?

Exercise 2.9: Advantages and Drawbacks of Reflective Practice

Considering your own conflict practice, how would reflective practice help improve the quality and effectiveness of your work? What would encourage you to adopt reflective practice methods? What might keep you from using reflective practice?

CHAPTER 3

The Attributes of a Reflective Practitioner

We are not going in circles, we are going upwards. The path is a spiral; we have already climbed many steps. —Hermann Hesse

Joyce is a phlebotomist. I love that word. When I was ten or eleven, an older cousin who was bound for medical school would show off by tossing around medical terms like "sphygmomanometer," "cardiopulmonary," and "phlebotomy." I was impressed with his knowledge; even more, I delighted in the resonance and rhythms of these words, repeating them, out loud, just to enjoy the sound of the words.

Joyce is the epitome of excellence—in attitude and skill. I interviewed her as part of a continuing exploration of excellence in practice. We sat together during her lunch break on a bench outside the medical facility in Sarasota where she works. This is her story.

Joyce was not destined to be a phlebotomist. In fact, whenever her children were injured and bleeding, she immediately called her husband or reached out to a neighbor who was a nurse. She recoiled at the sight of blood. Just as necessity can be the mother of invention, it can also lead us in paths we had never envisioned. That happened to Joyce.

Fate or, as Joyce would affirm, God led her to enroll in a training course to become a phlebotomist. Although initially resistant to the idea of being around blood, she gratefully accepted the opportunity, one in which she could live her faith through service.

Joyce is warm, kindhearted, attentive, meticulous, and skilled. The driving forces of faith and service guide her life. If you ask her how she's doing, she is certain to reply, "I am blessed and highly favored."

She is patient with patients who may be frightened of needles, people who fear what the blood analysis might reveal, or someone who is angry and scared about a recent diagnosis. She is adept at finding a vein, even in the most difficult circumstances. She acts confidently, efficiently, and with care.

"How did this come about?" I asked. "What distinguishes you from others who are good but not excellent?" She smiled warmly and replied, "God gives me what I need. I know He is there with me and will guide my hand."

> When you look at a field of dandelions, you can either see a hundred weeds or a hundred wishes. Anonymous

Joyce has been doing this work for many years. Experience does matter, but there is more. She reveals that the secret to her success is being able to step outside herself and focus on the patient's experience. She is concerned with what they need: a calm, stress-free experience. Joyce is unafraid of making small mistakes, knowing they will occur. She knows she is not perfect. And, with each misstep, she learns and becomes more confident, responsive, and effective. Faith gives Joyce the confidence to put these principles into action.

Joyce exhibits many of the attributes explored in this chapter. She is curious—always willing to learn, including from her mistakes. She is resilient—calm, confident, and secure. She pays attention to each detail of the process and to her patients. She is impeccable in her commitment to her patients and to learning from experience. And, guided by her faith in God, she embodies humility. Joyce reflects both the attitude or mindset and the behaviors associated with the attributes of a reflective practitioner.

James Joyce observed that a person's actions are "the best interpreters of their thoughts." Actions are noticeable—concrete, evident, and visible. Thoughts are conceptual, opaque, and hidden. Thoughts become visible through our actions. When we think about our practices, we naturally emphasize what we do, devoting limited attention, if at all, to the thoughts that shape our actions. Reflective practitioners, as I mentioned in the previous chapter, regard beliefs (theories) as the foundation for action. For reflective practitioners, thought and action blend together and are inseparable.

This chapter considers the intersection of thought and action by examining the attributes of a reflective practitioner—the attitudes and the behaviors that are hallmarks of reflective practitioners. The qualities of a reflective practitioner are expressed in both their way of thinking and their way of acting. Reflective practice is more than the tools required. In fact, as you will discover, nearly all practitioners are familiar with and repeatedly use the skills essential to reflective practice. What distinguishes a reflective practitioner is the integration of those skills with the mindset embodied in the ten attributes.

> Action without thought is empty. Thought without action is blind. —Kwame Nkrumah

The Ten Attributes of a Reflective Practitioner

Exercise curiosity—maintain a boundless and childlike sense of wonder.
Be resilient—remain calm and confident in the face of doubt.
Nurture simplicity—avoid unnecessary complexity; seek the core.
Value ambiguity—do not be bound by limiting assumptions.

Pay attention to detail—exercise the power of noticing what may be new.
Learn ceaselessly—be willing to explore the unknown, even at the risk of failure.
Resist certainty—remain open to new perspectives.
Balance commitment and flexibility—be thoughtful and confident while remaining humble.
Embrace failure as your mentor—actively seek to learn from experience.
Practice humility—acknowledge our uncertainties and welcome opportunities to learn from them.

Each attribute is a distinct quality yet is an integrated and inseparable part of a whole. There are specific behaviors associated with each attribute, and we will explore them individually, identifying their characteristics to understand their function. Similar to looking at someone's face, we may pay attention to one feature—color of eyes, hairstyle, or a dimple—yet our impression of the person results from the combination of these features.

> I think, at a child's birth, if a mother could ask a fairy godmother to endow it with the most useful gift, that gift would be curiosity. Eleanor Roosevelt

Curiosity is the first attribute and humility the last because they are central to each of the others. Like the warp in a loom that is the foundation for the weft (the design of the threads), the other attributes are bound together by curiosity and humility. It would be difficult to imagine the impact exerted by the other attributes without the unifying force of curiosity and humility.

Exercise Curiosity

Curiosity is the pure sense of wonder expressed, almost ceaselessly by young children, in the question, "Why?" Recall a conversation with a child, perhaps five or six years old, and you will understand the beautiful, tireless, and insistent nature of curiosity. Children are voracious learners. What may seem common or conventional to us is extraordinary and new to a child. As a result, they are un-self-conscious and unrepressed, asking a never-ending cascade of questions about whatever fascinates them.

For example, a child may ask a simple question, usually prompted by something they have just seen or read:

Child: Why is a fire truck red?
Adult: Fire trucks need to be visible.
Child: What does visible mean?
Adult: It means that people can easily see them.
Child: Why do they need to see the fire trucks?
Adult: Because when fire trucks are going to a fire, people should get out of their way.
Child: Oh. Do they come in any other colors?
Adult: Yes, some are yellow-green.
Child: Why?

This exchange might continue for ten minutes or longer until the child tires of the topic and shifts to another (Why aren't police cars red?), thinks your answers are silly (There's no such color as yellow-green), or you become worn out.

Children have no filters or limits. They are uninhibited and ravenous learners. Their curiosity is boundless. They are developmentally programmed to seek out and absorb as much information as possible. Children want to understand their world; they are gathering information to learn about and make sense of their environment. Childhood, as John Banville observes, is "a state of constantly recurring astonishment." They relentlessly want to touch, taste, hear, smell, and feel, occasionally with surprising and unpleasant consequences.

What happens to us as we become established professionals? Banville wistfully notes that "the process of growing up is, sadly, a process of turning the mysterious into the mundane." Our curiosity becomes tempered by the obligations of adulthood. We become deliberate and strategic rather than playful and spontaneous.

As adults, there are fewer and fewer unfamiliar ideas and experiences. As professionals, having completed academic courses and professional training programs and having attained a status—licensed or certified—we are assumed to have adequate knowledge and skills to act ethically, creatively, and competently. We are experts. We are presumed to know the answers—and we know many. Yet that sense of certainty, proficiency, and confidence that propels our professional work often inhibits our sense of wonder. As a result—and unsurprisingly—curiosity diminishes dramatically as we age.

> I have no special talents. I am only passionately curious. Albert Einstein

Especially in our professional lives, we self-monitor. By that, I mean that our curiosity, unlike that of a child, is bounded by utilitarian concerns. We seek information because it is significant, relevant, useful, necessary, or consequential. Our curiosity and therefore information we seek are based on timeliness (fits within the context of a conversation), suitability (not likely to embarrass either us or the other person), and appropriateness (not obtuse, insensitive, or tactless). We want to avoid sounding ignorant, fumbling, or confused.

In our conflict work, our curiosity is channeled into the questions that we ask to learn about the participants, experiences that led to their dispute, ideas and proposals for solving the dispute, and the parties' hopes and goals. Information gathering is purposeful, efficient, and practical. Some practitioners contend that asking questions to compile relevant and useful information exemplifies an attitude of curiosity. I disagree.

There is a considerable difference between curiosity and inquiry. The form of the questions may be similar, but the intention is not. The purpose of inquiry is transactional—gathering information to support analysis and problem solving. The process of inquiry is investigative and analytical. Inquiry involves seeking answers to questions such as who, what, where, and when. Inquiry involves the search for truth. As Schön (1983) notes, "Professional activity consists in instrumental problem solving made rigorous by the application of scientific theory and technique" (21). Inquiry is an essential component of every conflict resolution intervention.

Curiosity is an attitude or mind-set as much as a set of behaviors or techniques. It is not necessarily utilitarian, although it might be in certain situations. The objective of curiosity is not to establish facts required for evaluation and decision making. Instead, it is inquisitiveness without a predetermined goal. As in the example of the child who wants to know about the color of fire engines, curiosity is un-self-conscious and uncontrived. The curious mind wants an explanation for how apparently disconnected elements might fit together to provide a more complete picture. Curiosity involves an effort to understand why they are (or should be) connected:

> CQ stands for curiosity quotient and concerns having a hungry mind. People with higher CQ are more inquisitive and open to new experiences. They find novelty exciting. . . . They tend to generate many original ideas and are counter-conformist. . . . Individuals with higher CQ are generally more tolerant of ambiguity. This nuanced, sophisticated, subtle thinking style defines the very essence of complexity. (Chamorro-Premuzic 2014, 3)

A brief practice example illustrates the distinction:

> Eighteen participants in a facilitation that lasted several hours, having resolved various contentious issues, were on the verge of reaching a comprehensive agreement that would successfully address serious and long-standing logistical and communication problems in their workplace. Their next step was to consider a draft proposal for the final and, by their measure, least controversial issue on the agenda. Unexpectedly, the proposal proved to be contentious and divisive. After nearly an hour of passionate debate, the participants were unable to reach consensus. Individually, they were dismayed. As a group, they felt disappointed and discouraged.
>
> As the meeting facilitator, I asked questions such as the following:
>
> Does anyone have a fresh take on the proposal?
> [Silently, they shook their heads.]
> Is there a problem with a specific provision of the proposal or with the language used?
> [They weren't able to pinpoint the problem.]
> Does anyone have an alternative to present?
> [None was offered.]
> Would it make sense to take a fifteen-minute break?
> [No significant interest was expressed.]
>
> I scanned the room. I was puzzled that an ostensibly marginal matter was threatening to upend their progress and leave them unsettled and troubled. My efforts to help them resolve the impasse seemed to reinforce their pessimism. I was curious. How could this happen? Had I overlooked earlier signs of discord that were now emerging? Was the issue as uncomplicated and uncontroversial as they had imagined, or had it been deferred to the end because they feared it would prove impossible to resolve? Could there be a straightforward explanation for the collapse of their negotiations?
>
> Of course, the solution to this apparent impasse rested with them. I thought they might find a path forward if they could regain the optimism and confidence in their ability to find answers. With this in mind, I offered an observation: "This may be the first time many of you have participated in this type of process. Despite initial skepticism, you persisted. How did you manage to come this far and achieve so much? What did it take for you to stay at the table?"
>
> Not everyone responded. Those who spoke acknowledged that they had accomplished more than most had predicted. Everyone was nodding in agreement. They had put off this final issue, confident that it could easily be resolved. Dealing with the contentious issues had depleted their energy and drained their momentum.
>
> Listening to one another, the participants acknowledged their accomplishments, affirmed the value of their work, and, with renewed vigor, set about finding a workable solution for the remaining issue.

When the group's work came to a standstill, I (and they) had asked questions—inquired—in an effort to collect and share ideas and information and to identify alternative solutions, all in an effort to resolve the problem. It became obvious to everyone that relying on inquiry-type questions was not helpful. A different approach was required.

The question I asked helped shift the participants' focus from lamenting the setback to reflecting on their achievements. Why is the exercise of curiosity such an important attribute of a reflective practitioner?

- It produces a different kind of knowledge than that obtained through inquiry.
- The orientation shifts from practitioner centered to participant centered. The practitioner's prominence is reduced, and the participants' interactions assume greater importance. They become more actively and directly engaged rather than merely responding to questions and reporting information.
- It is infectious; it stimulates a similar approach in the participants. They become more fascinated by the process of exploration and discovery. Brainstorming that infuses curiosity into a stalled conversation can have a similar impact.
- Curiosity promotes creativity. Ideas that had been bottled up emerge, including thoughts and reactions that participants had not been aware of.
- Curiosity promotes learning—for the participants and the practitioner.

When asked about an important trait, Bill Gates and Warren Buffett have the same answer: curiosity. For both, curiosity plays an important role in their success. (A link to this conversation is in the bibliography.)

There is more information about the use of questions, including examples, in the appendices.

Resilience is all about being able to overcome the unexpected. Jamais Cascio

Be Resilient

We all experience moments when something unexpected, perplexing, or disruptive occurs. Reflexively, we stop and wonder, "What in the world is going on?" "You've got to be kidding me!" "This shouldn't be happening." "I haven't a clue what to do." Adrenaline surges through our bodies, heightening our attention, increasing our heart rate, readying our muscles, and stimulating deep breathing. Our primitive brain is activated; we are primed to act.

These are moments requiring resilience. The word "resilience" has been so often used in a wide array of circumstances to describe an extensive range of behaviors that it has become a cliché. So let me start by explaining how I understand and use the term. Resilience is a particular kind of strength, like the willow that sways and bends, pliable yet sturdy in defiance of strong winds. It neither yields nor submits. Like the willow, when we are resilient in the strong winds of an unexpected situation, we absorb the surprise, manage our reactions, and respond thoughtfully and decisively. To be resilient, we don't need to push back. We don't need to engage in a contest of wills. Nor do we need to give way or give in. We are flexible yet durable, supple yet resolute. Despite being puzzled and uncertain, we remain steady, composed, and focused on our task.

The following practice example illustrates resilience—being calm and confident—in response to an unexpected and bizarre situation. As you read this annotated account, note not only what occurred—the events—but also how my actions were shaped by my attitude, my mindset. My thoughts appear in brackets.

Presented with another in a series of motions in a twelve-year-long postdivorce parenting dispute, the magistrate ordered the parties to mediation, appointing me as mediator. We convened at 10:00 a.m. in the offices of the father's attorney. After ten minutes in joint session and despite no apparent rationale other than the attorney's repeated insistence that we do so, the mediation continued in separate rooms. By 4:30 p.m., the parties had a workable plan. The mother and her attorney were reviewing the proposed agreement and fine-tuning the language. The revisions were minimal in number and scope and did not affect the principal terms of the revised parenting plan. Without knocking, the father's attorney opened the door to the meeting room and, without entering, announced, "The office will close at 5:00." I stepped outside the room and found him in the corridor walking to the other conference room. During the daylong mediation, neither of the parents or their attorneys mentioned a cutoff time:

> Me: [This is stupid. How dare you set an artificial deadline.] She needs more time. The agreement is nearly complete. We may not finish by 5:00.
> FA: Your approach is taking too long. I am sending my staff home at five.
> Me: [Seriously? You're being unprofessional and a jerk. The mediation will finish when we finish. The magistrate put me in charge, not you.] Do you want to jeopardize this agreement? The parties haven't been able to settle their differences in twelve years. There will be a signed agreement today, but I need time.
> FA: [Gruffly and with obvious contempt] I'll give you until 5:15.

He turned away and marched down the corridor like a general who had issued orders to his troops and expected their obedience.

Before returning to the mother and her attorney, I spent a few minutes considering the attorney's behavior. I took a few deep, calming breaths. Infuriated by his arrogance and coldness, I felt powerless because we were meeting in his office and because I did not believe I had the authority to order the mediation to continue. His irrational and irresponsible attitude might squander a long-awaited and much-needed resolution to a twelve-year-long dispute.

[What did he mean by "my approach"? Maybe he was referring to an earlier comment about "therapeutic mediation." Today, the parties have come closer to ending this cycle of dispute than this blustering fool has been able to do in twelve years of litigation. He's trying to be in charge. If anyone should be in charge, it should be the mediator. But there's nothing to be gained by arguing over control.]

With patience and persistence, the mother and her attorney pressed ahead with their review of the document, fully aware of the looming deadline. The mother was cautious and deliberate, as she had been throughout the day. She would not be rushed. Minutes passed. My attention was divided between my conversation with the mother and her attorney and the relentless movement of the hands on the large clock located above the door.

At 5:10, again without knocking, the attorney poked his head into the room and announced the following:

> FA: I'm closing the office now. I'm not getting a divorce over being late. Call me about rescheduling.

And he left. I rushed out to speak with him. He was halfway down a long corridor, emptying wastebaskets into a large plastic trash bag. [I was livid and felt disrespected. And I was incredulous as the sixty-year-old senior partner of the law firm emptied the office waste bins.] As I rushed down the hallway, I shouted at him:

> Me: What are you doing?

He ignored me and continued his evening housekeeping chores. As I walked toward him, considering what to say, he turned and quite calmly reaffirmed his decision:

> FA: I told you I was closing the office. You're taking too long. I sent my client home thirty minutes ago.

[I calmly considered my response to this man's arrogance, his foolishness, and his disrespect—for the parties, me, the mediation process, and the order from the magistrate. Despite my fury, I knew I was powerless to reverse his decision, nor could I order him to ask his client to return.]

Without comment, I returned to the conference room. As I walked down the corridor, I consoled myself with an observation generally attributed either to Mark Twain or George Carlin. It fit the moment perfectly: "Never argue with an idiot. They will drag you down to their level and beat you with experience."

[I don't need to engage in a contest of wills. The issue isn't who is in charge. It's pointless to battle him or allow personal reactions to affect my judgment. I will do my job—focus on the parties and what they want—an opportunity to resolve a persistently troublesome situation. I smiled (at last), realizing I had leverage. The father who was seeking more time with his son could not pursue his request in court until I filed a mediator's report.]

I explained the situation to the mother and her attorney, including my authority to withhold my report to the magistrate, and proposed that we continue the mediation via an exchange of e-mail messages. They agreed, and, as I anticipated, the minor language issues were easily resolved by the two attorneys two days later.

> Always behave like a duck—keep calm and unruffled on the surface but paddle like the devil underneath. Jacob Braude

In my initial reactive mode, I saw myself in a seemingly impossible situation. I could see only two options: capitulate or resist. Neither response was likely to help the parties—and that was my singular objective. With resilience, however, bending but not yielding, I was able to help them find a solution that put an end to years of acrimonious and costly litigation.

For conflict resolution practitioners, every situation is unique. There are no "standard" categories of conflicts that can be resolved through a systematic application of a predetermined series of interventions. Understanding this reality, we need to be flexible and resilient. We need the mindset of resilience that allows us to adapt our techniques and strategies to respond to shifting and sometimes ambiguous situations. To accomplish this, we must be pliable yet resolute. Like the willow, we bend but never break. This is resilience.

Nurture Simplicity

> Entia non sunt multiplicanda praeter necessitatem. [No more things should be presumed to exist than are absolutely necessary.] —William of Occam

Widely referred to as Occam's razor—and generally interpreted to mean that with all things being equal, the simplest explanation is usually correct. When I first heard of this principle (explained by Jodie Foster's character in the 1997 film *Contact*), it upended my thinking.

> Ellie Arroway: Occam's razor. You ever heard of it?
> Palmer Joss: Hack-em's razor. Sounds like some slasher movie.
> Ellie Arroway: No, Occam's razor. It's a basic scientific principle. It says all things being equal, the simplest explanation tends to be the right one.

I had been acting on the assumption that conflicts, so entrenched as to require a third-party intervenor, are complicated and troublesome and therefore demand an intricate and carefully shaped approach. Occam's razor suggests that instead of assuming that the response to intense and thorny conflicts lies in complexities, there might be more down-to-earth, straightforward explanations. If that is true, it would follow that interventions might be modest.

Thinking of the scene from *Contact* and the value of simplicity, I revised my philosophy and my approach to conflict work. I determined I would be the smallest pebble tossed into the pond—meaning that when I intervened in a conflict situation, I wanted to produce the fewest ripples and the faintest traces of my engagement. I would do everything ethically and professionally responsible but as little as necessary to help the participants accomplish their goals. As a consequence of this revised philosophy, an idea occurred, obvious once I took note yet new to my way of thinking. We are outsiders, invited guests. We know so little about the participants, the history of their conflict and its effect on them, and, most important, what solutions might best achieve their implicit and explicit goals. Our efforts are concentrated on the immediate situation—what the participants present to us. Yet it's possible—and in many instances quite probable—that our involvement will significantly influence them beyond the conclusion of our engagement. We complete our work, our connection ends, their lives continue—as neighbors, coparents, or workplace colleagues—and to my mind, that is as it should be. If we are like a pebble, then the small ripples created through our interventions will quickly disperse, leaving few traces of our presence. But a boulder creates ripples that become waves, and the pond and its edges may be dramatically altered in ways that neither we nor they could predict.

> To be really great in little things, to be noble and heroic in the insipid details of everyday life, is a virtue so rare as to be worthy of canonization.
> Harriet Beecher Stowe

Not long after learning of Occam's razor, I had a chance to test my theory of limited intervention:

> As defined by the company's senior vice president, the twin objectives of my engagement were "to resolve a complaint of a hostile work environment and to restore collegiality and productivity among the workers." Given my mediator's mindset, I initially considered whether convening a mediation with the complainant and other affected parties would be the least complicated and most efficient approach.
>
> I interviewed the complainant and the three men she held responsible for creating a hostile environment. She was reluctant to participate in mediation. As one of two women in an office of thirty, she viewed the entire male work group as complicit in the rude and repulsive behavior of the three she had accused of harassment. She accused the trio of making vulgar and suggestive comments directly to her and posting lewd cartoons on the notice board in the coffee room. In separate interviews, each confirmed her allegations without a hint of embarrassment or remorse. The complainant also mentioned the behavior of several other men who had passively

condoned the offensive behavior; they hadn't told an offensive joke or made a rude comment but never confronted those who did. The manager's apparent indifference to her initial complaint ("Ignore them and they'll soon stop") and his tacit acceptance of some of the behavior ("It's just guys being guys") had permitted the behavior to continue without recourse. Viewing the circumstances, the workers, and behaviors through the lens of systems thinking, I concluded that my initial idea about a limited and tightly focused intervention, even if by some chance it resolved the specific complaint, was unlikely to achieve the objective of restoring "collegiality and productivity among the workers."

With authorization from the executive vice president, I enlarged the scope of my activities. I interviewed the manager and each person in the work group. My hoped-for small pebble was rapidly taking on the properties of a good-sized rock.

One question nagged at me: Was a large-scale, intensive and intrusive approach really warranted? Was there a more discrete and tightly framed method that could accomplish the twin goals set by the senior vice president?

A potential answer emerged during a lengthy second interview of the manager in his office. Our first meeting had taken place in a conference room in a separate building, chosen to provide privacy and confidentiality. For this second meeting, I wanted to be in the manager's office, situated on the same floor as the work group but isolated from and largely out of sight of the workers' cubicles—which meant he was out of their sight as well. His door was almost always closed.

He offered coffee. I noticed he had his own coffeemaker. That explained why he seldom went to the communal break room. In our earlier conversation, I learned that he used e-mail to distribute announcements of work assignments, meetings, and policies. As a result, to the workers, he was mostly invisible, communicating indirectly. To them, he was a disembodied voice to which they gave little heed and no respect. Several of them used the phrase "Indispensable but useless."

I proposed an intervention: the manager would relocate his office to the general work area, where he could be seen and where he would be able to observe the workers. He reluctantly accepted after receiving strong and not-at-all-subtle encouragement from the executive vice president. He also agreed to convene occasional face-to-face staff meetings to review policies or discuss assignments. Lastly, and as if it were punishment, he agreed to use the break room coffeepot.

My rationale was that, by altering the physical arrangements, the manager would be more likely to interact with the workers and they with him. Proximity and visibility, I hypothesized, might eventually lead to his becoming a more involved and relevant manager. If the intervention was successful, the structural changes and increased engagement from the manager could result in a more professional and productive work environment. Antics such as those that led to the complaint would be more readily noticed, confronted, and deterred. Merely altering the structural conditions, without further efforts, would not change the workplace environment. Achieving a collegial and productive workforce would require the manager's active, sustained, and effective engagement. Changing the structure created the opportunity for meaningful management. Furthermore, having acknowledged that he needed to develop managerial skills, he enrolled in a series of courses on leadership and management.

Three months later, following an extended leave of absence, the complainant returned to work. She declined an offer to engage in mediation. The offenders offered a limited written apology, which she acknowledged.

We explore the unfamiliar world of the participants' experiences, seeking clues that invite us to probe further, pursuing an explanation for the situation. As we follow each hint and clue, there is a risk that our inquiry might become an unrestrained exploration of details that, while fascinating and even illuminating, may be unrelated to the central issues for the parties. Succumbing to the temptation to collect ever more information about the situation and the participants, we may miss the "big picture," somewhat like concentrating on the myriad dots of color in a Seurat painting rather than observing the overall image.

It would be reasonable to wonder whether there is an inherent contradiction in urging practitioners to *pay attention to details* (another of the attributes) while advocating for *simplicity*. Often, a thorough exploration of details is required to become aware of the simplest explanation. Rather than being contradictory, the two attributes are complementary. In the example above, the simple explanation (that the manager's physical absence and lack of leadership contributed to discord among the employees) could not have emerged without awareness of key details (closed door, remote office, individual coffeemaker, and method of communication).

> Making things complicated is commonplace; making the complicated simple, awesomely simple, that's creativity. —Charles Mingus

Highly effective practitioners take careful notice of details without becoming obsessed by the prospect of an extended and intensive search for information. Reflective practitioners search for elegant and most obvious explanations without becoming lost in competing details.

Value Ambiguity

If ambiguity corresponds to confusion and uncertainty, then, without a doubt, being in conflict is an inherently ambiguous condition. When in conflict, the outcome is in question, the route is undefined, the perils and opportunities are often hidden, and the undertaking is demanding.

Many in our profession—I among them—regard "tolerance of ambiguity" as an essential quality of conflict professionals. For me, this involves the ability to remain calm, thoughtful, and resolute in the presence of messy, confusing, and unsettling situations. When interactions become muddled, chaotic, or intense, when a perceived impasse emerges and prospects for a successful outcome dim, we remain focused on the issues at hand and attentive to and engaged with the participants. We don't become unnerved or, at worst, throw in the towel. We are patient and attentive, unruffled and steadfast. We can't prepare for these moments of upheaval. No training course can teach us to be calm amid the storm of others' discomfort, doubt, and confusion. A few of us may have developed these skills by observing and modeling family members, teachers, or friends. Or perhaps it's not nurture but nature that produces this quality, though it's a distinction that matters little to clients who are unsettled and intensely anxious. People in conflict seek our help because of the ambiguity of their circumstances, because the acrimony, distress, confusion, and messiness of conflict overwhelms them, and as a result, they have been unable to sort out their differences.

> Life is about not knowing, having to change, taking the moment and making the best of it, without knowing what's going to happen next. Delicious ambiguity. Gilda Radner

Becoming dextrous and adept at managing these moments, to be calm in the midst of confusion, is an invaluable skill. We glide along waters like the swan, appearing serene and unruffled (forgive the pun), the movement seemingly effortless, while beneath the surface, we are paddling like mad. This behavior exemplifies tolerance for ambiguity.

The attribute of valuing ambiguity encompasses more than the ability to maintain composure in the midst of the conflict storm. It is an attitude as much as a set of behaviors. Let me explain the crucial differences between the two seemingly equivalent attitudes, differences much more significant and relevant than mere semantics.

Faced with moments of ambiguity, common responses include the following: calm the participants (take a break or meet separately), apply logic and reason (concentrate on and review facts and the issues at hand), offer reassurance (acknowledge the uncertainty and their frustration), confront them with the consequences of failing to secure an agreement (remind them of what's at stake), redouble attempts at problem solving (restate their progress, affirm their ability to work together), relieve them of the ambiguity (offer possible solutions), and raise the alarm (propose ending the session).

Do these strategies and techniques work? Are they helpful? Sometimes, possibly often. But the source of my disquiet with these approaches is not the techniques themselves but rather the attitude that prompts their use. As a rule, conflict resolution practitioners regard ambiguity—these chaotic and confusing experiences—as problems, predicaments, challenges, or hindrances, in other words, as situations to be managed, surmounted, worked through, dealt with, or handled. And this mindset regarding ambiguity leads to the techniques I've cataloged and to the determination to push through this moment of ambiguity, viewing it as a speed bump along the road to achieving a settlement.

Exploring why ambiguity has created a difficult moment and understanding what it means for the participants are a low priority, if addressed at all. When the practitioner's efforts are concentrated on managing or overcoming the ambiguity, the opportunity to see and then explore the potential for learning why this experience of doubt and turmoil occurred and what its significance is for the parties is eclipsed. Why, as most practitioners would likely wonder, would we want to learn about the significance and impact of the ambiguous circumstance; how will that improve the parties' circumstances and enhance our ability to assist them? My response is that, just as learning other vital information about the dispute and the parties' attitudes and goals, when we understand the source of the ambiguity, we are better positioned to guide our strategies and methods to address the root causes of the ambiguity. Although exploring ambiguity and its influence on the parties may seem like a detour from the primary goal of achieving a meaningful and relevant outcome, paradoxically, by making this effort, there is a heightened chance the parties will reach their desired destination.

Reflective practitioners have the mindset to see ambiguity as an abundant and influential source of information. In the chaos and disorder of intense conflict is a rich vein of opportunities for parties to gain insights about themselves and their dispute. Shifting from tolerating to embracing ambiguity requires no special techniques or skills; competent practitioners have these skills in abundance and know how to apply them capably and effectively. The difference between tolerating and embracing ambiguity requires a shift in attitude, a different mindset that can be learned. We can learn, for example, with the benefit of conflict theory as our guide, that divergence contains a rich source of self-awareness and understanding, that pressing for convergence (agreement) in the face of ambiguity results either in an impasse or a limited and incomplete (or, worse, flawed) settlement. We can learn to be patient and not immediately rush to harmonize distressing and disconcerting conditions. We can learn genuine tolerance and unflappability not simply to calm the turbulent waters but to help the parties explore and learn from these messy and unpleasant moments. Because we understand this potential, we are able to value and embrace ambiguity.

To illustrate, let's return to an example from the previous chapter—the case of the hesitant business partner reluctant to accept an ostensibly ideal settlement and the frustrated mediator who had "used a variety of techniques to conclude the mediation with a settlement." That settlement was frustrated by the partner's need for more information (he couldn't specify what she might require) and additional time to consider the latest and hopefully final proposal. Ambiguity confounded the mediator: why would a business partner who wanted to sell his interest and who had been offered settlement terms that matched his requirements be reticent to accept and sign the agreement? Characteristically, the mediator viewed the situation as a problem to be overcome, a roadblock of sorts that prevented the parties from concluding an agreement. With that mindset, that ambiguity is a condition to be handled or resolved; the mediator employed time-tested techniques to break up the logjam of ambiguity. And the mediator was frustrated because none of these familiar intervention approaches produced a hoped-for response from the partner, who remained implacable.

What if, rather than trying to battle ambiguity and wrestle it into submission, the mediator had instead embraced ambiguity and sought to understand the contours of the partner's thinking and decision? What if the mediator had embraced ambiguity as hinting at or pointing to a significant and troubling issue for the partner. And what if he then talked with the partner and said, "I'm curious. As the mediation began, you had a number of demands with respect to the dissolution of the partnership. The proposed agreement addresses each of your requirements. And yet you are unwilling to accept those terms—at least for the moment. As you consider the agreement and the end of the business partnership, what are you thinking? What continues to puzzle you or needs further explanation?"

Would the fog of ambiguity have lifted? Perhaps. Would the partner have revealed and discussed the reasons for her hesitation? Quite possibly. And imagine if he said, "This agreement marks the end of a successful ten-year partnership. The terms are probably okay, I just need some time to accept that our partnership is over." This is only one of a dozen possible explanations he might offer for his reticence. Embracing ambiguity and exploring its contours rather than trying to wrestle it into submission allow crucial information to emerge.

Uncertainty, confusion, and chaos are inevitable consequences of conflict and are the roots of ambiguity. Reflective practitioners don't attempt to manage the uncertainty; instead, they embrace the disorderly and unpleasant confusion—the ambiguity—as a source of information about the participants and their approach to the conflict. Reflective practitioners believe that ambiguity can be a teacher, a guide; it's not an impediment to progress. Through patience and persistence, reflective practitioners "gain insight and perspective that help shape interactions and interventions" (Gatti, Watson, and Siegel 2011, 34). Practitioners are most likely to experience these "insights and perspectives" if first they acknowledge and embrace the ambiguity.

Do not quench your inspiration and your imagination; do not become the slave of your model. Vincent Van Gogh

Pay Attention to Detail

Has this ever happened to you? You are in a familiar place. You notice—as if for the first time—something different and surprising, and you wonder, "Was that there the last time? How did I miss that?" Moments of temporary disorientation occur because we have become accustomed to certain patterns. Routines tend to focus our attention on the same markers. Ellen Langer (2015) says that such moments fit the category of mindlessness. "When you know something absolutely, there's no reason to pay any attention to it."

How does this notion of mindlessness—and, more important, the character of mindfulness—relate to the quality of conflict resolution practice? Consider an element common to nearly every conflict resolution intervention: the introductory statement.

Whether presented in a joint meeting or individual conversations, the introductory statement is generally viewed as a prelude (setting the stage, creating expectations, establishing boundaries) to the real work ahead. Preliminary comments are most often delivered as a monologue, the practitioner reciting prepared statements as if on autopilot, a mechanical repetition of instructions, guidelines and compulsory elements we have conveyed hundreds of times. The presentation can become tiresome, even numbing, for both us and the participants. When the importance of checking off required items becomes the primary objective, the introduction can seem like the obligatory (and generally ignored) preflight safety instructions delivered by flight attendants. Robert Parkinson, writing in the *Sarasota Herald Tribune* on October 14, 2017, observes,

> Habit (saying the same thing over and over) and focus (attention given to the audience) can be boring and repetitive. . . . Habit can result in speedy delivery, use of unfamiliar language. . . . The agent must "cover the material" and does so as quickly as possible in order to move on to other important tasks. The focus is on getting through it rather than on the waiting passengers who need to understand the information. . . . The announcements are busywork for the crew, and the delivery is by habit.

The process itself, the language we use, and the guidelines and principles are largely unfamiliar to participants. We speak about confidentiality with the ease and confidence born of experience. But do the participants really grasp its significance both in general and as applied to them? How likely is it that after ten or fifteen minutes, they will understand what they can expect from you—are there exceptions—and how it might affect them? For example, they may wonder whether it's permissible to talk with family members about what occurred in mediation. Or perhaps they're thinking, "I can keep this confidential, but what happens if the other party breaks confidentiality?" Except for parties who have participated in a similar process, every element is unfamiliar, like the first-time air traveler. Implicitly, they understand that success in the process will require them to trust us as reliable and competent professionals. Trust depends, to a significant degree, on receiving—and grasping—relevant information about a range of important topics that are presented not merely to them but for them. Much like flight attendants, we are less concerned with whether they have been paying attention and whether they have understood our presentation than we are with completing this tiresome yet obligatory aspect of our work. If we knew how little our clients grasp, we would be shocked. The following story illustrates the value of paying attention to detail:

> In extensive phone conversations with each of the divorcing parties prior to convening the mediation, the mediator described mediation, invited questions, and confirmed that each was prepared attend an introductory session. At the outset of the initial joint meeting, the mediator repeated much of what she had discussed separately with each of them, including an explanation of confidentiality, a description of her role (not a therapist or attorney), and the objectives of mediation.
>
> During the mediator's opening statement, the husband was busily consulting his notes, and the wife sat impassively, arms crossed over her chest, looking away from both her husband and the mediator. After concluding her remarks, the parties were invited to discuss their situation. The husband spoke first, describing their living

arrangements, plans for their daughter, and their finance situation. The mediator noticed that as he spoke, the wife was impassive, sitting rigidly, her gaze fixed at a spot on a wall above and behind the mediator. Curious about this behavior, the mediator interrupted the husband and turned to the wife and said, "Betty, I'd like to ask a question. I noticed that when I spoke and now while your husband was speaking, you weren't looking at us, and you seemed to be miles away. May I ask if you are okay to continue?"

First a quiet sob and flood of tears, then in a quavering voice hinting at bitterness and fear, she replied, "How could I possibly be okay? Two weeks ago, he told me that for the past year, he'd been having an affair with one of my closest friends, that he wanted a divorce, and that we should come to you for mediation!"

Her rigid posture and flat, emotionless stare might have passed without notice. Habit can become our nemesis. Like flight attendants completing preflight announcements, the mediator might have focused on the initial mediation routines with minimal attention to the wife's apparent impassive behavior. However, the mediator was attentive, and the mediator sensed that proceeding without addressing the wife's perplexing behavior could have had serious consequences, including the wife's abrupt decision to end mediation or, having reached an agreement, her ultimately repudiating the arrangements.

Of course, there could have been less consequential explanations for the wife's posture and appearance. For example, she might have replied that she was simply listening attentively and mentally rehearsing her own presentation. What matters is that the mediator paid attention to the unexpected behavior, was curious, and sought an explanation.

> There are two possible outcomes: If the result confirms the hypothesis, then you've made a measurement. If the result is contrary to the hypothesis, then you've made a discovery. —Enrico Fermi

Details matter. Reflective practitioners pay attention to what is novel and unexpected, resisting the pull of habit, avoiding the rut of routine. They are not indifferent to behavior or comments that do not fit an expected pattern of behavior. Reflective practitioners protect against allowing themselves to become complacent and unfailingly wedded to a routine; instead, they are attentive and responsive to new, unusual, and surprising behaviors and events. With fresh eyes, they allow themselves to see details that might otherwise be played down or disregarded—small details that can have a sizable impact.

Learn Ceaselessly

If asked, most of us would readily affirm the value of ongoing learning. We participate in professional development and continuing education programs, attend conference workshops, and discuss our work with colleagues. In addition, many practitioners improve their skills and extend their knowledge by reading books, journal articles, and professional newsletters. Without question, our success as practitioners—professional growth and evolution—is connected to and dependent on continued learning.

Genuine lifelong learning requires more than engaging in professional development activities; it begins with a mindset about learning. It is a drive to explore unfamiliar situations and risk mysterious and uncomfortable moments. It is the determination to question our biases and test the assumptions that shape our practice choices. It is an aspiration to experiment with a novel approach or attempt an untried technique. The mindset of lifelong learning involves a willingness to temporarily suspend self-assurance in order to gain knowledge.

> Take advantage of the ambiguity in the world. Look at something and think what else it might be. —Roger von Oech

Have you been in a situation where applying proven techniques and strategies was ineffective yet you persisted without any change in the results? This occurs because you have become comfortable with your style and methods and with the model of practice you regularly (and successfully) use—your routines. When you follow a well-worn path, you feel confident, poised, and at ease. But how do you respond when familiar practice routines are impractical or unsuitable or simply don't work? Do you persist, confidently and doggedly adhering to your habits? Or are you willing to experience a degree of confusion and discomfort and then adjust your approach in light of this foreign situation? Reflective practitioners consistently follow the unfamiliar path. Not as rebels, pushing back against convention, but as explorers eagerly seeking discoveries.

The next practice example reveals ceaseless learning as an attribute of a reflective practitioner:

The minute one utters a certainty, the opposite comes to mind. May Sarton

A twenty-six-hour journey, with four intermediate stops, brought me to a First Nations village in Nunavit, Canada's newest and most northern territory. It was early December; "the last day of the sun," as the locals explained. Daylight, as such, was a soft, diffuse light lasting about six hours. When I arrived at the B&B around noon, the desk clerk, laughing so hard she had difficulty speaking, announced to a small group in the lobby, "Hey, here's that guy from Florida." One of the patrons took my arm and, without speaking, led me to an array of weather gauges set into the pine-paneled wall beneath the stretched skin of an enormous polar bear. He silently pointed to the thermometer and grinned: –25 degrees Fahrenheit—one hundred degrees colder than at home. Three days later, the temperature had dropped another thirty degrees.

I was confident I could figure out the problems and design a useful approach to address the interpersonal and intragroup workplace conflicts that were affecting the employees' productivity and undermining the manager's authority. In the small and close-knit community, conflicts within the work group had become the source of gossip. Friends and relatives of the employees were drawn into the situation, battle lines drawn, relationships perilously strained.

After a few hours in the group's offices, I wondered whether I was the right person for this work. Techniques and strategies I had used in similar workplace settings might not be suitable. I was in an unfamiliar location, wearing a borrowed parka along with newly purchased long underwear, woolen hat, and mittens. More important, I was American, not Canadian; I was Caucasian, not First Nations; I knew nothing of the history, culture, and traditions of the Inuit people. In every respect, I was a foreigner. I became aware that if there was any chance to be helpful, I needed to be a curious and ardent learner.

For the first two of my five days, I was an eager student, hungry to learn about the people in the department, their lives, and their workplace. I was a sponge, absorbing as much information as I could. Instead of a more conventional interview process, I met informally, sometimes over coffee and pastries, individually and in small groups, and asked about their lives in the village. Naturally, countless stories about the workplace were woven into the threads of these informal conversations.

The staff and the manager were enthusiastic teachers, proud of their heritage and their homeland. They wanted me to hear about Inuit history, traditions, and customs and about the activities that shaped their daily lives. One worker provided a tour of the community on the back of a snowmobile (another first for me). I learned about the importance of seal hunting to provide food for the people and for their working dogs. The eldest member of the work group described the nomadic pattern of life in the years before the hamlet was established. Her family moved onto the ice in the winter when rivers froze over and animals hibernated and where fishing was their source of food, then back to land in spring to hunt large ruminants and fish in the pristine streams. I ate caribou stew and politely declined the offer of a delicacy—seal flipper. An unanticipated offshoot of my "lessons" was that we developed a mutually respectful working relationship. I used what I learned to design an approach I hoped would be relevant and helpful. On the afternoon of the second day, I met with the workers to present my proposal, explain my analysis, and ask for feedback. Only then did the "work" really begin.

I don't want to give the impression that my approach was imaginative or special. Many practitioners, with equal or greater knowledge and skill, have successfully worked within other cultures. My reason for telling this story is to provide an example of learning ceaselessly. It was crucial to understand the history, extent, and impact of the conflicts that had affected the staff and manager. But to truly understand what had occurred, it was crucial to learn about the context—the culture—the crucible in which everything occurred.

I can't be certain that taking the time to learn about Inuit culture, history, and traditions had an appreciable impact on the outcome. I believe that my attitude of honest, authentic curiosity was crucial to my ability to prepare and implement a conflict intervention process that was respectful of and responsive to the culture and to the people themselves. As a result, the staff and manager were receptive to my approach, I felt more relaxed and prepared, and I was more confident in my ability to adjust and adapt methods as required.

Resist Certainty

This attribute may sound like a slogan on a counterculture T-shirt, as if certainty is a peril to be avoided, opposed, and overcome. While certainty has an unquestioned and valuable role in professional practice, it can lead to overconfidence and even carelessness when not tempered by humility and curiosity. We may become complacent and overly reliant on our expertise with the result that our curiosity is supressed, we ignore clues that suggest something that doesn't fit our model, and we feel challenged (and, at worst, offended) when parties fail to respond as we expect. Indeed, Schön's (1983) advocacy for reflective practice was in significant respects a response to the model of "technical rationality" that characterized professions, a standardized knowledge base that is "specialized, firmly bounded, scientific, and standardized" (23).

Doubt is not a pleasant position, but certainty is an absurd one. —Voltaire

In professional education programs, we acquire knowledge of principles and theories, processes, and methods. We learn about and become proficient in the use of an assortment of technical skills and strategies. We read articles and books, attend lectures and seminars, participate in experiential learning activities, and engage in discussions with colleagues. Over time and through experience, we sharpen our analytical skills, refine our techniques, and create practice habits and procedures.

> The only man I know who behaves sensibly is my tailor; he takes my measurements anew each time. . . . The rest go on with old measurements and expect me to fit them.
> George Bernard Shaw

Even with limited information about the participants and their circumstances, we develop a seemingly intuitive ability to interpret a conflict situation. We recognize patterns quickly, and from those patterns, we develop a tentative explanation of the situation (hypothesis), and from that hypothesis, we design a plan for the intervention and act accordingly. Problems arise, however, when we fail to test our hypothesis, when we assume that our understanding of events is accurate and therefore that our interpretation is correct, and we become yoked to our hypothesis and as a result ignore or discount other possible interpretations. We are certain of our analysis and confident of our approach. Certainty becomes our nemesis, not a guarantee of effectiveness.

Chris Argyris (1990) observed the phenomena by which we use facts to generate meaning—an interpretation of those facts—and then act on our interpretation, a phenomenon he labeled the ladder of inference. The bottom rung represents reality and facts. We observe and respond to those facts based on our beliefs—our Constellation of Theories (see chapter 4). Through the lens of our beliefs, we produce an interpretation, incorporating our assumptions about the circumstances and events. We then draw conclusions that become set in a framework of conclusions. At the top rung is the action we take based on the foregoing steps. The progression from facts to action appears sensible, except there is no mechanism for testing whether our interpretation may be based on an unreasonably limited view of the facts or whether our assumptions are valid, so that when we act with certainty, our choices may be flawed.

Now consider the phenomenon of the ladder of influence repeated over time, dealing with similar situations, learning from and through these experiences. Schön (1983) describes this experience as the process of developing practitioner specialization. If the learning process is tested repeatedly by examining our assumptions and inferences, then the repetitive process results in expertise:

> A professional practitioner is a specialist who encounters certain types of situations again and again. . . . He develops a repertoire of expectations, images and techniques. He learns what to look for and how to respond to what he finds. As long as his practice is stable, in the sense that it brings him the same types of cases, he becomes less and less subject to surprise. His [practice] tends to become increasingly tacit, spontaneous, and automatic. (1983, 60)

How can professional specialization and efficacy be bad if the result is that our practice becomes "spontaneous and automatic"? What is the downside to our being skillful, knowledgeable, prepared, confident, and certain about our practice decisions? The answer is that any weaknesses are few as long as our practice is "stable" and our cases fall within a familiar (predictable) range of conflict situations. All is well if we have employed a helpful feedback loop to test the validity of the conclusions resulting from our climb up the ladder of inference. And all is well if cases are indeed comparable—a circumstance that occurs as frequently as a blue moon. Complications arise when we are surprised by unforeseen behavior that falls outside our customary practice routines or that challenges our operating beliefs or when our inferences are faulty.

Schön (1983) points to an adverse consequence of professional specialization. "In the individual, a high degree of specialization can lead to a parochial narrowness of vision" (60). In other words, we may become hidebound, wedded to our routines, or, worse, closed-minded.

A brief story from a reflective practice group session may help explain the limitations and, at times, the flaws of certainty. To protect confidentiality and privacy, I altered details while remaining true to the essence of the group member's story.

Reading the case coordinator's notes of the intake interviews, the co-mediators saw this as a typical neighbor dispute—loud parties late into the night, an unleashed dog frightening the neighbors' children, neighbors unwilling to speak with one, and a succession of complaints to the police. The parties (each couples) entered the room, did not look at the other pair, and sat as far from one another as the small meeting room allowed. The parties were a wife and husband in their early thirties, dressed informally in jeans and collared shirts, seemingly relaxed, and frequently whispering, and, in contrast, a wife and husband, slightly older, unspeaking, appearing anxious, and dressed in distinctive clothing that the mediators assumed was characteristic of the couple's background or culture.

Seeing the older couple's attire, the mediators questioned their initial assumptions (inferences) about the dispute. In addition to noting the parties' clothing, they noticed their more formal posture, somewhat proper greeting, and slightly accented speech. They now assumed that cultural differences might be the cause of or have exacerbated this dispute.

So following their introductory comments and after each "side" had related the basic facts of the dispute, the mediators asked the older couple how long they had lived in the town. They wondered but didn't ask whether they were immigrants. (In a subsequent debrief, both mediators acknowledged that they had made this assumption.) The mediators also asked about the names and ages of their children and their favorite activities, whether the family had pets, about the size and nature of the area around each residence and whether there were fences or hedges between the homes, about the distance between the two houses, and about their employment and working hours. Taking turns, the wife and husband politely and briefly responded to each question. The mediators did not notice that the couple's answers were increasingly terse, nor were they aware that the couple were becoming increasingly upset.

The mediators' questions for the younger couple, while lightly touching on some of the same topics, focused on their dog's breed, disposition, and behavior.

The mediators then asked both couples, "Have you tried to work out these problems?" The older couple looked at one another, then quietly stood. The husband calmly said, "This is not what we came for, to be seen in this way. You are no different than the police who didn't take our complaints seriously." And they walked out.

One of the mediators followed the couple. She asked whether they would talk with her, explain what occurred. In a caucus room, the visibly unsettled mediator asked, "I am confused by your decision. Would you be willing to explain why you ended the mediation?"

In a soft yet sure voice, the wife said, "We have lived in our house for twelve years. We know everyone in the neighborhood. Those two moved in six months ago after our friends next door moved to a retirement home. These people are unfriendly and unpleasant. They have been invited but never attend our monthly events in the park. They have no respect for us or our friends in the neighborhood."

So much for the mediators' assumptions that this couple were the more recent arrivals to the neighborhood and might have different expectations because of their background or culture. In one sense, the mediators were correct: cultural differences were a significant source of the conflict—culture in the sense of "the way we do things here." But it was the other couple who were disrespectful of the neighborhood culture.

> I have noticed that even people who claim everything is predestined, and that we can do nothing to change it, look before they cross the road. —Stephen Hawking

There are at least two possible shortcomings to practitioner specialization. The first, noted by Schön, is the possibility that our perspective—our practice routines—becomes fixed and confined. When faced with a novel situation that does not conform to assumptions born of prior experience, we may become confused and uncertain how to proceed. As a consequence, we may ignore or dismiss such a discrepancy as an anomaly. Then, when we do respond, we shape the contours of the situation to conform with those assumptions. Relying exclusively on experience and practice routines, our response will be limited to familiar tactics and strategies. Paradoxically, the factors that led to past success can weaken and undermine us:

> It used to be the case that people had living rooms that were never lived in. Then some smart person recognized, mindfully, maybe we should make the kitchen much bigger, because that's the room in which we spend most of our time. (Langer 2015)

The second downside lies in complacency born of the conviction that we are right. Because complacency can lead to a feeling that we're doing the same case over and over, simply waiting for the participants to discover a solution we knew all along would suit them. We may become bored, even disenchanted. Further, complacency may lead to carelessness. Because we already "know" what the participants will say and how the case will unfold, we minimize or disregard data or fail to notice relevant details. Our actions become predictable and unvaried. This sounds dreary, joyless, and depressing. And it is. I refer to this condition as being in a rut. Unfortunately, it is a common if unacknowledged condition, especially for experienced practitioners. We can avoid or get ourselves out of a rut by remaining open to new perspectives.

Reflective practitioners recognize that conflict resolution practice is not an assembly-line process predicated on repetition, predictability, and certainty. Participants are never alike despite having notable similarities. No matter how analogous problems may appear, each is unique. Every intervention, no matter how comparable to others we have managed, is a "one-off." The only certainty in our profession is the inevitability that every engagement is inimitable. The willingness to acknowledge this condition and a commitment to act accordingly is an attribute of a reflective practitioner.

> Absolute certainty is not something I strive for anymore. I've learned the hard way that destiny usually looks upon our most strident convictions with amusement, or perhaps even pity. —Elizabeth Gilbert

If your practice is stable and the problems you address are similar, well-honed techniques and strategies may produce excellent results. However, you may lack the flexibility and resilience to respond to the unexpected. If tunnel vision limits your perspective, you will underestimate the importance of surprising incidents. Your response is likely to be clumsy and inept. Conviction, born of unexamined self-confidence, is the nemesis of a reflective practitioner. Reflective practitioners learn to overcome that adversary and thus resist certainty.

Balance Commitment and Flexibility

> The possession of knowledge does not kill the sense of wonder and mystery. There is always more mystery. —Anais Nin

In conflict resolution practice, *balance commitment* refers to the intentional process of generating a working hypothesis based on observation of phenomena and the application of theory. *Flexibility* refers to the willingness to alter or abandon a hypothesis that, on examination and reflection, is deemed insufficient, unsuitable, or irrelevant. To accomplish these twin (and seemingly paradoxical) goals, we must be both confident and humble, self-assured and modest.

Think of the child's toy often called the Chinese finger trap. After inserting your index fingers into each end of a woven bamboo tube, you attempt to withdraw your fingers. Pulling—the instinctive response—causes the woven fibers to tighten, and your fingers are gripped more tightly. Resist, and you're trapped. Yield, and it's possible to release one finger at a time.

> *I couldn't repair your brakes so I made your horn louder.* Steven Wright

Practitioners often experience something quite similar. They generate a working explanation (hypothesis) for the conflict situation after listening to participants describe their experiences and express their goals. Relying on that hypothesis, they chart a course for the engagement and embark on the journey as if their explanation provided an accurate map. Along the way, participants appear to be making progress, and then there is an unexpected snag. New information that might prompt an adjustment in the hypothesis and thus a shift in its direction is overlooked as unimportant or dismissed as anomalous, and the intervention moves forward on the basis of the practitioner's initial assessment and explanation.

The following example is loosely based on an experience presented during a reflective practice group:

> It seemed to be a simple dispute between a contractor and a homeowner. Over the course of the six-week renovation project, there had been various discussions about delays, increased materials costs, and changes to the original plans. At the end of the project, the homeowner withheld the final payment (an amount less than 10 percent of the total cost), demanding that the contractor replace a bathroom sink and faucet that had been switched for out-of-stock items. The contractor had persuaded the homeowner to accept the substitutions rather than delay the project.
>
> The discussion was tense, initially concentrating on the decision to install replacement items for fixtures originally selected by the homeowner. As the exchange became more heated, each referred to former disputes that had been contentious at the time but ultimately seemed to have been resolved.
>
> The mediator attempted to refocus the discussion to the disputed payment. In response to the mediator's efforts, the participants stopped talking, sat back in their chairs, and glared at one another in stony silence.
>
> [The mediator thought, well, that didn't go as I expected. This should be a simple case. Neither of them wants to go to court over this modest sum. They were making progress, then wham, stalemate. Perhaps they want to talk about past grievances.]
>
> The mediator said, "There seem to have been a lot of conflicts during this project. Would it make sense to talk about these other situations?" In near perfect unity, the

participants responded, "No. Those issues are dead and buried. Let's get this done." And in a short period of time, that's what happened.

In the mediator's experience, disputes like these proceed in a straightforward manner. Problem solving is the best strategy because the amount in dispute is modest, and participants are motivated to reach a settlement and want to spend as little time and effort as possible.

Unexpectedly, the homeowner and contractor deviated from that predicted path, dredging up grievances related to the project but unrelated to the replacement fixtures, and withheld payment. When the mediator attempted to guide them back to their original goal, they resisted his suggestion and continued quarreling about disputes long since resolved. Reflecting on this unexpected reaction, the mediator considered whether to remind them—again—that they were in mediation to resolve a specific dispute or to acknowledge the changed circumstances and adjust his response. He realized that his assumptions about the parties and their motivation were at odds with their behavior. Faced with this odd situation, the mediator let go of his expectations. Revising his explanation for their behavior, the mediator concluded that sometimes parties who want to resolve a dispute need to rehash frustrating incidents not pertinent to that dispute. As a result of this recalibration, the mediator invited them to continue bickering about past issues.

To be flexible requires humility as well as self-confidence. Consider that, as practitioners, we know little about the participants and the nature, history, and impact of their dispute. We have an idea of their goals, some understanding of the dispute, and little more. Our picture of them is like a movie trailer: a few scenes, snippets of dialogue, and a voice-over describing the story line. As a result, our initial explanation for the dispute is a charitably considered working hypothesis or "best educated guess." It is not based on complete data. It is, however, a crucial and necessary starting point. We begin, acting as if our initial explanation—hypothesis—is accurate. As the intervention moves ahead, we learn more about the participants and their dispute; have a clearer understanding of the situation, their motivations, and their objectives; and, accordingly, alter our hypothesis. Reflective practitioners continually seek out and assess new information or changed circumstances, then, as necessary, reconsider their hypothesis. Reflective practitioners are willing to be flexible and adjust their actions in light of this revised explanation.

Embrace Failure as Your Mentor

In the cartoon *Peanuts*, Charlie Brown represents the triumph of hope, determination, and spirit over gloom, discouragement, and frustration. Whether attempting to kick a football, fly a kite, or manage a baseball team, he tries again and again despite repeated failures. "Good grief," he mutters, staring up at his kite hopelessly tangled in a tree or lying on his back after Lucy has once again pulled away the football. His heart and courage overcome memories of painful and frustrating experiences. Undaunted, he repeats the behavior, hoping for different results.

> Lucy: You learn more when you lose.
> Charlie Brown: Well then I must be the smartest person in the world!!! —Charles M. Schulz, *Peanuts Treasury*

Practitioners rely on polished routines involving a repertoire of practiced tactics and strategies that over time have proved successful. That makes sense. They validate their approach:

"I've got a 90 percent settlement rate. These methods have worked." Yet, no matter how reliable and valuable they may have been, practice routines are not flawless.

None of us is eager to acknowledge a mistake, and as a result, we sometimes overlook or minimize moments when a proven strategy has failed. Errors are unwelcome reminders of our human fallibility. Nevertheless, the uncomfortable reality is that we all make mistakes. We may misjudge the timing of an intervention or rely on a mistaken set of assumptions. We may simply be clumsy or inept, distracted or bored. In most instances, any slipups have limited or no adverse consequence to the participants or to the process.

Mistakes are the portals of discovery. —James Joyce

Most of us can instantly recall one or more moments when practiced and productive routines bump up against a surprising and confusing situation. Here's one I recall because I was caught completely off guard by the participants' response to an observation I routinely made in the early years of my mediation practice during the introductory phase of a divorce mediation:

Talking about the order in which they might discuss the various topics or issues in their divorce and trying to be helpful and efficient, I often said to participants, "It may make sense to put aside for the moment talking about how you want to handle furniture, furnishings, and other household items, as that tends to be less contentious."

Without a word, they handed me a meticulously prepared, sixteen-page, single-spaced, room-by-room list of artwork, collectibles, and antiques in their home, along with dates and places where the items had been acquired and the original purchase prices. I was taken by surprise. I stammered. I wasn't sure what to say. Fortunately, they were amused and not dismayed. Eventually, I regained a measure of self-control, and we continued.

I could have dismissed this encounter as a one-off, an aberration. "I guess I'll never do that again!" Instead, as a result of that "jaw-dropping" moment, I came to realize (1) that I can never know enough about participants to make assumptions about their objectives and that being curious and asking them is both logical and respectful and (2) that encouraging participants to identify their priorities recognizes the principle of self-determination. An added bonus—following these principles is not only good practice; it will likely prevent me from looking foolish. The lessons from this experience were not limited to that incident; I have applied them to every engagement, process, or intervention in the more than thirty years since that awkward moment.

To remind myself of the errors I've made and the lessons I learned from those experiences, I create role-play scenarios based on these situations to use in training courses. Each time these stories are presented, I am reminded of the original situation. I can see and hear the interactions, recall my reactions, and remember what I learned. There is an additional benefit to recalling the experiences and my reactions, humility—the notion that expertise is not limitless, that past success does not guarantee future achievement, and that there is always more to learn.

> I've missed more than nine thousand shots in my career. I've lost almost three hundred games. Twenty-six times I've been trusted to take the game-winning shot and missed. I've failed over and over in my life. And that is why I succeeded. Michael Jordan

We all fail sometimes. We deal with confusing and frustrating situations that leave us questioning our knowledge and skills. And we vow never to repeat that mistake. To a point, that familiar "trial-and-error" method works well, as shown in these common situations, where mistakes are an essential part of gaining proficiency:

- Learning to ride a bicycle, we tipped over, resulting in bruised knees and elbows.
- Preparing a lengthy report, spreadsheet, or multi-slide presentation, we lost material because we neglected to save our work.
- Planting a vegetable garden, we fail to protect against rabbits and other critters, and our seedlings become their supper.

Sometimes the cause-and-effect connection is so obvious that vowing never to repeat the mistake is sufficient. It doesn't require intense reflection to know what happened and how to avoid the mistake. We only need to lose one report or suffer one bunny assault on our garden.

Cycling offers a closer parallel to the web of behaviors required for success in conflict resolution practice. If we tip over, we can't correct the mistake until we understand the cause or causes. Were we riding too slow or too fast? Were we distracted by the sudden appearance of a child running into the street? Did we brake too suddenly or lose our sense of balance? Is there a mechanical problem? Knowing the cause allows us to adjust our future behavior. Simply telling ourselves we won't fall again doesn't prevent a recurrence. Similarly, to learn from a practice mistake, we need to understand not just what occurred but also why. And that is the benefit of reflective practice—learning from and through our experiences.

Reflective practitioners accept their fallibility—they know they will make mistakes. They don't dismiss, minimize, or overlook them or shift the blame to others (it was the client's fault). More important, reflective practitioners commit to learning from those mistakes in order to improve their effectiveness.

> To assess the quality of thoughts of people, don't listen to their words, but watch their actions. —Amit Kalantri

Quotation by Samuel Beckett; image by Jacob Lang.

Practice Humility

Following the publication of the first edition of this book, I wondered whether there is a tenth attribute of a reflective practitioner, a characteristic, much like curiosity in that it is central to the other attributes yet distinct. I believe the tenth attribute is humility. On first seeing the word "humility," you might assume I mean the qualities of modesty or restraint, being self-effacing, unpretentious, or deferential. For the reflective practitioner, these may be admirable traits, but the act of humility does not involve being submissive, self-deprecating, or yielding our well-earned expertise. Let me explain what the quality of humility means for reflective practitioners.

To become competent, effective, and resourceful practitioners, we prepare for professional practice by attending undergraduate and graduate schools and participating in specialized training courses in mediation, facilitation, and other conflict resolution principles and practices. In addition, we add to our foundation of knowledge and skills through years of practice. At some stage in our careers, we view ourselves as experts—knowledgeable and skilled, well versed in principles and techniques, proven in countless conflict interventions. In fact, we are experts. We know this because respected professionals rely on and repeatedly refer cases to us, clients regard us with deference and appreciation, and consistently successful interventions attest to our skill, creativity, and knowledge. Yet there is a surprising downside to seeing ourselves as experts. When we consider ourselves experts, we may begin to think and act as if we have achieved an esteemed status, and as a result of our position in the professional hierarchy, there is little more to learn. And it is in this belief that the danger lies—in an inflexibility born of unexamined and unreserved self-regard.

Humility is the first step in self-reflection. It makes us have second thoughts. It opens us to our ignorance, to our flaws, to our weaknesses. Christopher M. Bellitto

The "expert," according to Schön (1983), projects expertise, exudes self-confidence, maintains professional distance, and seeks deference to and respect for her reputation and status. In contrast, the reflective practitioner acknowledges uncertainties and embraces the opportunity to learn from them, respects that clients have expertise that bears on and will aid in the matter at hand, and dispenses with the facade of unwavering self-confidence.

To act, as Schön (1983) describes the reflective practitioner, requires humility. Acting with humility is not an abandonment of our expertise. It's not thinking less of yourself but rather thinking of yourself less. A personal example illustrates the dangers of seeing oneself as an expert:

> One afternoon when I returned home from the office, as I entered the house, I could hear loud, angry shouting coming from the living room. Curious and concerned, I walked into the room to see my older son (age twelve) holding the TV remote in his hand over his head as my younger son (age ten) jumped in a frenzied effort to grab it. Relying on my "dad voice," I told them to stop. When they turned to me, I asked why they were arguing. Having their attention, I calmly, following proper mediation practice, tried to help them resolve their dispute. Ten minutes later, having made no progress, my younger son turned to me, hands on his hips, smirking, and said, "And you call yourself a mediator!" In one sentence, I was leveled, my sense of competence dissolving as quickly as sugar in hot tea. Humbled. Later, on reflection, comforting myself as I put the humpty-dumpty pieces of my ego back together, it was obvious that as a dad, I couldn't be neutral—I wanted the fighting to stop. That was my goal regardless of their purpose. Further, yes, I am their father and wanted to assert my parental role, but I had not been invited into their conflict. I had inserted myself without their request or permission. Lessons learned. Be a mediator or be Dad (whatever that might signify), but I couldn't mix the two roles.

Reflective practitioners acknowledge that they are "not the only one in the situation to have relevant and important knowledge . . . uncertainties may be a source of learning" (Schön

1983, 300). Faced with a seemingly insoluble dilemma, the practitioner turns to the parties for their perspective. Why? Because there are as many experts involved in the process as there are participants. Each person has expertise—about themselves, of course, also about the history, impact, and nature of the dispute and of the terms of a suitable settlement. Reflective practitioners do more than acknowledge the parties' expertise; they enlist that expertise:

> *Spiritual Companionship is a one-to-one relationship between a trained, experienced guide and a seeker who experiences a longing for something beyond the daily reality of a busy life. Meeting with a spiritual companion who uses questions and deep listening can help you to discern your own answers and find a sense of balance on your spiritual path.*
>
> *Over the past few years, I have participated in a reflective practice group for divorce mediators facilitated by Michael Lang. Frankly, I was not very skillful in applying and implementing reflective practice in my mediation cases. Now that I am retired from divorce mediation, I find that reflective practice as a way of listening and questioning is the foundation of my approach to Spiritual Companionship. —Georgia Daniels*

Reflective practitioners restrain their impulse to offer solutions on matters in which they may have ample experience and knowledge, as when parents struggle to construct a time-sharing plan. Patiently asking questions to uncover the source of the indecision or uncertainty respects the parents' ability to find a workable time-sharing arrangement, even though the mediator could have readily provided an answer to their dilemma.

When the hesitant partner finds reasons not to accept an agreement that meets all her goals, reflective practitioners inquire—reflective practitioners don't assume they understand the partner's motivations, concerns, or strategies. They don't take on responsibility for pushing through the logjam; they engage the participants, who are far more knowledgeable about their situation than most practitioners allow. When participants in a multiparty engagement appear to be acting against their own interests by behaving contrary to their stated goals, reflective practitioners invite the participants to reflect on their experience rather than pointing out the discrepancy between aspirations and actions. In each of these examples, reflective practitioners act with humility, gathering information from those at the table who have a special expertise in the dispute and in the process that would best suit them.

Humility is an attitude toward others—that their ideas, goals, and preferences matter. Humility is reflected in the action of inquiring about and incorporating the expertise of each person involved.

You may see these examples as reflecting good practice as much as illustrating humility. And you would be correct. The attributes of a reflective practitioner—mindset and actions—are the building blocks of competent, resourceful, and effective practice.

The exercises below will stimulate your curiosity and nurture the mindset of being an enthusiastic and persistent learner.

Exercises

Exercise 3.1: Exercise Curiosity

Recall a recent intervention in which a comment or behavior aroused your curiosity. What sparked your curiosity? Identify three "impertinent" questions you might have asked but did not.

Exercise 3.2: Be Resilient

Recall a moment when something that occurred was unexpected, disorienting, or disturbing. What were you feeling? What were you thinking? How did you respond?

Exercise 3.3: Nurture Simplicity

Thinking back on a recent engagement, imagine how you could apply the principle of Occam's razor.

Exercise 3.4: Value Ambiguity

Recall an impasse where you acted purposefully and decisively to break through the logjam of uncertainty, indecision, or a seemingly intractable conflict. Can you now envision an alternative approach?

Exercise 3.5: Pay Attention to Detail

Picture a recent intervention. Recall your opening statement: both the substance and how you conveyed the information. What do you think the parties learned about you, the process generally, your style and methods, and their roles? As you were delivering this introduction, were you attentive to reactions? What did you discern?

Exercise 3.6: Learn Ceaselessly

For the next three months, invest at least thirty minutes each week reading a professional book or journal article and make a note of something you wonder about. In the next six months, sign up for a course, webinar, conference or similar that you do not need. At the end of twelve months, reflect (mentally or in writing) on what you learned during the year.

Exercise 3.7: Resist Certainty

This exercise helps counter the tendency to remain comfortably cocooned in the certainty of your practice patterns and routines. Write the following on a piece of paper and place the note prominently beside your computer or notepad during your next professional engagement: "What is new, surprising, unforeseen, and different?" Refer to this note often.

Exercise 3.8: Balance Commitment and Flexibility

During a conflict engagement, have you thought, "I see now what this conflict is all about." Were you ever mistaken? How would you know? What would you do if you learned that your view of the conflict was off the mark?

Exercise 3.9: Embrace Failure as Your Mentor

Recall a time when applying a technique or strategy you've used often and successfully proved to be a mistake. Perhaps you asked the wrong question of the wrong person at the wrong time. Or maybe you separated the participants unnecessarily and unhelpfully. How did you respond to this apparent mistake? As a result of this experience, what did you learn?

Exercise 3.10: Practice Humility

At your next session (mediation, facilitation, etc.), as you learn about the participants, make a note of their expertise—their knowledge and experience about the conflict, the others involved, and themselves. How can you enlist their expertise? As that engagement proceeds, make note of any time you think (or say), "If you want to get this resolved, then this is what you should do."

Practice Tips

Practice Tip 3.1: Learning from Mistakes

Accept the idea that you will make mistakes. Everyone does.
Do not dismiss, overlook, or minimize these errors. You can't learn from your mistakes unless you acknowledge them.
Use reflection-in-action or reflection-on-action to explore the basis for the mistake.
What did you learn from your reflection? How will you use this lesson in the future?

Practice Tip 3.2: Introductory Comments

For your next introduction—whether presented in joint or separate meetings:
Speak conversationally and avoid acting on autopilot.
Look at the participants as you speak and pay particular attention to their reactions and responses.
Stop and engage with them frequently, especially if you notice behavior that suggests the need for a response.
Remember this as your first intervention into the conflict.
Treat the opening statement as you would any other action—be intentional and have a goal.
Invite the participants to ask questions about what you've said. It's not enough to ask whether they understood you.
Ask about their expectations for the intervention—for the process, not the outcome.
Through your introductory comments, you are building rapport. You are helping them learn about you. Because you talk with (not at) them, they are gaining confidence in you and the process.
Use the opportunity wisely and mindfully.

Practice Tip 3.3: Questions to Inspire Curiosity

For example, consider the different types of questions asked during an intervention. Two of these categories (closed ended and open ended) are consistent with the goals of inquiry—focused on realizing a solution; the other (elicitive) reflects the practitioner's curiosity.

Closed-ended questions:

What is your role in the company?
Where do you live in relation to the proposed shopping center?
Have you previously participated in a dispute resolution process?
Is there additional information you want to present?

Open-ended questions:

What are your expectations about participating in this process?
Is there anything you need to help you to reach a decision?
Can you identify any part of the proposal that would be acceptable?
Has anything you've heard so far helped you to better understand the situation?

Elicitive questions:

Is there anything that might help you see the problem from a different perspective?
As a parent, what do you want for your child?
How do you think your coworkers view the conflict between you and your manager?
What influences your perception of the neighborhood?

CHAPTER 4

Theory
What We Think Shapes What We Do

Do you know why you do the things you do . . . the choices you make? —Rick to Merle, *The Walking Dead* (AMC television series)

When I talk about theory as part of a course or seminar, the audience tends to react—at least initially—in a predictable manner. Deep sighs signaling resignation that they can't escape this segment of the presentation. Eyes close in guarded anticipation of something like medicine—it may taste bad, but it's good for you. They listen respectfully, hoping for some juicy or humorous stories while tolerating the dry parts in between. And that's how I have organized this chapter.

A professor must have a theory as a dog must have fleas. H. L. Mencken

The stories I offer will help you realize that theory influences your countless ordinary decisions of the day, from the moment you wake and throughout your professional work.

Examples and illustrations from our common activities and from our conflict work will illustrate the pervasive—truly essential—role of theory in our lives. Therefore, my objective in this chapter is to present theory as accessible and relevant to our practices—indeed, as necessary for all our practice decisions. My goal is that by the end of the chapter, you will begin to find your own answer to Rick's question of Merle:

> Jacob had been on my roof, repairing broken clay tiles, in the intense heat of a Florida summer, unshaded by nearby trees, for four days. Several factors made his work particularly challenging—the tiles are fragile, broken tiles were situated all over the roof, we had a limited supply of replacement tiles, and preserving existing tiles that might be cracked but could be repaired was imperative. The job was fussy and exacting and strenuous and exhausting; it required patience and care. Jacob was meticulous in his preparation, always thinking and planning before he hauled the next load of tiles up the ladder. Although a young man, probably mid-twenties, Jacob had been "on the roof," as he put it, since he was a young boy helping his father and learning from him. We spoke each day when he arrived and as he prepared to leave. Jacob is an easygoing person, friendly, intelligent, eager to satisfy the customer, and always ready to talk about his work. We fell into an easy rhythm during the week. On the fourth day around 3:00 p.m., after he had cooled off, rehydrated, and put on a clean shirt, he was giving me a daily report of his activities, I asked him to explain how he went about his work, how he knew what to do.
>
> To paraphrase a line from a popular film, he had me when he replied, "Well, here's my theory." Jacob explained how he used cement to support the arched (barrel) pieces, working meticulously to ensure that they were well anchored. He would experiment. He knew how to use all the materials; that was never an issue for him. But this situation was different. He wondered whether the mortar (cement) would serve as a support for the tiles so that he could secure them to the roofing underlayment with special adhesive. He tested the mortar. Was it too wet and then take too long to set and then dry? Was it too dry and might crumble under the blistering summer Florida sun? He used one hand to hold the mortared tiles in place and applied the adhesive with the other hand. He used a trowel, sliding it repeatedly over the surface of the mortar to draw out liquid.
>
> He said, "I used to be impatient. When I encountered a situation that I couldn't resolve easily and quickly, I'd be frustrated and walk away. Now I am patient. I work as slowly as I need to in order to solve the problem."

As he pulled out of the driveway, I rushed into the house to make notes of our conversation and later obtained his approval and from his employer, Nick Zoller, to use Jacob's story in this book.

Can we as practitioners explain the analysis and thought process that leads to our actions as clearly as Jacob described how he puzzled through the challenge of using materials he knew and understood well in a situation he'd never encountered? Can we describe the theories—the beliefs, principles, and values—that shape our thinking and in turn influence our practice decisions? This is the central theme of this chapter—understanding how theory shapes practice. To begin, I want to define theory, then explore how theory acts to influence our decisions, and, finally, I will describe how we can identify and then consciously and purposefully use theory to guide our actions.

Defining Theory

A common understanding of theory, one that I am using in this book and that shapes my practice, is that theory explains phenomena and gives meaning to events, structures, patterns, and behaviors. Moreover, when I speak of theory, I don't restrict my definition to academic models and conceptualizations, the sorts of systems taught in professional schools, such as theory of jurisprudence, conflict theory, or communications theory. My notion of theory—especially in connection with professional action—includes the vast, interconnected and integrated collection of beliefs, principles, biases, models, doctrines, philosophies, and standards (even maxims and proverbs) that shape our perceptions of the world around us and influence our decision making and actions. To Argyris and Schön (1974), "Theories are theories regardless of their origin: there are practical, commonsense theories as well as academic or scientific theories" (4). I concur.

David Brooks, a *New York Times* columnist, although not explicitly exploring notions about theory, nevertheless proposed an explanation for the operation of theory on our perception of objects to create meaning and knowledge. Brooks, reflecting on the phenomenon of seeing and perceiving, as viewed by John Ruskin, the Victorian art critic, comments,

> Ruskin intuited something that neuroscience has since confirmed: Perception is not a simple and straightforward act. You don't open your eyes and ears and record the data that floods in, the way in those old cameras light was recorded on film. Instead, perception is a creative act. You take what you've experienced during the whole course of your life, the models you've stored up in your head, and you apply them to help you interpret all the ambiguous data your senses pick up, to help you discern what really matters in a situation, what you desire, what you find admirable and what you find contemptible. (*New York Times*, January 25, 2024)

Reading this essay, I recognized in Ruskin's proposition something analogous to my own understanding of the process of producing meaning through filters of our beliefs—our theories. It is, as Brooks notes, more than the mechanical act of the optical lens gathering light and producing an image on film (or digital media). Yes, our theories are lenses, but their function in the process of creating meaning are active, not passive, intermediaries. The application of theory requires intention, choice, and purpose. It's not just what we believe but also how we choose to apply those beliefs to our experiences.

Before you tell your life what truths and values you have decided to live up to, let your life tell you what truths you embody, what values you represent. Parker J. Palmer

In *The Making of a Mediator* (Lang and Taylor 2000), Alison Taylor and I proposed a conceptual model, the Constellation of Theories, to illustrate this wide-ranging, interrelated and integrated collection of ideas. Each person's constellation is unique, consisting of theories drawn from life experiences, guided by family values and traditions, shaped by education and training, inspired by professional experiences, and influenced by cultural and contextual circumstances. The elements that form each person's constellation are unique, and each component may have a greater or lesser influence on us. Some are dominant and have a significant impact on our perceptions and our decisions. Others are weak, and their influence is irregular and infrequent. Some operate continually and affect nearly every aspect of our lives; others are situationally dependent.

Like the sun in our solar system, each of us is at the center of our personal Constellation of Theories. Orbiting around us and interacting are five types of theories: personal beliefs (core values), applied theories, models of practice, professional experience, and contextual factors. Their orbits are not parallel; they intersect. They combine in various configurations, and they affect one another—each influencing the others and being influenced by them.

Core values orbit nearest the center. Their placement does not necessarily imply prominence or greater relevance. These values are tied to self-identity and are nearly always deeply ingrained. Changes in these values are slow to emerge and less common, yet when changes occur, they are likely to have profound implications for how we perceive and engage with the world around us. Core values consist of life lessons passed to us from our families, teachings learned in school or in religious or spiritual education, or values, rituals, and traditions embedded within and commonly accepted as part of one's culture. They may be initiated, shaped, and altered through relationships with peers, participation in athletics or art programs, employment, significant life experiences, and historical or current events. Examples of core values are moral and ethical principles, such as honesty, self-respect, justice, dependability, kindness, compassion, loyalty, self-reliance, generosity, and fairness. Other examples of core values include how we understand and respond to goodness and decency or to venality and malice, whether we tend toward optimism or skepticism, also our experience with and beliefs about autonomy, faith, love, friendship, interdependence, respect, and trust.

The next orbit comprises *applied theories*. In academic courses and professional development programs, we learn broadly applicable models and philosophies, such as theories applicable to conflict analysis and management, economics, critical analysis and writing, scientific principles, systems analysis and design, and interpersonal communications. We may also learn theories related to specific disciplines, such as philosophy, biology, literature, psychology, history, sociology, and astronomy. As preparation for professional practice, we learn theories pertinent to disciplines such as law, education, medicine, international relations, education, or business management. Of particular significance to conflict resolution professionals, concepts in this orbit include theories about conflict formation and transformation, power, justice, negotiation, interpersonal communication, decision making, and human development.

Models of practice, personal styles, and norms of professional behavior include standards of practice; professional ethics; best practices; articulated models of practice, such as narrative, insight, and transformative; and personal approaches, such as facilitative and evaluative.

This orbit encompasses the broad framework of and strategies for intervening in conflicts generally and includes specific notions regarding conflict areas, such as workplace, community, family, commercial, labor-management, public engagement, and environmental. Also in this orbit are laws, regulations, and other public policies that affect the nature of conflict practice and the certification and regulation of practitioners.

Within this orbit, I include theories evolved from *practice experience*. Argyris and Schön (1974) refer to this as implicit or tacit knowledge. "Tacit knowledge is what we display when we recognize one face from thousands without being able to say how we do so, when we demonstrate a skill for which we cannot state an explicit program" (10). Through practical experience, we establish practice routines (preferred strategies and tactics) and a framework for our interventions (e.g., joint or private sessions, in person or online). We develop an intuitive sense of what works. In subsequent chapters, I will say more about the crucial importance of tacit knowledge, its relevance for and application to practice, and how it can be strengthened or altered through reflective practice.

> The world can doubtless never be well known by theory: practice is absolutely necessary; but surely it is of great use to a young man, before he sets out for that country, full of mazes, windings, and turnings, to have at least a general map of it, made by some experienced traveler.
> Lord Chesterfield

In the outer orbit are a collection of *contextual factors* affecting our practices. Among these are operational policies and procedures (our own or those promulgated by organizations and agencies that contract for our services such as courts, government departments, and businesses). Additional elements in this orbit include forms and documents, norms of practice (use of joint or private sessions), and expectations (length of session, settlement rate). Other contextual factors include our role (mediator, facilitator, coach, arbitrator, or convener), whether we are serving as internal or external consultant, and expectations of those requesting our assistance (e.g., attorney, agency director, human resources manager, participants, or judiciary). Finally, our understanding of and response to conflict situations is directly affected by the nature of the conflict itself. How we think about and address disputes between neighbors over the placement of a fence involve different principles than responding to a multistakeholder situation involving the siting of a major industrial facility.

To further understand the constant and vital impact of theory on our thoughts and actions, let's consider how our Constellation of Theories is meaningfully and continually influenced by the common and routine events of our lives.

Theory in Everyday Life

If you drink tea or coffee, you likely have a preferred variety of teas or beans, use particular equipment, and employ a favored method for making the perfect brew. If you manage, supervise, or mentor others, you likely have a preferred style based on ideas about the role and responsibilities of leadership developed through experience and based on principles you learned in university courses or professional development programs. You may hold beliefs about the proper way to organize and delegate work, motivate and supervise employees, and demonstrate leadership. If you exercise, you choose a unique goal (aerobic capacity, strength, flexibility, balance, or endurance). Then, to achieve your objectives, you choose routines that incorporate certain techniques, use various pieces of equipment, and determine the frequency, duration, and intensity of your exercise routine. These choices are influenced by your "theories" about the value of and methods for exercise and conditioning.

In each of these situations, we make choices based on a set of beliefs, theories, assumptions, or principles. These beliefs are often tacit, running in the background. Like the operating system in your computer or smartphone, you can see the results even if you aren't aware of the mechanics and processes. In each of these situations—and in our personal and professional lives generally—theories have a direct and instrumental impact on our actions and are fundamental to our sense of ourselves and our world.

There is no single set of theories that distinguishes accomplished practitioners from those who are skilled and less proficient. What I believe is true is that skilled and effective practice can be achieved only through conscious awareness of the theories that shape our perceptions and guide our actions and thoughtful and purposeful application of those beliefs.

I often use this exercise when talking about the relationship between theory and practice. I present the basic facts of a conflict situation and ask for an explanation (hypothesis) for the behaviors and circumstances therein—"What's going on here?" Predictably, there are nearly as many answers as there are participants in the training program. Most responses are reasonable, compelling, relevant, and valid; a few are off the mark, and one or two are just plain goofy. That there are multiple explanations to a simple description of an uncomplicated conflict situation isn't surprising. In developing their hypothesis, each person focuses on and makes use of selected facts and relationships and then filters the information through their unique Constellation of Theories to produce individual, distinctive (and plausible) explanations.

I want to acknowledge an apparent contradiction and explain how two seemingly incompatible statements can be true. I have said that, for the most part, theories operate outside our conscious awareness. I have also said that being aware of and intentionally applying our theories is crucial to professional decisions. Can both be true? The answer to this seeming paradox is yes:

> Studies of dual cognitive processing and developing expertise confirm that system 1, automatic, unconscious intuitive judgments dominate expert decisions. System 1 processing relies on the recognition of patterns stored in the memory, while system 2 processing is conscious, deliberate, analytic, and restricted by working memory capacity. Within the fast and tense mediation context, judgments are likely to be automatic. (Peleg-Baker and Lang 2022, citations omitted)

Interactions in conflict work are generally rapid, and conscious processing (system 2) is less frequent; instead, we respond automatically, relying on tacit knowledge (system 1) to guide our actions. But the next obvious question is, how can we be confident that our reflexive and instinctive judgments are linked to and supported by our beliefs? In *Blink*, Malcolm Gladwell (2005) describes a process used by Thomas Hoving, former director of the Metropolitan Museum in New York, to develop the ability to make apparently instinctive, automatic judgments about the authenticity of works of art. Quoting Hoving, Gladwell reports,

> "We spent evening after evening taking things out of cases and putting them on the table. . . . There were thousands of things. . . . It was really poring and poring and poring over things." . . . What he was building, in those nights in the storerooms, was a kind of database in his unconscious. He was learning how to match the feeling he had about an object with what was formally understood about its style and background and value. (184)

Tennis players exhibit this ability to respond in the blink of an eye. The time from one player's stroke until the ball passes the net is less than one second. In this time, the opposing player must assess many elements, including the ball's trajectory, speed, and spin, and identify the likely spot where it will first bounce. To respond, the opposing player must immediately begin moving into position and decide how to play the return. There is little opportunity for system 2 processing of the event. The player must rely on system 1 thinking, an instinctive, automatic response—adjusting her position, calculating where the ball will land, and determining how best to respond. She develops the ability for instantaneous response through years of systematic, structured, and purposeful repetitive practice (often coached).

In theory there is no difference between theory and practice. In practice, there is. Yogi Berra

In other chapters, we will delve more into the process of how conflict intervenors can develop their own "database." For now, let me note that experience alone will not produce the tacit knowledge required for system 1 responses to fast-paced interactions in a conflict setting. Achieving a reliable and effective database requires purposeful reflection and a commitment to learn from our experiences. Reflective practice produces that type of learning.

Theory in Practice

Ellen Barry, in an article in the *New York Times* on March 10, 2018, reports on an experiment in England that illustrates the use of theory to guide action:

> Educators in Britain, after decades spent in a collective effort to minimize risk, are now, cautiously, getting into the business of providing it.
>
> Four years ago, for instance, teachers at the Richmond Avenue Primary and Nursery School looked critically around their campus and set about, as one of them put it, "bringing in risk."
>
> Out went the plastic playhouses and in came the dicey stuff: stacks of two-by-fours, crates, and loose bricks. The schoolyard got a mud pit, a tire swing, log stumps, and workbenches with hammers and saws.
>
> Limited risks are increasingly cast by experts as an experience essential to childhood development, useful in building resilience and grit.
>
> Outside the Princess Diana Playground in Kensington Gardens in London, which attracts more than a million visitors a year, a placard informs parents that risks have been "intentionally provided, so that your child can develop an appreciation of risk in a controlled play environment rather than taking similar risks in an uncontrolled and unregulated wider world."
>
> "It's about exploring controlled risk, risk that we've carefully designed," said Chris Moran, manager of Queen Elizabeth Olympic Park. "We've got the gorse bushes, which are quite spiky," he said. "The child will touch it and learn it is a spiky bush."

If you don't know where you are going, any road will get you there. Lewis Carroll

The proponents of the playground plan explicitly specified the values and beliefs supporting the decision to create managed risks. They based their actions on theories of cognitive development and experiential learning. Among other considerations were the (theoretical) benefits of developing resilience and grit and the possible risk of injury. The designers also determined that to minimize the risk of harm to the children, the plan would require increased adult supervision.

This approach to playground design is an experiment that, if successful, will result in outcomes predicated on the applicable theories. By deliberately basing their choices on identified theories, the designers have a basis for assessing their results—whether successful or not. Recall the description of reflective practice offered by Linda Finlay (2008):

> In general, reflective practice is understood as the process of learning through and from experience towards gaining new insights of self and/or practice. This often involves examining assumptions of everyday practice. . . . The point is to recapture practice experiences and mull them over critically in order to gain new understandings and so improve future practice. (1, citations omitted)

To examine our assumptions, we must first know what they are. The designers identified the beliefs (assumptions) that supported the choices of materials and equipment. Monitoring the children's experiences, they will learn whether their assumptions are valid or ought to be adjusted in light of certain behaviors.

How Theory Shapes Actions

The metaphor of a lens—as in telescopes, cameras, and eyeglasses—helps explain the process by which theory affects our perception of and response to events. The lens captures and concentrates rays of light and creates an image. The lens determines the field of view. Adjust the focal length of the lens (from normal to zoom), and your perception will change dramatically. Use a "fish-eye" lens, and the image will differ markedly from one produced by a telephoto lens.

> We must look at the lens through which we see the world, as well as the world we see, and the lens itself shapes how we interpret the world. —Stephen R. Covey

Consider the digital camera in our smartphones. We use this camera to record events, scenery, and people. The operation is simple: point, press the shutter button, and, magically, a digital image is captured and stored on the device. Apart from choosing and framing the image and perhaps adjusting the zoom feature, we rely on a mysterious and intricate web of sensors, circuits, and chips, carefully integrated, to create the image. We don't need to think about focal length, shutter speed, aperture opening, and ISO setting. All are embedded within the camera's digital components. Each feature is based on theories of light and photography. We may not understand these theories or see how they impact the design of the camera; we experience the effect whenever we take a shot.

Too often, opinion is a lens polished by the grit of bias. And as I stare through my own lens, I might ask how much polish can the grit of bias actually create? Craig D. Loundbrough

Like the camera lens, theory operates by capturing and concentrating information (behaviors, ideas, language). Instead of creating a photographic image, theory produces a hypothesis, a possible explanation for what is observed. Theory allows us to create meaning—an explanation—by organizing the data and producing an interpretation. That interpretation determines how we respond. If we use a different theory (change lenses), the meaning (image) changes.

The notion of theory as a lens may seem self-evident, especially with respect to choices such as diet, exercise, and playground materials. The interrelationship between what we think and how we act is obvious. In other situations, this connection is not as apparent. Instead, the process is opaque and mysterious (digital photography). It doesn't matter whether we are conscious of our beliefs or unaware of their influence; they affect our actions to the same degree.

The Role of Theory in Making Practice Decisions

In practice we rely on theories each moment. Mostly, they operate in the background (system 1), and our actions appear to be guided by an intuitive sense. We do what seems appropriate and responsive, moving from moment to moment, applying one tactic or strategy after another, responding to rapidly unfolding events, adjusting our approach to meet what we perceive as the needs and interests of the participants. We seldom interrupt the moment-to moment flow of the interaction to consider what theory may be influencing our judgments. Yet, like the sensors and chips in our smartphones, our beliefs actively affect our actions, even when we are not actively aware of their effect.

In a *Sarasota Herald Tribune* article on June 22, 2018, financial adviser Lauren Rudd observes,

> What about trying to mimic the moves of successful investors? . . . Many people have tried to mirror the strategies of investors such as Warren Buffett of Berkshire Hathaway. The problem is that, by not understanding exactly how someone makes decisions, you cannot fully duplicate the process.

Rudd's observation points out the inherent downside of accepting advice from well-meaning colleagues for resolving a practice dilemma. In part, the problem stems from their lack of direct knowledge of the situation and the participants. More important, however, no matter how thoughtful and discerning they may be, your colleagues do not know how you make decisions; they don't have your brain, they have their own. That's why the exercise I described previously results in multiple explanations for the same set of facts:

> *A perception, an assumption, a knowing — all traits and traps that can distract from the task of partnering with the practitioner to help them find their own dawning of wisdom. Finding the questions that brings them deeper and deeper to a stillness of inward reflection. Holding them there, until a spec of light appears in their search, that suddenly brings perfect clarity. The answer appears, the practitioner now has the "knowing" — the next steps are clear. —Frances Stephenson*

Likewise, when seminar and workshop presenters enthusiastically describe an intriguing or knotty practice situation and explain how they navigated the troubled waters, their story is incomplete. It lacks an essential element (their reasoning), how they chose their strategy and tactics, and, most crucially, why. Without explaining how they made the decisions, it's not possible to learn from their experience. We are left with a captivating tale of an interesting practice challenge.

The following example illustrates this key element—the decision-making process that connects events, analysis, and response:

> Ninety-five days into a projected five-month construction project, the general contractor halted the job, idling his workers and the subcontractors. This decision followed an argument—loud, angry, and unfortunately overheard by most of the

workers—involving the three principals: architect, developer/owner, and contractor. This was not the first dispute among these longtime business associates, but it was the first to remain unresolved after twenty-four hours. Continued delays could imperil the economic viability of a project based on an aggressive construction schedule. Failure to resolve differences among the principals could upend a decade-long and profitable collaboration. No one wanted to back down. The only thing they could agree on was the need for a prompt resolution.

Even with this limited information, can you develop a working hypothesis that would explain this situation? Why are these longtime partners unable to resolve their conflict? Can you connect your explanation to your theories? Are you influenced by prior experience with construction disputes? Is your explanation affected by theories about interpersonal communication, power, or conflict?

The three principals sought my help as a mediator. I was acquainted with them but had no professional relationship with any of them as an attorney, a mediator, or a client. The dispute arose over the design for and installation of patio railings. Given the scale of the entire project, the issue itself was minor. The remedy was obvious and relatively simple to achieve—reinforce the railings. The additional work would extend the 150-day construction schedule by no more than four or five days. The associated costs for labor and materials were estimated to add $25,000 to a construction budget exceeding $2 million.

As I listened to their stories, I was puzzled that three experienced and accomplished people with a long association were unable to solve this problem. They had successfully completed numerous projects. I wondered why their dispute arose at this moment. Also, why had one relatively minor item in a major construction project taken on an importance that was threatening the venture and undermining their profitable business relationships?

To answer these questions and develop a working hypothesis, I applied several theories to the information provided.

First, they sought my help because I had experience in and knowledge of real estate development and construction. I understand architectural drawings and specifications—important because construction disputes are frequently resolved by reference to these documents. I assumed that they tried this method and were still unable to find a solution.

Second, when an inexplicably passionate response to a seemingly minor conflict arises among people with an ongoing relationship, its intensity is often aggravated by prior disagreements that had been ignored, dismissed, or played down.

> I needed to change the lens through which I viewed everything familiar. Gretchen Rubin

Third, I often refer to the "Circle of Conflict: Causes and Interventions" (Moore 1996, 60–61). Moore contends that the cause (or causes) of conflicts generally fits into one of five categories: data, interests, values, structure, or relationships. In more complex disputes, there may be multiple overlapping causes.

Theories from other orbits of my constellation also shaped my understanding of the situation, including the following:

Core values—commitment to fairness in process and outcome; belief in people's capacity to find their own successful outcomes.
Applied theory—management of interpersonal communications and active engagement to help them communicate effectively, purposefully, and candidly.
Model of practice—facilitative; encourage interactions and dissuade them from looking to me for answers; businesslike and cordial.

Professional experience—knowledge of construction documents; experience in how this type of dispute arises, intensifies, and is eventually resolved.

Applying Moore's sources of conflict, I formed a preliminary assessment (working hypothesis) that *interests* (economics of the venture, professional reputations, and future opportunities for collaboration) were a likely source of this dispute. The amount of money and effort to "fix" the problem would increase overall costs and delay completion but to a seemingly minor degree.

The partners' inability to find a solution in the face of economic and time pressures suggested they may have lost trust in one another and perhaps confidence in their partnership. In addition, admitting an error could affect their professional reputations.

I considered whether this situation might be the result of conflict involving *data* (inaccurate or incomplete information, miscommunication, misinterpretation), *structure* (time constraints, lack of proper documents, imbalanced power relationships), *relationship* (persistent negative interactions, stereotypes), or *values* (ideological differences, reliance on differing benchmarks for assessing the situation). As these factors seemed less likely to have spawned the conflict, I put them aside.

Focusing on interest differences as the source of the dispute, I developed the following working hypotheses:

- A simple misunderstanding becomes overblown because of the intense pressure of time and economics.
- Conflicts are a natural and predictable part of any construction project. They arise because of differing interests, roles, and perspectives despite shared goals.
- The partners are implicitly renegotiating their working relationship, recasting their roles, and redefining the degree of their relative influence and power.
- Relying on their successful working history, the partners have made decisions assuming that any problems that arise will be readily resolved.
- Factors such as expected profits, professional reputation, and ability to meet commitments for other projects may be influencing their respective perceptions of and responses to the underlying problem.

To test these working assumptions, I asked them to describe the project, its origins, and their reasons for working together on this venture. This kept the focus on their mutual interests. I kept their conversation away from the dispute itself. I anticipated that talking about their original intention to work together might induce a more collaborative attitude.

They described the development process, from selecting a site to obtaining government approvals and financing and then beginning construction. They were animated and engaged, often interrupting one another to add a forgotten detail. When eventually they turned to the thorny problem of the railings, their attitude and behavior had shifted from contentious to problem solving. Data became their focus. When the discussion bogged down, when one tried to assess blame rather than find solutions, another would refocus the discussion, reminding the others of the consequences of continued conflict. Spreading the construction documents on the conference table, they concentrated on creating the most practical and cost-effective solution. In the end, they settled on a solution that was, as one of them noted, "not perfect but definitely good enough."

Could they have achieved the same result if I had considered that either data or relationship was the primary cause of their conflict rather than interests? It's possible. A different mediator with a different perspective and with a different Constellation of Theories would almost certainly have taken a different path with an equally positive outcome.

This story offers two lessons. First, it demonstrates the purposeful and step-by-step progression from observation to hypothesis to action. Theory, acting like a lens, focused attention on and illuminated key elements that yielded an image (explanation). Second, it illustrates the integration of theory and action. The intervention strategy resulted from a conscious process of analysis and deliberation.

A child of five would understand this. Send someone to fetch a child of five. Groucho Marx

Purposes of Theory

Argyris and Schön (1974) propose that theories have three purposes: they "are vehicles for explanation, prediction or control."

In the construction dispute, theories helped explain what occurred. Applying theory to the facts produced a hypothesis that led to the design of an intervention. This is theory as a vehicle for explanation.

Theories about the impact of conflict suggest that if the conflict persisted, the partners' positions would likely harden, and the principals would become more committed to their separate points of view and solutions. Trust would diminish. Effective communication would be diminished. As a consequence, they would challenge one another's recollections and dismiss the others' arguments, and their principal strategy would be to assess blame. Frustration would intensify. Individual needs would eclipse common goals.

> Problems rarely exist at the level at which they are expressed. If you are arguing for more than ten minutes then you are probably not discussing the real conflict. —Kare Anderson

I concluded that they might resolve their substantive conflict by starting with what unites them, their common interests, and then leveraging their long-standing working relationships. This view of the situation and the principals prompted my decision to "control" their conversation—not manage their interactions. By intentionally inviting them to tell the story of this project, the focal point became their common aspirations. Problem solving became an extension of that conversation about common interests rather than the continuation of the "blame game" that had produced the intense conflict. As a result of concentrating on their mutual goals and concerns, they reaffirmed their partnership, reinforced their trust in one another, and created a foundation for problem solving:

> *Reflective Practice has made all the difference to the way I practice my craft. Over the past six years I have had the privilege of being part of a dynamic group of reflective practice mediators—this has profoundly shaped my approach to mediation and significantly enhanced my professional journey. Participation in the group has helped me hone my skills as a mediator. Whether I am the one undergoing the reflective exercise or supporting a colleague in their journey, each debrief session has brought with it the opportunity for professional growth. Critically, it has also provided me with an opportunity for vicarious learning, gleaning insights from the unique challenges and experiences shared by my fellow group members. Reflective Practice is not just beneficial, it is indispensable for any mediator committed to excellence in their chosen profession. —Tracey-Leigh Wessels*

Practitioners become more effective when they know what they believe (their theories) and intentionally apply those beliefs to guide practice decisions. They know why they do what they do.

Espoused Theory versus Theory-in-Use

Argyris and Schön (1974) propose that professional competence stems from a practitioner's ability to integrate thought and action; the result of this effort is what they term theories of action. There are two categories of theories of action: espoused theories and theories-in-use:

> When someone is asked how he would behave under certain circumstances, the answer he usually gives is his espoused theory of action for that situation. This is the theory of action to which he gives allegiance, and which, upon request, he communicates to others. However, the theory that actually governs his actions is his theory-in-use, which may or may not be compatible with his espoused theory; furthermore, the individual may or may not be aware of the incompatibility of the two theories. (6–7)

The construction dispute illustrates espoused theory. I purposefully applied a set of beliefs to generate a hypothesis and then design and carry out an intervention. Like the playground designers, I was aware of the theoretical basis for my actions and the intended outcome.

Whether my actions (my theory-in-use) matched my espoused theory could be determined only by an independent observer. I believe there was congruence, but was there?

Lab studies of mediators' behaviors (Kressel et al. 2012; Peleg-Baker 2012a, 2012b) have revealed a general lack of congruence between the mediators' approach and intervention choices during a mediation simulation and the mediators' stated beliefs expressed in interviews prior to conducting a mediation simulation. The following are two examples from the research:

> A mediator who described her work before and after the mediation as facilitative and emphasized her goal to facilitate win–win solutions primarily sought compromise from the very early stages of the process. In most cases, mediators did not take the time to examine the parties' underlying concerns and consequently seemed unable to help the parties develop mutually acceptable solutions. . . . In his pre-mediation interview, another mediator presented himself as eclectic in style and emphasized his goal is to help parties improve their relationship. He talked about providing counseling, if needed, and promised not to make any decision for the disputants. In contrast, this mediator was observed using an evaluative style, was judgmental, and had no tolerance for relational or emotional expressions. (Peleg-Baker and Lang 2022, 4)

The incongruence between espoused theory and theory-in-use can be disorienting and confusing for us as practitioners and for our clients. To be effective, we must walk our talk; we must achieve a consistency between what we say we do and what we actually do. Without this congruence, we are fumbling, off balance, and ultimately less effective than when our beliefs match our actions. Consistency between what we say we believe and what we actually do is a hallmark of professional competence. Consider this common situation:

> The parents have established (and enforce) a household rule that digital devices may not be brought to the dinner table. Often, however, one of the parents will place

their phone on the table, explaining to the skeptical children, "Sorry, I'm expecting an important call. It won't take a minute."

In theory, the rule protects family time. In practice, it is ignored when an adult decides that there is a compelling reason to respond to a text message or to answer a phone call. The implicit—and dissonant—parental message is, "Do as I say, not as I do." How often does this occur—when espoused theory gives way to theory-in-use with the justification that it's expedient, pragmatic, or necessary? Is this what occurred in the lab study of mediators' methods and beliefs: that the irresistible desire for a satisfying end—"the deal"—prevailed over the mediators' avowed intentions and aspirations? Did espoused theory give way to the allure of theory-in-use?

Consider the incongruence between words and actions in managing a work project:

"I called this meeting," declares the delighted IT manager, "to announce that we have a new client and a major project. We need to complete the research, design, testing, and implementation of a website. The deadline is three weeks. I assured the client we could complete the project on time. You know your assignments. I'm available to troubleshoot problems. Send me one-page updates weekly."

The manager believes in delegating authority, relying on capable and self-reliant employees. She sees her role as providing encouragement and (when asked) advice and not micromanaging their efforts. Two days later, she joins a few of the workers in the coffee room and asks, "How are things coming along with the research? Any questions?" The following Monday morning, walking around the workspace, she stops and interrupts several employees to request "a brief progress report on this big, important project." Later that day, she invites the four team leaders to meet in her office "for lunch and a complete update."

> To believe in something, and not to live it, is dishonest. Mohandas (Mahatma) Gandhi

Yes, despite her commitment to delegation and encouraging independence, it would be difficult to avoid the conclusion that she is micromanaging. Does she see an inconsistency between her espoused theory and her theory-in-action? Does the staff? What are the implicit assumptions in her theory-in-use?

The manager might justify her actions (to herself) for any of the following reasons:

This is a new and important client, and as a result, she is experiencing increased anxiety about her team's performance.
Even though she expresses confidence in the staff's skills and professionalism, she may wonder whether they share the same commitment to the work schedule.
She misses hands-on work and finds that the role of manager distances her from those experiences. She feels insecure in her position because the role is not an ideal fit for her.

Serious problems may occur when espoused theory is incongruent with theory-in-use. Staff may wonder whether they should take their cues from her actions or her words. Do they patronize her, treating her interruptions as "that's just how she is"? Or, despite contrary instructions, do they provide frequent updates on their progress? Inconsistency creates uncertainty. Uncertainty results in anxiety. Anxiety may affect productivity and in turn lead to conflict. That's the experience of the employees. Incompatibility between stated intentions and actual behavior produces a similar anxiety within the manager. She is uncertain, hesitant, off balance, and less effective:

> We cannot learn what someone's theory-in-use is simply by asking him. We must construct his theory-in-use from observations of his behavior. (Argyris and Schön 1974, 7)

When the difference between what we say and how we act produces adverse consequences serious enough to demand a response, then either self-reflection or feedback from others can provide the incentive "to confront inconsistencies between their thinking and their practice and promote a conceptual change in [their] views" (Zalipour 2015, 1).

We can observe the benefits of a congruent relationship between espoused theory and theory-in-use, as well as the adverse consequences when the theories of action are incompatible, in the following example from conflict resolution practice:

> Under the rules of the family court, parties are required to attend and participate in a two-and-a-half-hour mediation session to address and, hopefully resolve arguments regarding the parenting of minor children. The mediator, an employee of the judicial system, convened the session, introduced herself, described the mediation process and her role, explained the principles of confidentiality, and stated that the ideal outcome would be a comprehensive parenting plan. (I had been invited to observe the mediation and to offer feedback following the session.)
>
> Mindful of time limitations, the mediator quickly gathered information—names and ages of the children; whether all were in school; whether any was involved in music, sports, or other after-school activities; how long the couple had been married; where each was residing; and whether they had already agreed on financial support. She then asked them to describe the current parenting arrangements.
>
> She next identified key topics (issues) to be discussed, including allocation of time with the children, transportation plans, and responsibility for decisions about the children's health, schooling, religious instruction, and participation in non-school activities. Child support, payment for health care, and other expenses would be discussed once they had agreed on a parenting plan. The mediator took each issue in turn:
>
> Mediator: What plans have you put in place for spending time with the children?
> Father: Well, I haven't seen them but once in the last two weeks. That's not good enough.
> Mediator: What's your proposal?
> Father: I've got a decent apartment. I work long days, but I was thinking they could spend two or three weekends each month with me.
> Mediator: [to Mother] Will that plan work for you too?
> Mother: I guess so, but what's he going to do with them for a whole weekend? He's never had that kind of responsibility.
> Mediator: That would be his problem to solve, wouldn't it? If you think he can properly look after them, then why not go along with this plan?

The session proceeded in this fashion as the mediator helped them build a co-parenting plan. Finally, the mediator prepared a memorandum of understanding, reviewed the plan, and answered their questions. At the end of the allotted time, the parties walked out of the room with a signed document. Later, the mediator, Sara, and I talked about the session:

Me: Was this a typical parenting mediation?
Sara: Pretty much. Some parents have just separated and have no plan in place; others, like this couple, have at least given some thought to how they want to parent their children.
Me: Do you use the same approach in private mediations?
Sara: No. I have more time. The participants can talk about interests, goals, hopes, and anxieties. In my private practice, it often takes four to five hours to create a parenting plan.
Me: What's different about court mediation?
Sara: It's just a function of time. The court administrator determined how long we can meet based on the number of cases filed and available funding for the mediation program.
Me: I noticed you were directive. You allowed little time for give-and-take between the participants. You pressed them for decisions, even when they seemed hesitant or unsure.
Sara: You're right. When I mediate in the court program, I just focus on getting an agreement. That's what the judges want. And that's all I can do in the time I have. It's not ideal, but for the parents, it's better than a court battle.
Me: I know you believe in the principle of self-determination where parties can exchange information and engage in a thoughtful discussion of various issues and proposals. That didn't happen in the mediation I just observed. How do you reconcile what you believe with what you're required to do?
Sara: At least half the couples I see will end up in court, no matter what happens. If I can help the other half avoid that calamity, I'm okay. I don't necessarily feel good about what I have to do to help them. The parties probably feel they have to accept the agreement because I am part of the court system. I do whatever I can to get them to reach an agreement. It's not great for any of us. I can't fight the administration, so I focus on achieving the best possible outcome.

Mediating within the court system, Sara is aware of the unfortunate and distressing divergence between her espoused theory and her theory-in-use. By being aware of this discrepancy, she believes that she limits any adverse effects on the participants and lessens any impact on herself.

What are the consequences when practitioners are unaware of the inconsistency between their espoused theory and theory-in-use? Often, practitioners act in a way that is inconsistent with their espoused beliefs. A common example is practitioners who assert that they use a facilitative approach, as in the research projects I cited. Judged by their actions, however, they are directive and at times even evaluative.

Wisdom is not what you know, but how quickly you adjust when the opposite proves true.
Robert Brault

You may question why this is important. After all, if the parties are satisfied with the process and outcome, why should you be concerned? There are three reasons:

1. Being unaware of your theory-in-use, you have no foundation for understanding why your actions are well received and successful or why your choices are ineffective. Without knowing the reasons for your actions, you won't be able to connect what you did with what occurred. If you lack the ability to evaluate your decisions, you are unable to learn from your experience. And when you are unable to learn from your experiences, the spiral of professional growth and evolution is stalled, and your practice becomes repetitive and stale.
2. Congruence enhances confidence and conviction. These qualities give you assurance that your interventions will be relevant, timely, and effective. Divergence creates instability—you feel out of balance.
3. If your strategies and techniques are limited to those with which you feel comfortable and which you sense have been helpful, every intervention looks the same. You lack the capacity to adjust your approach to meet the unique needs of the participants.

Learning from our experiences is the most direct and effective method for improving the quality of our work.

Single-Loop and Double-Loop Learning

According to Argyris and Schön (1974), learning from experience occurs through one of two methods: single-loop learning or double-loop learning. In single-loop learning, we apply a cause-and-effect method for resolving a problem as in the following example:

> Alicia is experiencing sleep deprivation—unable to fall asleep, insomnia, waking in the night, restlessness. She has researched all the common remedies, including prescription and over-the-counter sleep aids, homeopathic or natural products, warm milk, limiting caffeine intake, a new pillow, reading a paper book rather than a digital reader or watching television before bedtime, and meditation. In search of relief, Alicia decides to try several of these remedies.

Habit is necessary; it is the habit of having habits, of turning a trail into a rut, that must be incessantly fought against if one is to remain alive. Edith Wharton

These therapies address the symptoms but not necessarily the underlying cause. She tries one or more possible solutions until hopefully she finds a suitable remedy. Through trial and error, she may discover an effective treatment.

In another example of single-loop learning,

> The practice manager of a medical group has been receiving complaints from patients about delays in scheduling appointments with their physicians. Waits of two to three months are common. After consulting the medical staff, the manager institutes a policy that directs routine patient contact to nurses and nurse practitioners, with physicians addressing more acute problems.

In these examples, the response to the problem maintains "the field of constancy by learning to design actions that satisfy existing governing variables" (Argyris and Schön 1974, 19). This is cause-and-effect thinking—treating the presenting symptom.

Conditions of sleeplessness may be remedied by one of the therapies noted above on the assumption that the problem is most likely episodic and situational. If this is true, then addressing the symptoms is an adequate and effective approach. If the condition continues, however, symptomatic remedies may have limited value. Similarly, the new policy about patient visits may be sufficient without further deliberation.

Imagine applying double-loop learning. The process begins with an examination of the "governing variables" (Argyris and Schön 1974)—the assumptions and beliefs that influence our response to the condition. The governing variable may be that sleeplessness is the result of external stressors (work, family, finances) or a medical condition (sleep apnea, depression, side effects of medication) and that normal sleep patterns will resume once the source of stress is addressed or the medical issue is treated. If this is the case, treatments will address the stressors.

Governing variables applicable to the situation in the medical practice might include the system of scheduling all appointments for the same amount of physician time even though there is great variation in the time actually required; because some physicians spend more time with each of their patients, they are unable to see their allocated share of patients; or the number of patients seen in the practice has significantly increased through advertising and other promotional efforts without a corresponding boost in the number of clinicians. Using double-loop learning, the practice manager can identify which governing variable is at the root of the problem and design a response most likely to address the source:

> In a profile of Rebecca Onie in the *New York Times* on May 27, 2018, Karen Weintraub recounts the story that Dr. Onie tells of "a teenage boy who was mysteriously losing weight. His doctor, stumped, huddled with several other caregivers to decide which medical tests to run. Then someone asked the boy a simple question. 'Are you hungry?' It turned out the teen had been homeless for weeks and had eaten almost nothing. He had been too embarrassed to speak up but was relieved someone had finally asked."

The medical personnel relied on a recognized and dependable process for diagnosing the likely cause of the patient's weight loss. The governing variables were the identification of symptoms and the use of medical tests to search for a condition for which treatment could be prescribed. With a single question and without requiring a series of tests and further consultation, the explanation for the patient's condition became obvious. Looking to the patient for an explanation challenged the "governing variable" of the assessment protocol.

The benefit of double-loop learning is evident in the following practice situation, described by a participant in a reflective practice group:

> The mediator was exasperated with one of the parties who was troublesome and disruptive and repeatedly interrupted the other party and the mediator. This behavior was impeding progress and disrupting any meaningful discussion of the dispute and its possible resolution. On the rare occasions this party was silent, he was either muttering to himself or fidgeting with documents.
>
> Group members offered advice, including the following: avoid joint sessions and meet only in caucus, invite the attorneys to help in dealing with the behavior, or confront the person about the impact of his actions. Their suggestions were in the nature of single-loop learning, addressing the symptom—the party's behavior. Contrast those responses with the double-loop learning approach in a conversation with the group's facilitator (debriefer):

Every man is a damn fool for at least five minutes every day; wisdom consists in not exceeding the limit. Elbert Hubbard

Mediator: I tried every technique I could think of. His behavior was upsetting the other party. I was unsettled, discouraged, and bewildered.
Debriefer: What do you know about the dispute and about this party?
Mediator: The difficult party owns a company that produces specialty valves. The other party's company incorporates these valves in its products. The purchaser rejected a shipment claiming the valves failed to meet the required specifications. The supplier refused to replace the valves and canceled the contract.
Debriefer: What troubles you about the behavior?
Mediator: I have been mediating commercial disputes for more than ten years. I don't expect people to be completely logical and unemotional. Conflict is upsetting, and being in mediation isn't easy. However, I do expect people to be prepared, deal constructively with one another, and seek a settlement. They may get upset, even angry, but this person was being childish, self-indulgent, and distracting.
Debriefer: What are your assumptions about the party's behavior?
Mediator: He is stubborn and a bully. He likes to keep things stirred up. I don't think he's interested in settling the dispute.

Debriefer: When a participant acts this way, what is your role as a mediator?
Mediator: It's my job to help parties to identify the central issues, gather and discuss relevant information, explain their points of view, present and discuss proposals, and assist them in problem solving. This person was making all that impossible. We can't have a discussion on anything because of his troublesome and distracting behavior.
Debriefer: How do you explain his behavior?
Mediator: I can think of three possible explanations for his actions. He's embarrassed that his company failed to meet the standards required for these products. He knew the valves weren't perfect but hoped they could still be used. Second, he doesn't want word to get out about the mistake because he could lose customers. Lastly, he has previously bullied other people into settling their disputes with him.
Debriefer: Which explanation seems most plausible?
Mediator: The first. He doesn't want to admit that the valves were deficient. For him, any settlement would amount to an admission of fault.
Debriefer: Is it possible for you to address this issue with him?
Mediator: I could speak privately with him and his attorney. I could ask about his company, its history, the products it produces, and its successes. Then I could ask about this specific dispute. Depending on his responses and his mood, I could ask whether he would continue even if there was the possibility of a resolution that would not adversely affect the reputation of his business.
Debriefer: And if you spoke with him in this way, how would this help you in managing the mediation?
Mediator: I can't assume that difficult behavior necessarily means he is unreasonable and unwilling to participate. I need to consider other possible explanations. He might be a bully and a difficult person. Or there could be other reasons for his behavior.

The differences between this conversation and the offers of advice are obvious. Offers of advice represent single-loop learning. Any of the proposed recommendations might have been helpful. However, if that occurred, it would have been fortuitous and inadvertent because the advice, like the mediator's assumptions, was based on incomplete information about the reasons underlying the disruptive behavior. Each proposed intervention addressed only the party's actions—the symptoms, not his purpose or motivation. Through a reflective process of double-loop learning, the mediator discovered an intervention that might be suitable and successful because it was based on understanding the reason for the party's behavior:

> Both single-loop and double-loop learning methods have value. Both have limitations. Long-run effectiveness requires single- and double-loop learning. We cannot be effective over the long run unless we can learn new ways of managing existing governing variables when conditions change. In addition, we cannot be effective unless we can learn new governing variables as they become important. (Argyris and Schön 1974, 24)

The upside to single-loop learning is economy of effort and time—a direct and clear response to symptomatic behavior. It's a process we use frequently in our daily lives as well as in conflict resolution practice, often with success. Focus on the symptom, the observable behavior or impact, and then identify and apply an applicable solution.

The advantage of single-loop learning can also be its shortcoming:

> In single-loop learning, we maintain the field of constancy by designing actions that satisfy existing governing variables. (Argyris and Schön 1974, 19)

If the intervention effectively addresses the party's behavior, we move forward, having satisfied the "governing variable." In our example, the mediator may conclude that she has discovered an effective tool for dealing with the party's disruptive behavior. If her intervention (trying to exert control through vigorous and persistent steps to halt the behavior) is unsuccessful, what does she do next? Try another and another method until she (hopefully) discovers one that is helpful. This is the shortcoming to single-loop learning. Each effort to restrain the party's disruptive behavior is based on the mediator's governing variable (participants behave in a certain way). Unexamined obedience to assumptions that result in seeking a solution through trial and error that involves single-loop learning can leave the mediator and the parties exhausted, frustrated, and, in the worst case, without a solution.

Here's where double-loop learning can be constructive and advantageous:

> Double-loop learning changes the governing variables (the "settings") of one's programs and causes ripples of change to fan out over one's whole system of theories-in-use. (Argyris and Schön 1974, 19)

> *I have a simple philosophy. Fill what's empty. Empty what's full. Scratch where it itches. Alice Roosevelt Longworth*

Making use of double-loop learning, as occurred in the reflective debrief conversation, the mediator is able to critically assess the relevance and usefulness of the governing variable, adjust her thinking to allow for alternative causes for the disruptive behavior, and discover a practical and suitable approach.

The drawbacks to double-loop learning include the following:

1. The process may require more time as compared to single-loop learning. The rapid pace of interactions may limit opportunities for this degree of analysis and decision making.
2. In many situations, we are faced with the need for prompt, almost intuitive responses to unfolding events. Double-loop learning requires thoughtful analysis and reflection.
3. The double-loop process may unnecessarily complicate a situation. Some problems are better suited to a simple solution. Replacing a lightbulb often solves the problem; we don't need to evaluate the entire electrical system.

Theories—in the broadest sense—are the foundation for action. Whether we are aware of our beliefs and explicitly apply them or whether they are tacit and function without our awareness, theories influence every element of our practice. They determine what we pay attention to; shape the meaning we ascribe to events, behaviors, and circumstances; and determine the timing and choice of our interventions. As we become aware of our beliefs and how they direct our actions, we can use this knowledge to ensure that our decisions are more relevant, suitable, and effective.

> Experience without theory is blind, but theory without experience is mere intellectual play. —Immanuel Kant

Exercises

Exercise 4.1: Lenses

Choose a photo taken with your smartphone or camera. Examine the image. What influenced your choices of image, setting, composition, lighting, and perspective? Can you identify these factors?

Exercise 4.2: Beliefs

Recall the dispute among the architect, contractor, and owner. Consider the statements below. Do you agree with any of them? How do your beliefs affect your view of the conflict and influence your response?

- Instead of shutting out what is different, we should welcome it because it is different and through its difference will make a richer content of life. —Mary Parker Follett
- For good ideas and true innovation, you need human interaction, conflict, argument, debate. —Margaret Heffernan
- Change means movement. Movement means friction. Only in the frictionless vacuum of a nonexistent abstract world can movement or change occur without that abrasive friction of conflict. —Saul Alinsky
- If you want to bring an end to long-standing conflict, you have to be prepared to compromise. —Aung San Suu Kyi
- I always believe you should try to find peace and reconciliation before conflict. That has been the approach I've taken. —Colin Powell
- I don't like a tremendous amount of conflict. I don't think that fighting and passion are the same thing. —Tina Fey
- The most difficult thing in any negotiation, almost, is making sure you strip it of the emotion and deal with the facts. —Senator Howard Baker
- Quiet, calm deliberation disentangles every knot. —W. S. Gilbert, *The Gondoliers*

Exercise 4.3: Constellation of Theories

Identify factors that shape your perspective and influence your choice of strategies and tactics.

1. What are your core values or beliefs? What are the sources for these core values?
2. Do you consciously use theories as lenses for making sense of conflict situations? Which theories do you rely on most frequently? Think theories in the broadest sense.
3. How would you describe your approach to practice? Is your method facilitative, evaluative, directive, or something else? Do you subscribe to the theories and related techniques of conflict transformation, narrative mediation, transformative practice, or some other system?
4. How does past experience inform your current practice? Do you make use of lessons from previous practice situations?
5. Do you work with prescribed forms, procedures, or expectations? How do these factors affect your tactics, strategies, and other practice methods?

CHAPTER 5

Research Improves Practice

Progress has not followed a straight ascending line, but a spiral with rhythms of progress and retrogression, of evolution and dissolution. —Johann Wolfgang von Goethe

In previous chapters, I described the spiral of evolution and growth of professional development, and offered examples to illustrate that our practices are nourished and stimulated by continuously learning from and through experience. In these examples and illustrations, we concentrated on learning that arises out of practice experiences through the application of reflective practice principles and methods. As practitioners, we give little time to research studies and their implications for practice. In this chapter, I want to describe the crucial role of research in the growth and evolution of our practices by shaping our understanding of conflict, enhancing our skills, and expanding our knowledge.

Research matters to practitioners, and practitioners matter to research.

You might be skeptical of this statement. Reports of research can read like a foreign language unless we are familiar with the esoteric terms and complicated methodologies common to research studies. Practitioners also tend to dismiss research studies as academic exercises grounded in speculation, relevant only to other researchers, and largely disconnected from the day-to-day work of practitioners. As a result, we are likely to ignore the work of researchers, and the loss is ours.

Research isn't always based on complicated statistical analyses with formulas that look like this:

> *Research: The distance between an idea and its realization. David Sarnoff*

The joint profit scores for EML negotiators ($M = 13.87$) and FTF negotiators ($M = 14.68$) did not significantly differ, $t(37) = -1.15$, $p = .13$. (Morris et al. 2002, 92)

Making sense of the factors (how would I know what "M" or "t" signifies?) and their significance stumps most of us; this is the realm of statistics—a territory few practitioners will attempt to visit. This example is taken from a quantitative research study, a methodology that explores numeric patterns and relationships. In addition, there is a broad assortment of methods, such as interview, questionnaire, observation, action research, and case study, that may utilize non-numeric analysis. The point is that we should not assume that reading papers and articles describing research studies necessarily requires a sophisticated and esoteric knowledge of mathematical formulas.

Numerous studies that directly affect conflict resolution practice rely on such nonmathematical methods and present results that are accessible and comprehensible. For example, an early key study utilized qualitative methods to investigate and define the knowledge and skills of an effective mediator (Herrman et al. 2001). Additionally, the report on mediator techniques and approaches conducted under the auspices of the American Bar Association Section of Dispute Resolution (2017), and relying on a survey method is another relevant and readable research paper. Just because a journal article includes the word "research" in its title should not deter you from reading and learning from the study's approach, findings, and conclusions. Learning from research, like learning from and through practice experiences, advances our developmental spiral. As that spiral expands outward and upward, we grow in competence and effectiveness.

> Research is formalized curiosity. It is poking and playing with a purpose. —Zora Neale Hurston

I have two goals in this chapter. First, I want you to consider the results of research studies to be a valuable, even essential, part of your professional development. Second, I want to demonstrate the practical benefits of reading and applying the results of research studies for improving the quality of your practice. In pursuing both goals, I want you to consider the results of research projects that have practical implications for the strategies and tactics we use as conflict resolution professionals. For this book, I am not undertaking an analysis of the more complex and sophisticated aspects and methodologies of these research projects; I lack the knowledge and experience to do so. Rather, I want to show you what the research can teach us as practitioners and learn to integrate the results into the practitioner's day-to-day activities. This chapter is an orientation to research and a road map to an intriguing and valued means for developing your practice, a method equally as crucial as the tools and strategies you learn in training courses and professional development workshops.

I love doing research. It's like cheating, but with permission. Greg Rucka

Before we proceed, let me reveal a surprising piece of information: every time you engage in a conflict intervention, you are conducting research. With apologies to proper researchers for this brief and crude description, let me explain.

Our research begins with questions about interactions, our own and those we have observed, that we would like to understand. We wonder, what is happening, and why?

Our curiosity generates questions that lead to one or more explanations or hypotheses, from which we choose the most plausible.

Next, we explore whether our explanation matches the parties' experience through experiments or interventions—for example, offering a comment, asking a question, or moving from joint to separate meetings. We observe and assess the responses and evaluate the results in order to evaluate our hypothesis—whether it is confirmed or disproven.

If our explanation is contradicted, we wonder why and consider an alternate hypothesis and conduct further experiments. If our hypothesis is confirmed, the spiral of inquiry and learning continues throughout the engagement: observation, curiosity, hypothesis, experiment, results. We are conducting research!

Before turning to research specifically applicable to conflict resolution practice, let's consider two lessons from a book on sales, *SPIN Selling* (Rackham 1988). Why use a book on sales and not on negotiation or some other area of conflict resolution work? Because the author's approach is transparent, allowing the reader to look behind the curtain at the cluttered, reflective, and purposeful process of creating, evaluating, and selecting the methodology; implementing the experiment; and being thoughtful and curious about the results and their implications, even when faced with unexpected findings. As a result, we both understand the details of what occurred and, even more significant, learn why choices were made: the description of the process—the researchers' successes and frustrations. Their unstinting and meticulous search for answers is more than a fascinating narrative, more than a voyeuristic peek behind the curtain. Because the author explains the thought process that underlies the researchers' actions, we understand their rationale, not merely the results and implications. We pay attention to why they do what they do.

> *I notice increasing reluctance on the part of marketing executives to use judgment; they are coming to rely too much on research, and they use it as a drunkard uses a lamp post for support, rather than for illumination. David Ogilvy*

In the candid and insightful assessment of the researchers' thoughts and actions, we see, perfectly illustrated, the iterative unfolding of the research process—the spiral of inquiry and learning. And that is my second reason for citing *SPIN Selling*. Research is not a linear process proceeding resolutely from hypothesis to conclusion. As Rackham shows us, research moves in an evolving and expanding spiral.

Research into Reflective Practice and Reflective Practice Groups

Before considering research projects with practical implications for practice and because this book is centered on reflective practice, a brief look at research projects that examine the effectiveness of reflective practice for professionals seems in order. Frustratingly, reflective practice for conflict resolution professionals is the subject of a single research study (Arms Almengor, 2018); in contrast, there has been considerable research involving the professions of nursing, education, and social work in which reflective practice methods and principles have been in use for decades. Arms Amengor (2018) notes,

> Despite its many possible benefits, a reflective practice approach is still not the dominant form of teaching mediation or of gauging one's own "success" in practice. The benefits of reflective practice may not be evident, in part, because our field lacks

adequate models of reflection at the transformative levels of reflexivity and critical reflection; many practitioners still limit "reflection" to trial-and-error (single loop) thinking, storytelling, or advice giving. While useful to a degree, such forms necessarily limit self-reliance and variation in learning. (34)

The validity and effectiveness of reflective practice and its use in groups of professionals have been confirmed in numerous quantitative and qualitative studies. For example, the authors of one study of reflective practice and teacher training conclude,

> Reflective practice is an indispensable tool as far as effective teaching and learning are concerned when well practised can be regarded as a good option to create understanding in the teaching and learning process for attainment of educational goals. (Oduro et al. 2022, 2317)

In a review of relevant studies on reflective practice in nursing education, the authors concluded,

> The study results prove that reflective learning has a positive and effective influence in improving students' critical thinking, and it has some positive aspects for students in nursing education. (Uswahzulhasanah and Arotiati 2021, 1238)

Reflecting on the nature of reflective practice and its potential value for health care workers, the authors of a research study concluded,

> Reflective practice is valuable. Where group reflective practice is used for group reflection, resourced and facilitated expertly and related to external benchmarks, the potential benefits are extensive. (Quilty and Murphy 2022, 2)

Familiarity with reflective practice generally together with increased participation in reflective practice groups will hopefully stimulate greater interest in conducting additional research to examine the impact of reflective practice on conflict resolution practitioners and to learn whether and how it supports improvement in the quality and effectiveness of practice.

Do not be too timid and squeamish about your actions. All life is an experiment. The more experiments you make the better. What if they are a little coarse, and you may get your coat soiled or torn? What if you do fail, and get fairly rolled in the dirt once or twice. Up again, you shall never be so afraid of a tumble. Ralph Waldo Emerson

I approach research from the experience of a practitioner; I am not a researcher. I may not be able to distinguish between independent and dependent variables or know the meaning and significance of "chi-square analysis," but I can learn from reading research papers. I may labor to understand statistical analysis, but with persistence and patience, I can work my way though empirical studies.

For those of us unfamiliar with statistics, and I am among this group, our eyes might glaze over as we read this sentence. Yet even if we aren't trained in statistical analyses, we can appreciate and learn from research on conflict resolution practice. The citation above is from the report of a fascinating study that I'll discuss later in the chapter that explored the impact of rapport building on the effectiveness of e-mail negotiations. The report has important implications for our day-to-day professional activities. As in this research study and others highlighted in this chapter, there is a rich vein of practitioner gold to be discovered.

The Interaction of Theory–Research–Practice

There is an essential interrelationship among theory, research, and practice. The synergy that develops from this three-way collaboration nurtures the development of our profession and supports the continued expansion of each individual's spiral of professional growth and evolution. Each element has a distinct role. Each employs a unique set of methods and language. Yet none exists independently of the others. In a synergistic partnership, each influences and in turn is influenced by the others.

No research without action, no action without research. —Kurt Lewin

Researchers are dependent on practitioners for raw material. Practitioners "furnish the researchers with problems for study and a ground for testing the utility of research results" (Velayutham and Perera 1993, 291). They examine and assess what we do—our styles, the skills and strategies we use, our values and beliefs. They investigate the reasons we choose certain strategies and techniques in response to particular situations. They examine the practice problems we encounter, how we respond, and the impact on the participants and the overall process:

> Researchers' findings and conclusions explain the effect of our interventions on participants and as a result pointing us to strategies and tactics that are the most relevant and effective in certain situations, and broadly to identify the skills and knowledge required for competent practice. "Researchers are expected to provide the basic and applied science to derive the techniques for diagnosing and solving the problems of practice." (Velayutham and Perera 1993, 291)

Theorists generate hypotheses through observation of the phenomena of practice. Research provides a means for theorists to test their hypotheses. Research may also lead to rethinking an existing theory. Theory is the basis on which practitioners understand conflict situations as well as design and implement appropriate interventions:

> Core to almost all discussions of the relationship between academic research and . . . practice is that they are two very distinct knowledge and practice communities. The academic community typically develops and publishes theoretically framed generalizable knowledge based on rigorously peer reviewed research. . . . Practitioners develop and refine knowledge in the course of solving problems and addressing challenges to accomplish their purposes in a particular setting. Each community develops its own language and frameworks of knowledge, its own methodologies for creating and applying knowledge, and its own standards of relevance and rigor. (Mohrman and Lawler 2011, 15)

Over the past forty years, conflict resolution practice has developed at an astonishing pace, creating extraordinary opportunities for practitioners, researchers, and scholars. As a profession consisting largely of sole practitioners, our "separate worlds" have for the most part developed independent of one another. Conflict work tends to be solitary and private, always a confidential process, and therefore not easily accessed by researchers. Not surprisingly, researchers have difficulty persuading practitioners to participate in studies. Parties too generally resist the intrusion of an outsider notwithstanding promises of discretion and privacy. As a result, theorists and researchers have limited access to the moment-to-moment interactions of conflict practice, permitting few opportunities to observe, explore, evaluate, and understand the day-to-day activities of practitioners and the effect on clients of their strategies and interventions.

If you don't synthesize knowledge, scientific journals become spare parts catalogues for machines that are never built. Arthur R. Marshall

The growth of understanding follows an ascending spiral rather than a straight line. Marion Milner

Benefits of Research for Practitioners

As reflective practitioners, we seek out the best techniques and strategies to use in various practice situations. We need to know what parties in conflict are looking for, that is, what it would mean for them if the process "works." Particularly true for those who design and deliver educational programs is knowing what skills and knowledge lead to resourceful, competent, and effective practice.

Research findings and conclusions often challenge our beliefs and practices and prompt us to examine our assumptions and our methods. Other findings may confirm what we have learned from years of experience (tacit knowledge). Whether research studies prod us to adjust our thinking and our strategies or affirm practices we know to be effective and reliable, research provides vital information for us as practitioners.

As I mentioned earlier in the chapter, for a fascinating account of a research project that reads like an unfolding mystery story, I encourage you to read *SPIN Selling* by Neil Rackham. The author describes the meticulous research process undertaken by researchers at Huthwaite (the author being the lead investigator) to examine a long-held belief about sales practices and negotiation. The narrative follows the researchers as they generate a hypothesis, test their ideas, and assess the results in a continuingly evolving process. It's an absorbing and intriguing story:

As well, there are implications for conflict resolution practitioners such as,

There is a clear statistical association between the use of questions and the success of the interaction. The more you ask questions, the more successful the interaction is likely to be. (Rackham 1988, 14–15)

The Huthwaite study further determined that open questions (rather than closed) are more likely to produce positive interactions and successful results. Think of the implications for your practice—open-ended questions are inviting and "are more powerful than closed questions because they get the customer talking and often reveal unexpected information" (Rackham 1988, 15). Translate "customers" to "parties." Aren't these conclusions stunning—and valuable? If asking and listening are keys to successful engagement, consider your current approach. Would you consider altering your methods in light of these conclusions?

In *Mediation Research*, Kressel and Pruitt (1989) assembled articles from more than thirty esteemed and experienced researchers, scholars, and practitioners in an extraordinary overview of the mediation process and its effects. These studies, now decades old, are relevant to current conflict resolution practice. In areas as diverse as public policy, family, and community, the articles are useful and encouraging. As the authors note, practitioners "often wonder if there is any 'scientific' evidence that what they do works; here they will find reassurance on that score" (xvi). The conclusions in a number of the reported studies have been eclipsed by the rapid growth and evolution in our profession, yet some of the chapters contain gems, equally if not more important to conflict work than when the book was published thirty-five years ago.

If at first you don't succeed, search, search again. That's why it's called research.

Research of Particular Importance to Practitioners

Following is an abbreviated review of a handful of research projects; their conclusions, methods, and outcomes; and their implications for practitioners. The few studies described here demonstrate the value of research to practitioners. I selected projects to illustrate the value of research for practitioners using four criteria:

1. The findings have a direct bearing on the tactics and strategies used in negotiation and conflict resolution practice.
2. No special knowledge of research methods is necessary to understand the research methodologies, findings, and conclusions.
3. The reports are accessible and comprehensible—in other words, readable.
4. The studies display a range of research methodologies.

In each, you will recognize the relevance of the research findings to your day-to-day conflict work.

References in the bibliography include a number and variety of research papers published in books and scholarly journals and on blogs and websites. This collection of materials merely hints at the range of topics on negotiation and conflict resolution studies conducted over the past forty years.

The first group of research studies falls into the broad category of outcome research. Often, we mark our own success and justify the value of our profession by referring to settlement rates or post-session reports that focus on participant satisfaction. These studies focus on why mediation might be deemed successful; they identify and analyze the results that, apart from outcome, indicate that our interventions work.

Court-Annexed Mediation Pilot Project

I conducted an evaluation of a court-annexed pilot mediation program. The research focused on two questions: What do participants in sixty civil (nonfamily) mediations think about mediation and their experience? What implications can be drawn from an evaluation of their experiences?

To be clear, I am not trained as a researcher, and as a result, the methodology was uncomplicated, unsophisticated, and straightforward. Every party and every attorney (nearly all parties were represented by counsel) completed a multipage questionnaire. Using a simple 1–5 scale, the participants rated various elements of the mediation process as well as the mediator's temperament, support, engagement, and effectiveness. They were also encouraged (and most did) to provide examples to support their assessments. Mediators completed a similar questionnaire for each mediation conducted.

I conducted hour-long lightly structured telephone interviews with three of the five mediators, two assignment judges, the court administrator, and the project administrators. Information from those interviews supplemented data collected from the questionnaires. Results from the questionnaires were compiled, and the scores were averaged to provide an overview of the participants' experience. I presented my observations, findings, and conclusions both in a written report and during a lengthy in-person conversation with the chief justice of the Supreme Court, who had backed the project and was himself a proponent of mediation. The following are some of the results I reported:

1. Eighty-nine percent of disputants believed that by participating in mediation, they were able to express themselves, their thoughts, and their concerns.
2. Two-thirds of disputants believed that mediation helped them understand the other person's point of view and helped the other person understand their point of view.
3. More than 90 percent of disputants and nearly 100 percent of attorneys indicated that they would use mediation again.
4. Disputants and lawyers, at a rate of 90 percent, reported that mediation helped clarify the issues in dispute.
5. Almost universally, the disputants reported that mediation provided an opportunity to talk about the issues that were important.
6. In more than 90 percent of the cases, the disputants believed the mediator helped them come up with their own solutions.

The results were stunning. Everyone involved in the project had anticipated favorable reviews but not the widespread and enthusiastic acceptance of mediation. Curiously, their near universal endorsement of mediation bore little relationship to the settlement rate of approximately 60 percent. I surmised from the extensive comments as well as the survey data that participants' clear-cut support for mediation resulted to a significant degree from their opportunity to talk to one another, to explain the history and impact of the conflict (to tell the story of their experience), and even to engage in vigorous, even heated, arguments.

Does Mediation Work, and Why? A Small-Claims Study

An early research study (also discussed in Kressel and Pruitt 1989) investigated the effects of mediation in small-claims disputes in Maine. The research included a comparison between disputes that went to court and those that were mediated. Among the study's results was a conclusion that underscores a benefit of mediation that is particularly notable:

> Small claims mediation still succeeds in producing agreements and encouraging compliance. The kinds of outcomes encouraged by mediation make compliance more probable. But, the consensual quality of the mediation process also powerfully promotes compliance by implicating the parties in enforcing agreements upon themselves. By consenting to outcomes that they had some part in achieving, parties to a settlement enlist their own sense of honor. (McEwen and Maiman 1989, 66)

This makes sense intuitively. We are more likely to live up to our agreements when we agree to do something than if the terms are imposed on us.

What does this mean for practitioners? The study's conclusions reinforce the practical effects that occur when practitioners reliably honor the principle of self-determination—a value embedded in nearly all published standards of practice and in legislation governing mediation practice:

> Self-determination is the act of coming to a voluntary, uncoerced decision in which each party makes free and informed choices as to process and outcome. Parties may exercise self-determination at any stage of a mediation, including mediator selection, process design, participation in or withdrawal from the process, and outcomes. Standard I, A. (American Arbitration Association, American Bar Association, and Association for Conflict Resolution 2005)

Knowing that compliance is more likely when parties consent "to outcomes they had some part in achieving," best practice suggests that we structure our interventions accordingly. On a practical level, this may lead us to ensure that participants engage actively in talking about their dispute, identifying and gathering information they deem relevant and useful, and creating and evaluating proposals, not merely consenting to the terms of a settlement. Dogged pursuit of a settlement, without resolute and persistent concerns for party self-determination, is unlikely to produce the lasting benefits described in the research.

What Is the Effect of Alternative Dispute Resolution on Participants?

In the report of a study to measure the impact of alternative dispute resolution (ADR) on the experience of litigants in the District Court of Maryland, the researchers concluded, among other significant findings, that participants who went through ADR are more likely than those who went through the court process to indicate the following:

1. They could express themselves, their thoughts, and their concerns.
2. All of the underlying issues came out.
3. The issues were resolved.
4. The issues were completely resolved rather than partially resolved.
5. They acknowledged responsibility for the situation. (Charkoudian 2014a, 46)

The researchers also learned that ADR participants are more likely to accept responsibility for the situation and less likely to believe that others need to admit they are wrong. Crucially, these findings were applicable regardless of the outcome.

You might wonder whether practitioners need a research study to prove what most of us already believe to be true. Consider this: because our attention is often intensely focused on helping participants realize a successful outcome, we may be unaware of (or, worse, unconcerned with) the experience of the disputants. The findings and conclusions of these several research projects suggest that regardless of the outcome, participation in mediation can produce a shift in parties' attitudes about the other person and increase their sense of personal responsibility for their part in the conflict. That disputants appreciate the quality of the process as well as the possibility of achieving an outcome has important implications for how we engage with our clients.

For example, given these findings, you might consider maximizing participants' opportunities to talk about the history of the dispute and its impact, their relationship (if any), and the basis for their positions and proposals. While never losing sight of the participants' desire for a successful result (a settlement), you ensure (1) that they have an opportunity to "express themselves, their thoughts, and their concerns" and (2) that "underlying issues" as well as the more obvious areas of dispute are identified and addressed. In a subsequent chapter my colleague Tzofnat Peleg-Baker (2014) explains why attending to the parties' implicit needs or goals is a crucial element in achieving their explicit goal—a reasoned and satisfactory outcome.

Measuring the Effectiveness and Efficiency of Mediator Approaches

> *There's nothing like looking, if you want to find something. You certainly usually find something if you look, but it is not always quite the something you were after. J. R. R. Tolkien*

Funded by the State Justice Institute with the support of the Maryland Administrative Office of the Courts, this study of practitioner behaviors in child custody mediation collected data through a variety of methods, including, pre- and post-mediation participant surveys, mediator questionnaires, and, most significant, observation of mediation sessions. The research project reached a conclusion (among several) that, for most practitioners, is a surprising, even counterintuitive, result:

> The greater the percentage of time that the mediator spent in caucus, the more likely the participant was to indicate that the mediator respected them and did not take sides. . . . More time in caucus also resulted in participants increasing their sense of hopelessness about the situation from before to after the mediation. In addition, greater time in caucus resulted in participants decreasing their belief that they could work together with the other parent to resolve their conflict or that there were a range of options that could resolve their conflict. It appears that while caucusing increases faith in the mediator, it decreases faith and problem-solving potential with the other participant. (Charkoudian 2014b, iv)

What are the implications for your practice when you learn that when mediators spent more time in private sessions, (1) the parties felt more "hopeless about the situation," (2) their belief that they could "work together with the other parent" decreased, and (3) they had greater respect for and rapport with the mediator? These findings challenge, if not upend entirely, practitioners' rationale for the default use of private sessions as well as for their nearly automatic reliance on caucus in response to contentious situations. In the face of these findings, practitioners might want to reassess their reliance on private sessions, being more inclined to make use of caucus sessions sparingly and strategically.

No single research study can provide definitive conclusions or resolve all questions regarding its subject. For example, this study's conclusions are based on research about mediating child custody matters in a court-annexed program. Would studies of private mediation of custody matters yield similar results? Would studies of commercial or workplace mediations reach the same conclusions? As with many research studies, the outcome suggests the necessity for further research. Nevertheless, practitioners would be wise not dismiss the results of this study simply because it involves conflict work in a different arena of practice or because more research is needed. As with the findings of any research study, we should thoughtfully consider the implications for our practices.

The Northern Ireland Peace Process—Case Study

Case studies are fascinating. We are intrigued by the developing story as we follow the narrative, paying careful attention to how the events unfold and to key actors in those events. Our interest is more than simple curiosity. We look for meaning in the stories, what they tell us about the events and the participants, the nature and history of the dispute, the implications for possible solutions, and what lessons they hold for us.

Most of us have read accounts of the prolonged negotiations between the Republicans and the Loyalists that led to the Good Friday Agreement (also known as the Belfast Agreement). That milestone accord brought a long-sought and much-needed measure of peace and cooperation to the people of Northern Ireland, one that has provided relief, if imperfectly. That remarkable achievement resulted from decades of persistent and diligent efforts on the part of countless partisans and from the meticulous work of courageous, dedicated, and skilled intervenors, such as Geoffrey Corry. Coauthored with Pat Hynes, "Creating Political Oxygen to Break the Cycle of Violence, 1981–1994" reflects on and examines the process and methods used in back-channel pre-negotiations that ultimately led to the parties' willingness to enter into peace talks (Corry and Hynes 2015).

Sectarian violence, rigid political positions reinforced by religious hatred, and a lengthy period of violence, discord, and dissention had resulted in a deeply divided country. The most notorious events were well known—Bloody Sunday, the prison hunger strikes, and bombings (estimated at ten thousand over a period of thirty years). Stories depicting these incidents appeared in books, dramatic films, documentaries, and television programs. Distressing, heartbreaking, and uplifting photos and articles describing the events appeared in the news media. During the peace talks facilitated by Senator George Mitchell, there were almost daily reports on the progress of negotiations, obstacles encountered, renewed hope, moments of frustration, and, ultimately, the remarkable achievement of an accord. The backstories, however, were known only to the participants and to a few who knew about these less publicized events.

The Corry and Hynes (2015) article recounts efforts over fifteen years to bring the fiercely divided factions to the bargaining table. The authors (and others who labored in the dangerous and harsh terrain of the conflict to move the parties toward peace) were concerned with these questions:

> But how do you stop the violence which blocks parties from entering into talks process? How do political negotiations get started? What are the political conditions that have to be in place before governments can begin to talk to groups engaged in violence? (1)

The authors are engaging and reflective storytellers. You must read this piece to appreciate the brilliance of their assessment. A couple of the ten "lessons" the authors propose may be useful to conflict resolution practitioners:

"Leaders must prepare the ground for negotiations and to see whether dialogue is possible." Preparation provides a critical foundation for the success of the substantive discussions (negotiations). The nature and extent of the planning activities will vary widely, depending on the type of intervention, and may include e-mail or other written communication, telephone conversations, questionnaires, and pre-meeting interviews.

Creating a "unity of hearts and minds acting in common purpose." Incrementally building trust is crucial to constructive bargaining—a principle pertinent to virtually every conflict resolution intervention. Unlike the circumstances in Northern Ireland and, mercifully, for most of us, the breach of trust between the parties has not involved the use of force. For every intervention, no matter the intensity, duration, lethality, and nature of the conflict, participants are understandably suspicious of one another. Too often, however, the end goal is so alluring that we and the participants may

> *"Excellent!" I cried.*
> *"Elementary," said he.*
> Arthur Conan Doyle

overlook opportunities to build a common framework before moving ahead with the substantive discussions to the ultimate detriment of the parties and the process.

Corry and Hynes insist that success in the negotiations also required the participants to *"manage the expectations of people on all sides."* In many conflict resolution interventions, the principals are influenced, to a greater or lesser degree, by others (constituents) who may not be directly involved in the discussions and who will be notably affected by the principal parties' decisions and agreements. Stepparents or new partners, the children themselves, other family members, and close friends are affected when parents decide on postdivorce parenting arrangements. Managers, employees, vendors, customers, and others associated with a business are affected by the terms agreed by the principals working to resolve a contract or other commercial dispute. In multiparty public policy or environmental dispute processes and in labor–management negotiations, everyone at the table represents the interests of constituents who have a stake (and often a voice) in the discussions and outcome. Ignoring or minimizing the interests of those directly and meaningfully affected by the decisions of the principals is an oversight that can spell disaster for the primary negotiations. On the other hand, attending to those individuals can, as Corry and Hynes explain, profoundly influence the success of the negotiations.

Action Research—Reflective Practice Groups

The principal elements of *action research* are action, evaluation, and critical reflection. In the following example, the researcher, a graduate student in conflict analysis and resolution, as a principal aspect of her dissertation research, collaborated in the action by organizing, structuring, and facilitating reflective practice groups. One goal of the research was to assess whether and to what extent participation in such groups results in shifts in assumptions about the nature of practice and the role of the intervenor and in changes to practice routines. She also wondered whether the quality of professional practice was positively affected as a result of those changes and insights:

> Through conversations before and after their conflict resolution sessions, ongoing roundtables or focus groups, and observations of cases when possible, this study aims to clarify the processes and influences surrounding how practitioners interpret their training once faced with their own cases, and how they can improve upon their interpretation and learning over time.
>
> Ultimately, the goal of this project is to provide empirically grounded recommendations for training and professional development of conflict resolution practitioners. (Arms Almengor 2017)

The findings and analysis provide valuable insights into the learning process that occurs through reflective practice as well as fresh ideas for structuring and managing reflective practice groups in order to maximize opportunities for learning and professional development. Moreover, as with most research, the findings point to additional areas of inquiry, particularly the long-term effects of the use of reflective practice on the quality of conflict resolution practice. I discuss reflective practice groups and their impact on professional development in subsequent chapters.

Workplace Mediation Research

In a further effort to persuade you of the relevance and practical value of research for conflict resolution practice, I want to describe studies that employ two additional research methods.

The first of these methods, testing the researcher's hypothesis about the effect and potential benefit of utilizing external mediators (not affiliated with the workplace) for addressing workplace disputes, involves the use of interviews and questionnaires and literature review. In two companion studies, the researchers surveyed the research literature on mediator skills and knowledge, wondering whether they could discover a consensus as the basis for developing training and credentialing standards.

Increasingly, private businesses, nonprofit organizations, and government agencies view mediation as a preferred method for addressing a variety of disputes that arise in the workplace. Often, the underlying rationale for these dispute resolution programs is that mediation is a more direct, speedy, efficient, and inexpensive process; that when successfully implemented, these processes result in agreements that are reasonable, responsive to the situation, and consistent with the values of the organization; and that the opportunity for disputing parties to engage directly and constructively has a positive effect on employees' attitudes and productivity.

We assume these assertions are valid, but the researchers wondered whether they are substantiated by the participants' experiences and by the results of the mediations. They also wanted to know whether a different outcome and impact result if the mediation is conducted by internal mediators who serve either as volunteers or as part of their employment contract or by private practitioners (external mediators).

People generally see what they look for and hear what they listen for. Harper Lee, To Kill a Mockingbird

A network of researchers in Ireland, the Kennedy Institute Workplace Mediation Research Group (KIWMRG), under the auspices of the Kennedy Institute at NUI-Maynooth, designed and directed these research projects. The mission of KIWMRG is "to critically inform the continuing development of workplace mediation practice in Ireland through cooperative research" (http://kiwmrg.ie). Full disclosure: I am a member of the group's Advisory Board.

Three of the group's research publications on workplace mediation offer important lessons for practitioners generally and especially for those who deal with workplace conflict situations. The first paper (Bouchier 2014) reports the results of a study examining the use of external mediators to address workplace disputes. KIWMRG also produced an extraordinary two-part study (Curran et al. 2016a, 2016b). In part 1 of that study, the researchers present findings from a comprehensive survey of published material on the skills and knowledge required of workplace mediators. Part 2 offers recommendations for training requirements, standards of practice, and mediator certification.

External Mediators

Margaret Bouchier's (2014) study examined the impact of the use of external mediators for workplace disputes. Her project centered on two questions:

> Question 1: Does external mediation result in satisfactory outcomes for the parties to mediation?
> Question 2: What is the value and benefit of external mediation to the contracting organization? (2)

To address the first question, Bouchier surveyed workplace mediation participants using anonymous questionnaires. To address the second question, she conducted semistructured interviews with human resources/case managers and external mediators.

Respondents to the questionnaire revealed overwhelming satisfaction with their participation in the mediation process. Nearly 90 percent of the mediations ended with an agreement of some nature. Participants affirmed that the mediation had a positive effect on their continued working relationships, and they attributed the successful outcomes to having the opportunity to talk directly. As one person remarked, "It cleared the air between me and my work colleague." Success rates were matched by the participants' belief that addressing their differences in a structured and facilitated setting allowed them to pay attention to the other person and, in that way, find an accommodation that suited them.

Responses from interviewees confirmed that, by talking out conflicts in mediation, employees were able to move past their difficulties, acknowledge their interdependence, and develop cooperative working relationships. One HR manager observed that "the quality of the working relationship where a mediation succeeds are [sic] likely to be far more functioning than following on from other processes." In addition to noting the impact on productivity—the ability of employees to do their jobs without the distraction and obstruction of conflicts—some interviewees commented that the mediation process could serve as a model for how the company addresses employee disputes.

Despite its limited scale and scope, this study provides both the rationale and an incentive for engaging in additional research to examine these findings and conclusions more fully. For practitioners, the study and its findings are encouraging. Mediation succeeds. There is tangible evidence in the rate of successful outcomes. In addition, there are lasting benefits in terms of employee satisfaction, cooperation, and productivity.

Shaping the Agenda

A team of ten KIWMRG network members conducted a two-part study, commissioned by the Mediators Institute of Ireland (MII), a national professional organization that accredits and certifies mediation training courses and mediators in Ireland. The goal for the study was to produce "a systematic review of published material on mediator skills, behaviours, and competencies." A principal goal of this project was the development and implementation of standards of practice for workplace mediators. Both reports may be downloaded without cost from the KIWMRG website (http://kiwmrg.ie).

"Shaping the Agenda, Part 1: Exploring the Competencies, Skills and Behaviours of Effective Workplace Mediators" reports on a thorough literature review of research findings that would aid in the development of training standards and certification procedures and would identify potential methods for improving mediator knowledge and skills in relation to workplace disputes. The results of the authors' extensive examination and analyses of existing research literature provide a conceptual framework for the second paper, "Shaping the Agenda, Part 2: Implications for Workplace Mediation Training, Standards and Practice in Ireland." As the authors note in Part 1,

> The partner document to this literature review, Shaping the Agenda 2, contains a systematic analysis of the implications of the material presented here for the field of workplace mediation in Ireland. The recommendations presented in the second document will be informed by the international body of knowledge presented in this document. (Curran et al. 2016a, 51)

The research studies reviewed by the KIWMRG team relied on research methods such as observations, interviews, questionnaires, case studies, and simulations. They first conducted a comprehensive review of published materials on mediator skills and knowledge. Next, they summarized, analyzed, and synthesized the findings and conclusions, producing an overview of the existing literature as a foundation for Part 2 of the project.

"Shaping the Agenda, Part 2" offers recommendations for "training, standards and practice of workplace mediation" (Curran et al. 2016b, 6). Termed "implications" in the report, thirty-six proposals are directed to the sponsor, MII. Among the implications presented are the following:

Implication 1: The MII should adopt a specific definition of "workplace mediation" such as the one provided in this report.
Implication 7: Research needs to be undertaken to enable mediators and mediation advocates to have a better understanding of the impact of specific aspects of context on the use and effectiveness of mediation.
Implication 8: It is incumbent on mediators to ensure that they have a clear understanding of how their role fits within the organizational context, including organizational policies and procedures, and that their actions are consistent with those policies and procedures.
Implication 14: The MII, as the accrediting body in Ireland, should ensure appropriate training standards and assessment of knowledge, skills, and competencies on the part of the workplace mediator.
Implication 19: Mediators should engage in ongoing reflective practice and skills development through, for example,
- Participation in a peer group for "learning and sharing."
- Engagement with a supervisor, particularly for recently qualified mediators or those returning to mediation.
- Maintaining a reflective journal during the initial period of training/mediation to support reflection on emotional intelligence development.

Implication 22: Mediator style, approach, and behavior are inextricably linked, so it is incumbent on mediators to understand their "actual stylistic proclivities" and the significance of their approach to the process.
Implication 24: Research is needed to inform understanding regarding the durability of mediation agreements within an organizational setting.
Implication 34: The MII should outline recommended training areas for workplace mediators. (Curran et al. 2016b, 34–38)

Why are these companion reports valuable, indeed crucial, for practitioners generally and especially for reflective practitioners who continually seek to learn, grow, and evolve in a spiral of professional development? Because these reports identify the skills, competencies, and behaviors that would enhance our practices, they put forward an urgent reconsideration of the path to becoming resourceful and capable professionals. In this regard, I encourage you to examine the catalog of mediator competencies in table 1 (Curran et al. 2016a, 28), the mediator skill set in table 2 (Curran et al. 2016a, 29), and the mediator skills project findings in table 3 (Curran et al. 2016a, 31). The last chart is from a study of mediator skills and knowledge by Margaret Herrman and colleagues (2001).

The conclusions in these studies suggest that mediation trainers may want to reexamine our course design, materials, and learning activities. Are we teaching the skills and knowledge required for competent practice? Are we providing trainees with the competencies they require to be effective workplace mediators?

> It often seems to me that's all detective work is, wiping out your false starts and beginning again. Yes, it is very true, that. And it is just what some people will not do. They conceive a certain theory, and everything has to fit into that theory. If one little fact will not fit it, they throw it aside. But it is always the facts that will not fit in that are significant. Agatha Christie, Death on the Nile

For leaders of professional organizations concerned with developing and ensuring adherence to standards of practice or designing criteria for certifying practitioners, these reports are a blueprint for action.

Experimental Research

The research study I mentioned at the beginning of the chapter was a controlled experiment, involving volunteer participants who enacted carefully constructed protocols to test their researchers' hypothesis regarding rapport building as a means of improving negotiation outcomes.

The principal focus of the research was, how should people effectively make use of internet-enabled communications technology when negotiating deals and disputes? (Morris et al. 2002, 99). In addressing this question, the study considered the impact of rapport (they use the term "schmoozing") on the outcome of simulated negotiations. The study involved two experiments.

The first experiment compared the results and the process employed as a number of negotiating pairs attempted to reach a settlement. Participants were divided into two groups; pairs in one group communicated only via e-mail, while pairs in the other group met face-to-face. Not surprisingly, the pairs who spoke directly were more likely to reach a settlement. Their conversations included activities, particularly nonverbal, that tended to increase their openness toward one another, allowing them to propose, consider, and evaluate proposals and then reach an agreement. Communication between pairs who relied only on electronic communication was almost exclusively limited to the task at hand—the negotiation.

The second experiment examined simulations conducted only via e-mail, assessing the nature of the participants' interactions as well as outcomes of the simulated negotiations. One group of pairs, however, were provided photos of their counterpart and were instructed to talk by phone for five minutes in advance of their negotiations, but they could not discuss the negotiation itself.

Among the key findings of this study are that

> e-mail can be used successfully in negotiating with people with whom one already has a relationship. Indeed there are many theories of trust based on the notion that prior relationships or common group memberships provide assurance and enable cooperation. However, negotiations often occur at the start of business relationships between geographically distant parties. . . . The current findings suggest that a simple preliminary act, a brief phone call, would greatly improve the outcomes to be expected in such cases from an e-mail negotiation.
>
> In sum, schmoozing greases the wheels of sociality and commerce, allowing relationships and deals to develop despite the friction involved in negotiations. (Morris et al. 2002, 99, citations omitted)

Participants in the study were instructed to conclude a negotiation. Similarly, in our practices, we are largely goal oriented—assisting parties to achieve a successful outcome. To that end, we set the stage for the ensuing process, establish ground rules, confirm conditions for privacy and confidentiality, and then proceed with the work of addressing the problem, issue, or conflict. Our approach is not necessarily formulaic or mechanistic, but it is goal oriented. In the same way, participants in the research study were instructed to achieve an outcome—a negotiated settlement. Imagine, however, if we applied the lessons from the study. We know that trust, in any measure, improves the quality of the parties' communication and thus increases the likelihood of a successful outcome. What if we engaged in schmoozing—a bit of personal interaction unrelated to the content of the dispute, might we have a similar experience? Could greasing "the wheels of sociality and commerce, allowing relationships and deals to develop," become part of our practices? How might we accomplish this while honoring the parties' goal of successfully achieving an outcome?

Even if everyone involved knows everyone "at the table," the findings of this study point to the importance of taking a few moments for conversation on a topic unrelated to the dispute or problem before diving into the substance of the dispute.

Perhaps we can take a lesson in this from trainers and workshop leaders who routinely conduct "icebreaker" activities before moving into their substantive presentations.

> Research is to see what everybody else has seen, and to think what nobody else has thought. —Albert Szent-Györgyi

Recently, I have been considering questions about the effectiveness of reflective practice as a process for learning from experience. I'm not qualified to design and carry out the research that might answer these questions. Yet they are central to the increased acceptance and widening use of reflective practice and to improving our reflective practice methods.

(1) Is reflective practice so rooted in Western values and professional and cultural traditions that its usefulness in other cultures may be limited? Is it possible that reflective practice is in some crucial aspects incompatible with commonly accepted forms of learning in other cultures and countries? Can we modify reflective debrief in response to these possible differences in learning methods and communication styles? Are there situations in which collective learning, as in reflective practice groups, is unsuitable and an individualistic learning approach is preferred? Is the prescriptive form of learning so generally accepted and embedded in a culture or nation that the elicitive form of reflective debrief is incompatible? Informally and anecdotally, I intend to test these ideas and questions (subjectively) as I and my colleagues introduce reflective practice and reflective debrief into new settings and other countries.

(2) Is it possible to assess the assumed benefits and positive effects of reflective practice—empirically, not just anecdotally? How do we know that reflective practice works, that it produces durable learning, or that it improves the quality of practice? We need to identify which methods are most useful and to understand why they work. And if reflective practice has the potential, as I believe, to nurture the spiral of professional growth and evolution, how could that progress be measured?

Let me conclude with one more exhortation to give research a chance. Reading and learning from reports of research studies benefits practitioners in two significant ways. First, research findings are data. Data can be used in whatever manner seems appropriate, responsible, and most likely to improve our practices. Take, for example, the finding that challenges the routine practice of extensive private sessions and that raises the possibility that such use could be counterproductive. You might decide to adjust the timing, frequency, and purpose for meeting in private sessions; limit the amount of time spent in caucus; monitor the parties' attitudes toward one another after meeting in caucus; or disregard the results because, after thoughtful consideration, you recognize that your experiences differ markedly. The point is that once you know the findings, you can choose whether, how, and when to make use of the data.

> If you try sometimes
> You just might find
> You get what you need. —Mick Jagger and Keith Richards

Second, reading research studies is part of our commitment to the attribute of learning ceaselessly and to the continued evolution of the spiral of our professional development. Conclusions from studies may provide ideas for altering your approach to practice. They may encourage you to think about what you do and why. Like reading articles and books and attending professional development courses, reading research papers introduces you to new ideas and strategies and expands your understanding of and approach to conflict resolution practice.

> You'll never know everything about anything, especially something you love. —Julia Child

Exercises

Exercise 5.1

Consider the following statement. If you accept this proposition as true, how would you behave, and why?

> Research shows that when we read words on paper, it reduces our stress levels by nearly 70 percent. We also read more carefully than on tablets or laptops. —Margaret Heffernan

Exercise 5.2

In what ways, if any, do these findings on the efficacy of private sessions affect your thinking about and future use of private sessions?

Exercise 5.3

If rapport building increases the likelihood of a successful negotiation, what steps might you take to incorporate this activity into your pre-negotiation (or pre-intervention) process?

CHAPTER 6

The Methods of Reflective Practice

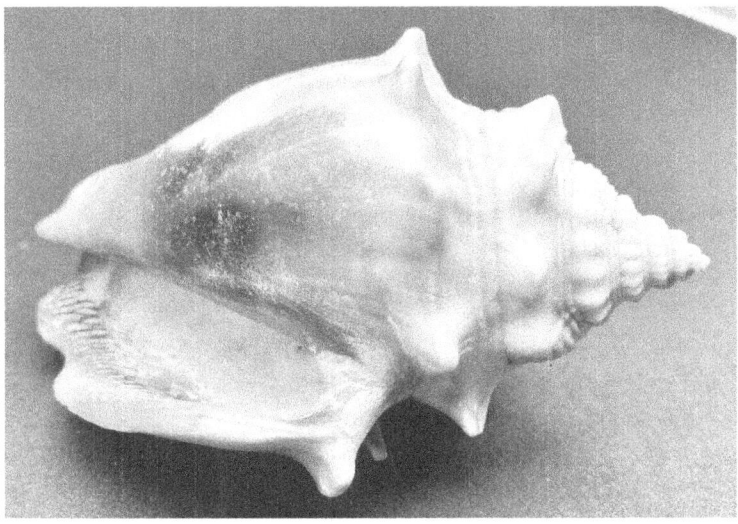

A circle in a spiral, like a wheel within a wheel
  Never ending or beginning on an ever spinning reel —"Windmills of Your Mind," Alan and Marilyn Bergman

How Will Reflective Practice Make a Difference to Me and My Work?

My objective in the previous chapters has been to provide a foundation for becoming a reflective practitioner. I want you to understand—as you hear so often in this book—the why of reflective practice. Before exploring the methods, it's crucial to have a grasp of the purposes and principles of reflective practice. In this chapter, I will present three methods of reflective practice and provide examples to illustrate their use in real time and to demonstrate the practical benefits of reflection. In addition, I invited my colleague Tzofnat Peleg-Baker to explain a tool she developed: the Structured Reflective Instrument®. As she notes in her section of the chapter, "My purpose in designing this reflective framework is to help professionals reconsider taken-for-granted, habitual ways of thinking and practicing." I conclude the chapter with another reflective tool: the learning journal. Each of these methods of reflective practice furthers the goal of becoming a more effective and capable practitioner. Because at heart I am a practitioner and a pragmatist, I always ask—whether reading a book or article, writing in my journal, or attending a course or training—how this approach and these techniques will strengthen my practice. With this as prologue, let's begin our exploration of these reflective methods.

> The capacity to learn is a gift, the ability to learn is a skill, the willingness to learn is a choice. Brian Herbert

Schön (1983) proposed two modes of reflection, and since *The Reflective Practitioner*, those of us eager to put the principles of reflective practice into action have adopted, occasionally with some modifications, these two methods. Reflection-in-action considers what is happening in the moment (the present), and reflection-on-action looks backward at what has occurred (the past). We will examine both methods in more detail. First, however, I want to describe a third reflective process that I (Lang and Taylor 2000) and other authors have proposed (Bassot 2023; Thompson and Thompson 2023). This additional reflective process is anticipatory reflection, future focused, and named either reflection-for-action or reflection-before-action.

> Perfectionism is the enemy of happiness. Embrace being perfectly imperfect. Learn from your mistakes and forgive yourself; you'll be happier. —Roy T. Bennett

Reflection-before-Action

Some degree of reflection-before-action occurs as practitioners plan and prepare for an engagement. The extent and nature of these preliminary activities and their purposes vary widely, influenced by factors, such as the practitioner's preference, style, and experience; the nature of the conflict or problem; the purposes and goals of the intervention; and the needs of the participants.

For example, prior to mediating a small-claims matter, preparation and planning might be limited to reviewing a judicial referral sheet that identifies the parties, the nature of the claim, and the amount demanded. Small-claims disputes commonly concern a single issue, uncomplicated-fact situations, two parties (usually unrepresented), a narrow range of possible outcomes, and a modest time limit.

Contrast this with the extensive and meticulous planning required to design and manage a conflict process involving multiple stakeholders, complex issues of law, complicated-fact situations, and often indefinite remedies or solutions and perhaps stretching over many sessions and possibly for months. Preparations routinely include extensive preliminary interviews with participants and nonparty stakeholders; review of the pertinent literature, possibly including court documents; and a conscientiously tailored design of a unique intervention approach. In both types of situations, there are opportunities to engage in and benefit from reflection-before-action.

In the appendices, you will find a guide to reflection-before-action. You can download a digital version of this guide from the publisher's website. Similar to preparations for any conflict engagement, the activities of reflection-before-action include the following:

1. Become familiar with the history, characteristics, impact, and scope of the dispute. Identify participants, representatives, and nonparty stakeholders.
2. Create a preliminary plan or approach.
3. Be aware of our theories and how they influence our perceptions and actions.
4. Prepare to learn from experience:

- Be attentive to novel, surprising, and puzzling situations
- Remain open to new information and multiple perspectives
- Pay attention to the unique qualities of the parties and nature of the conflict
- Thoughtfully and mindfully use prior experience as a guide
- Identify the parties' intrinsic and extrinsic needs and goals

5. Generate an initial "working" hypothesis

Conflict practitioners regularly attend to the first two items; they are largely objective and outward looking. The other preparatory tasks are internal, subjective, and quite literally the process of reflecting. For many practitioners, these interior, reflective tasks are seldom addressed; one likely explanation is a lack of familiarity with the reflective tasks.

To understand the process of reflection-before-action and its benefits, consider the following example provided by a colleague from Ireland.

Niamh Lehane, an Irish family mediator, generously contributed parts of a reflective paper she wrote in 2011 to fulfill a course requirement for the Masters in Mediation and Conflict Intervention program at the National University of Ireland, Maynooth. Niamh served as mediator for Patricia and Paul in a role-play simulation created and managed by faculty. In the scenario, the parties were discussing the terms of a parenting plan in connection with the dissolution of their marriage:

> *The path isn't a straight line; it's a spiral. You continually come back to the things you thought you understood to see deeper truths. Jaylene Moreau*

Predictable areas of concern that may require my attention include the following:

- The parties being at different stages in the process of separation, with Paul being further ahead (having left the family home two years ago).
- Paul returning for three months (after Patricia's encouragement) and leaving nine months ago may mean children have a fantasy of parents reconciling and an unwillingness to acknowledge end of marriage.
- Paul recently told Patricia he will be moving to live with his new partner.
- Patricia may need time to adjust to the news, to face the reality of the end of the marriage, and to emotionally detach from Paul.
- Patricia may have concerns around the children spending time with Paul's new partner.
- Paul is recently self-employed, without transportation, and having serious financial difficulties. Either or both parents may be stressed about how to support the family and emotionally unavailable to the children.
- Children may need routine and structure around the time they spend with each parent, considering their different ages.
- The financial and practical considerations around transportation will need to be explored.

I will aspire to be responsive to the likelihood that the parties will want to be sure that their issues, perspectives, and concerns are heard, acknowledged, and understood. I seek to be aware of moments when one of them appears not to be listening or when one of them seems hesitant or otherwise struggles to express themselves.

I will endeavor to ensure the parties' goals, resources, options, and preferences are fully explored in the process of mediation in as much as this is professionally and humanly possible. To do this, I seek to be mindful of how they interact with one another and how I might respond if it appears they are resisting a difficult conversation or if they are minimizing or exaggerating their differences.

The most appropriate skills will be listening, observation, empathy, normalizing, mutualizing, reframing, and questioning. Circular questioning is likely to be important in order to encourage them to be open and reflective.

My key objective is to facilitate and empower the parties to work collaboratively to create their own parenting plan in accordance with their balanced interests and the interests of their children. Although creating a workable parenting plan is an important goal, I want to be sure the plan reflects their own values, objectives, and commitments.

> Live as if you were to die tomorrow. Learn as if you were to live forever.
> Mahatma Gandhi

Let's explore Niamh's reflections in light of the activities that make up reflection-before-action.

Description of the situation and the parties:

Niamh gathered background information (married, separated following a brief reconciliation, four minor children, family is experiencing financial difficulties, parties are at different stages in emotionally accepting the divorce, Paul will be living with a new partner, and the parties' goal is to create a parenting plan).

Niamh focused on designing a workable parenting plan, with empathy for the children's possible anxiety and confusion, acknowledging the effect of Paul having a new partner, and addressing the practical aspects of the plan given their finances. Niamh would support their efforts to communicate—both speak and listen—by helping to "empower the parties to work collaboratively" and act in a manner "that their issues, perspectives, and concerns are heard, acknowledged, and understood."

Examination of possible concerns—hers and the parties:

She considers that they may be struggling because they are "at different stages in the process of separation," and Patricia may find it difficult "to face the reality of the end of the marriage and to emotionally detach from Paul." In addition, Patricia may have concerns about "the children spending time with Paul's new partner." Niamh considers whether their ability to create a plan may be affected by "financial and practical considerations," including Paul's recent decision to be self-employed. She decides that the most appropriate skills will be listening, observing, empathizing, normalizing, mutualizing, reframing, and questioning.

Reflection on areas for her learning:

Niamh wonders how she would respond if Patricia and Paul tried to avoid a difficult conversation or minimize their differences. She encourages collaboration and self-determination and considers whether her values will influence her choices and approach. She also believes her role involves facilitating effective communication; defining her role in this way will almost certainly influence her practice decisions.

The quality and detail of this preliminary reflection evidence the mediator's commitment to learning. She identifies potential areas of difficulty and considers the skills she may choose to address these concerns. While she has an overall plan for the mediation, she is keenly aware of the likelihood she will adjust her approach as the discussion between Patricia and Paul develops.

Niamh foresees several areas where Patricia and Paul may have trouble accomplishing their goal: their differing stages of emotional acceptance of divorce, the effect of Paul's new partner on Patricia and the children, the impact of Paul's unemployment, and conflicting ideas about what the children require from their parents. "My key objective is to facilitate and empower the parties to work collaboratively to create their own parenting plan in accordance with their balanced interests and the interests of their children."

Niamh isn't trying to produce a script that would inflexibly determine her interactions with Patricia and Paul. Preparing is not scripting. Her pre-session reflections orient her and give her a starting place, and she is well positioned to act and then readjust according to the parties' responses. Here Niamh demonstrates an attribute of a reflective practitioner: remaining balanced and flexible.

If people knew how hard I worked to get my mastery, it wouldn't seem so wonderful at all.
Michelangelo

In this reflection, Niamh demonstrates a reflective practice mindset and attitude about learning from experience. Her determination to use the reflective process means that she is much less likely to be attentive to the surprising and puzzling moments that are opportunities for learning.

Reflection-in-Action

Schön (1983) proposed that "both ordinary people and professional practitioners often think about what they are doing, sometimes even while doing it" (50). This is reflection-in-action. The notion of thinking while doing is captured in these common expressions: thinking on your feet, flying by the seat of your pants, thinking quickly, keeping your wits about you, and learning by doing (54).

In excerpted portions of the transcript of the mediation simulation, we see Niamh's reflection-in-action. Her reflections are shown in italics:

Paul: I don't want this to happen again. So, it's really important that they know that, listen, I'm not going to be shut out of their lives again.

Mediator: So, one of the things you really want your children to know is that you're going to be there for them. That you are separating from each other, and not from them.

Paul: Yeah, like I'd say they might even be wary, you know, of seeing me again, like you know. Wah.

Patricia: That's why it's important that they just have to see you, you know that I think this other person is going to be confusing, and . . .

Paul's emotions appear to be throbbing with fear, anger, and self-defensive urges. Aware of strong feelings in the room and feeling emotional self. Paul, and possibly Patricia, may need ventilation and emotional clearance before they will be ready to have an open-minded and loving discussion with each other about their children. Mediator interventions will need to enable fears to surface in order to enable Paul to move away from self-defensive urges.

Paul: Well of course they are just going to see me. I mean you're the one who brought her into it.

Patricia: You've just told me that you're going to live with her.

Mediator: What you are saying there, Paul . . .

Paul: Of course, I'm going to live with her.

Mediator: I suppose we haven't got to the specifics yet of how you are going to continue to build the relationship with your children. It hasn't been that long. You both clearly want this (meaning for Daddy to see the children). One of the things you've said there is that you have a concern about if the children might be angry at you?

Paul: I mean, who are they going to blame for this? What has she been saying?

Paul may be finding it hard to accept the children's negative feelings and may be seeking positive affirmation from the children. Wondering if questions around the children's need to express negative feelings safely might be useful after Paul's own emotions have subsided.

Patricia:	I need that to be completely clear. You know that I don't agree with that. I haven't been saying that. I've just said that we needed a break from each other.
Paul:	What am I going to say when they say "Why Daddy, Daddy. Why haven't you been spending time with us? Well, Mommy said . . ."
	Noticing Paul's anxiety about communicating realities to the children. Thinks that questions around the children's need to know what is happening might be useful later.
Patricia:	You can tell them that you don't have the car or . . .
	Mindful of the children's possible insecurity around lack of information.
Mediator:	One of the things . . .
Paul:	[cutting in] But I'm here right now. I've been here for the past three months. I haven't moved yet.
	I note Paul's impassioned statement. It's important, however, to keep a focus on the needs of the children, and help Paul and Patricia avoid an argument about Paul's on-again, off-again involvement with the children.
Mediator:	One of the things that you are highlighting is the question of how you explain to your children the reason Daddy hasn't been with them recently [change to an uplifting tone] and also how you assure them that Daddy is going to be there for them now, that both parents will always be there for them. It can be helpful for parents to communicate that to their children together. Is that something you think would be possible for you both to do? That once you create a parenting plan, that the six of you would meet together and . . .
Patricia:	I think they'd like that. I think they want the reassurance from the two of us that things are going to be ok, to be easier from now on. So I think that would be a good idea.
	Noticing Patricia's movement to a cognitive response that is considering the children. Paul's face looks anxious. Mediator turns to look at Patricia.
Mediator:	I'm sensing from you, Patricia, that you think it would be helpful to the children. [Mediator turns to look at Paul at this point.] What difference do you think it would make to the children if you could sit down together and talk to the children?
Paul:	It might be good. It just depends on how we answer their questions. 'Cause they're going to have loads of questions.
	Noticing Paul's movement. Thinks it may be helpful to slow it down at this point and normalize the children's need to know what is happening.
Mediator:	Ok, so one of the things you are recognizing [pause] is that the children might have questions.
Paul:	I think [looking at Patricia] they deserve answers. At this stage, you know, we tried to make it work. It didn't. We've been separated now for a good few months, and it's just I feel they deserve to be involved, particularly the older ones John, Ciara, Patrick. They understand, I mean Amy just thinks, you know, Daddy's not here, Daddy's away. I mean she knows something is not right. I think the older ones really need to understand. We need to explain it to them, and maybe yeah, doing that together is the best way.
Patricia:	Yes. I think they'll trust it more.
Paul:	That we're on the same page.
	Paul looks at Patricia at this point. Mediator noticing movement, sensing a possible shift in their interactions.
Patricia:	They'll believe it. I think if they hear the two of us talking about it, and if it's a plan that I'm happy with and that Paul is happy with, and that we both tell them, I think that would be very reassuring for them.
	Noticing the energy clearing.
Mediator:	It might give them a sense of security?
	Raising shoulders slightly, opening hands.
Patricia:	Yeah, 'cause we've not been agreeing, and while I've been very upset and I can't see another way of having done it this past time, I do see the impact that that's had on them.
	Noticing movement of both parties, aware of feeling compassion, empathy, sadness, identifying a "critical moment" in their interaction. Sensing opportunity to empower the parties. Looking at both, speaking softly and slowly.

Mediator:	So, you are recognizing that the transition has been difficult for you both. [Paul nodding. Pause.] [Mediator placing both feet on the ground, clear, assured energy.] Yet somehow you are willing to work cooperatively to be able to reassure your children. . . . [Pause.]
Paul:	Yeah. [nodding]
Mediator:	. . . To be able to give them that sense of security in a different, restructured family. And what kind of things do you think your children would like to know?

Every practitioner engages in moment-to-moment reflection, though we might not be aware that's what we're doing. To be competent in practice demands an awareness of our internal voice that is based on continually noticing, evaluating, and reflecting on the unfolding events of the process and that informs our responses. Reflective practitioners harness the power of their inner voice through reflection-in-action, initiating appropriate and effective interventions:

Spiral minds are harder to twist. Kris Saknussemm

> Reflection-in-action . . . a kind of thinking we do all the time and is thinking while we are doing other things. In practice, we all have thoughts as we go about our everyday lives and this kind of reflection is our ability to think about things and do something at the same time. Often this helps us to adjust our approach in the moment. (Bassot 2023, 3)

When I present reflection-in-action at conferences or in training courses, practitioners often comment with the following:

- I understand how this works. I'm sure it might be helpful. But I'm skeptical that it can really work.
- I can imagine using reflection afterward to help me learn, but I don't think I could use this during a session.
- With everything I need to pay attention to during an intervention, you want to add something else?
- You're seriously asking me to react in the moment to what's happening? The parties don't stop talking because I need to reflect-in-action.

In every conflict engagement, we are simultaneously tracking multiple threads: the unfolding process; body language; tone of voice; discussions of content, data, and decision making; and more. In the fast-paced interactions among parties and ourselves, we need to act quickly and decisively to rapidly shifting circumstances. Conflict interventions encompass a web of interrelated, integrated, and constantly changing elements. We need to monitor and be mindful of them all. As we act, our minds are actively engaged, making sense of the constantly shifting actions. As we pay attention, we are simultaneously looking for explanations, strategically planning ahead, and deciding what to do. We are thinking while doing, thinking on our feet. Reflection-in-action is the process of harnessing that many-faceted process of thinking and acting. It helps us learn to be deliberate and intentional about connecting thinking and doing, using what occurs innately (tacit knowledge):

> Our thinking serves to shape what we are doing while we are doing it. (Schön 1987, 26)

Do you ride a bicycle, drive a car, engage in sports, dance, or play a musical instrument? Each involves reflection-in-action. Each requires us to make continuous adjustments to our actions—adjustments that occur in a split second, seemingly without engaging in a deliberate thought process. How do we decide to respond while riding a bicycle or driving a vehicle when suddenly a red ball bounces onto the road between two cars? We have a second, at most, to determine whether there is a likelihood a child will follow the ball into the road, heedless of traffic. Driving a vehicle, riding a bicycle, playing tennis, and playing a musical instrument are activities in which reflection-in-action leads to smooth, un-self-conscious, competent, and successful action.

I'm not suggesting that reflection-in-action is easy. But consider this: was it effortless when you learned to play a musical instrument, ride a bicycle, or learn a sport? What I am saying is that reflection-in-action is crucial to our effectiveness and to our professional evolution and growth. The process of thinking and doing builds our conflict engagement muscles, developing our capacity and effectiveness. I am asserting that it's possible to train yourself to use your inner voice to guide your practice decisions and to act with intention. The bottom line is that your practice will be more resilient and effective if you adopt this method of reflection.

As you will observe in Niamh's example of reflection-in-action, her reflections are selective and purposeful. She does not continuously reflect-in-action, addressing every aspect of the mediation at every moment.

You can learn to reflect-in-action—in fact, as I have noted, you do it all the time. You can learn to adapt that process (thinking on your feet) to your conflict engagement work. Initially, you may feel awkward, and the process is clunky and clumsy. You will likely feel insecure and self-conscious—as we all do when learning a new activity or skill. With practice—and intention—reflection-in-action will become a natural and effortless part of your conflict resolution practice.

> Performers can sometimes train themselves to think about their actions. In the split-second exchanges of a game of tennis, a skilled player learns to give himself a moment to plan the next shot. His game is the better for this momentary hesitation, so long as he gauges the time available for reflection correctly and integrates his reflection into the smooth flow of action. (Schön 1983, 279)

The more reflective you are, the more effective you are. Pete Hall and Alisa Simeral

Writing about mediator decision making and exploring the connection between conscious and unconscious reasoning, Tzofnat Peleg-Baker (2014) notes,

Automatic, intuitive judgments are by their nature unconscious, fast, and involve an associative match. Simon described intuitive decisions as "analyses frozen into habits and the capacity for rapid response through recognition." Though many intuitive judgments are proficient and successful, it is not the case for all decisions. (7, citations omitted)

As part of any learning process, we acquire skills that we test through repeated, deliberate, and thoughtful practice. First attempts are tentative and awkward, insecure, and worrying. You know this from learning the skills required for your conflict work. At first, you were hesitant and unsure, afraid to fail, lacking confidence. After time, after learning from your experiences, your actions have become smooth and nimble; you have become proficient, poised, and self-assured. Once we develop skills and acquire a repertoire of responses to probable (or recurring) situations, we act deftly and confidently. Learning to reflect-in-action is no different from learning other skills and techniques. Intention and a commitment to learning from and through your experience will yield competence and self-confidence.

No technique or method is perfectly suited to all circumstances. Potential limitations or shortcomings are associated with every strategy, tactic, or process. For reflection-in-action, there is an inevitable tension between, on the one hand, the need to act quickly, almost automatically, and, on the other, the need for time required to deliberate—if only a few seconds. Some skeptics I've encountered questioned whether we have time to deliberate when an immediate response or intervention is required: "We need to be quick and responsive." Some jokingly imagine their clients sitting idly or checking their social media feeds as the practitioner methodically contemplates the situation, reviews alternatives, and finally responds. While the examples are a bit extreme, it is important to consider circumstances when reflection-in-action might inhibit or unacceptably delay action.

Schön (1983, 277) identifies situations in which reflection is unhelpful. I have added observations and examples from conflict resolution practice for each of the conditions where reflection may be impractical or unworkable:

- An immediate response is required.
  A participant pushes back from the table, stands up, moves to the door, and announces, "This isn't working. I'm out of here."
- Reflection adds unnecessary complexity and interferes with the smooth flow of the process.
  Responding to a question from a participant, "Have you ever seen a situation such as this one?" you become embroiled in a web of deliberation trying to discern the "real" purpose of the question.
- We engage in a series of reflections, each one leading to another in an endless loop, leaving us inert, immobile.
  I was confused during a workplace mediation when the complainant and the employer's representative refused to disclose basic information requested by one another.
- The context is one in which action is required and reflection may be inconsistent with the goals of the situation and therefore unlikely to prove helpful.
  You are concentrating on completing a number of prescribed tasks, such as delivering key introductory comments or methodically reviewing the proposed terms of an agreement, requiring scrupulous attention to essential details.

Like any of our techniques or strategies, reflection-in-action can be an asset or a liability.

Knowing when and why to make use of a tool is the difference between being relevant and effective or inappropriate and clumsy:

> Much reflection-in-action hinges on the experience of surprise. When intuitive, spontaneous performance yields nothing more than the results expected for it, then we tend not to think about it. But when intuitive performance leads to surprises, pleasing and promising or unwanted, we may respond by reflecting-in-action. (Schön, 1983, 56)

Reflection-on-Action

Reflection-on-action is "reflecting on a situation or experience after the event with the intention of drawing insights that may inform my future practice in positive ways" (Johns 2000,

2). According to Moon (1999), it "is the form of reflection that occurs after action and . . . has a role in learning, in informing action and in theory building" (47–48).

In essence, then, reflection-on-action is a process of looking back on a practice situation with the benefit of hindsight, disconnected from the immediacy of the interaction, identifying and examining puzzling and surprising moments. We aren't simultaneously thinking and acting. We aren't managing a host of tasks like a juggler who, with incredible concentration and astonishing skill, keeps a dozen items in the air. We aren't pressured by limitations of time or by the urgency to act:

> As well as identifying how we can improve and find solutions to problems we might identify, reflection-on-action also helps us to see what went well and to build on that. This in turn helps us to build our professional knowledge . . . as we think about how we could adapt our practice and approach things next time. (Bassot, 2023, 52)

Reflection-on-action begins as we mentally roam over the events of the intervention, identifying one or more instances when something unexpected occurred—a puzzling moment or an unsettling set of interactions. Perhaps the object of reflection is one or more of the following:

- We were surprised and unprepared to respond, and as a result, we reacted reflexively rather than fully considering our decision.
- Our actions did not elicit the response we predicted or hoped for.
- Perhaps we were confused or frustrated by the outcome of our tactics and strategies.
- We were taken aback by a surprisingly positive response or proposal from one of the parties.

There are no fixed or predictable criteria for selecting experiences for reflection-on-action. We are unique, and we experience and respond to situations differently; what is surprising and confusing to one of us may be common and unremarkable to another. The common characteristic of these objects for reflection is that after the engagement (and possibly for years), we replay the circumstances in our minds unendingly, like a recording set to repeat, feeling uneasy or unnerved, without coming to terms with the source of our distress. When this occurs, when we can't shake the memory or effect of an experience, it signifies an opportunity for learning from experience and a need for reflection.

Recall Niamh's pre-session and in-action reflections we previously reviewed. Now, detached from the events and with time to reflect, she examines the parties' circumstances and her responses in light of a persistent concern about how to address instances when parties are highly emotional. After meeting with Patricia and Paul, Niamh looked back on the session, searching for any lessons from the experience that might inform her approach to mediation in instances where one or both parties emotionally respond to one another:

> In Reflection On Action (post session) I had the overall sense that my key objective had been accomplished—that there was a readiness of both parties to work collaboratively/cooperatively to create their own parenting plan in accordance with their balanced interests and the interests of their children.
>
> The techniques/skills employed were listening, observation, empathy, normalising, mutualising, reframing, and questioning, especially the use of circular questioning. All were employed to facilitate an understanding of personal narrative and individual self-disclosure within the context of the changing relationship. This focused upon the

dual outcomes of personal ownership, mutual recognition, and deference to the needs of their children in the process.

As mentioned in my earlier Reflection In Action there was a specific point in the dialogue where I became intensely aware of the impact my interventions were having with Patricia. This may be pinpointed at the moment when I was confronted with the dilemma of allowing conflict to surface or assisting them, in my understanding, to focus upon their children. This reflects a greater dilemma that I often encounter. In one sense such an intervention is helpful in that it is goal focused. In another sense it is unhelpful in that it often involves the potential suppression of emotional energy within the process. The deflating of an emotional balloon is perhaps my best attempt at conceptualising this. Would or should I have approached this situation differently?

Without reflection, we go blindly on our way, creating more unintended consequences, and failing to achieve anything useful. Margaret J. Wheately

The answer as always is maybe, but then I must make the point that I was drawing upon my professional intuition here, and in mitigation may rely upon the fact that I was approaching the situation with honesty and an open heart, therefore may claim my interventions to be authentic. It is interesting however to note, with hindsight, that the emphasis of my interventions became more focused upon the readiness to facilitate collaborative engagement with the expressed issue at hand when I experienced less resistance in the emotional dialogue. This poses a very specific, and very human, question about my engagement with strong emotional resistance and defensiveness in others. Am I seeking to create an emotional comfort zone in order to pursue an outcome, or am I facilitating the stabilization of potential chaotic conflict in order to enable an outcome?

My insight here is that this existential question is at the heart of the mediation process, and I clearly remember asking it in one of my first reflective essays during my Higher Diploma in Mediation Studies at University College Dublin in 2005. My understanding now is very similar to my sense then, and it is that this question is more important in the asking for the professional mediator than in the answering. It must act as a constant presence in what I do, just as for me every mediation encounter must have some of the same trepidation that I sensed in my first encounter. This personal reality provides me with a very tangible sense of authenticity.

Would I have done anything differently? Upon reading my Reflection In Action there is one sentence that has really given me pause for reflection. "I pace my communication to enable the emotion to be released 'constructively.'" What does this mean for me. For me it means awareness/honest expression of emotion with "compassion for the self and compassion for the other" (Sweeney 2010, 21), without harm to the self or the other. So my desire within this would, I sense, be that I seek the naming and framing of emotional response within the authentic expression of genuine, heartfelt compassion for the self and the other. Overt expressions of anger and aggression that seek to overwhelm and diminish the other provoke within me a desire for "constructive," rather than destructive expression. What do I do with this insight? In that sense this Process Recording has served a very important purpose in my ongoing personal and professional development. The continuing embrace of my "Gestalt + Whole." (Sweeney, 2010)

Niamh searched her memory for a moment when she decided to intervene in a particular way and examined the reasons for her action. She acknowledged the implicit dilemma for mediators (and especially for her): to focus on helping the parties achieve a practical outcome, with the possible consequence of "suppressing the emotional energy" or acknowledging their strong emotions, with the possible consequence of heightened conflict that could imperil any agreement. Through reflection-on-action, Niamh came to understand that, in nearly every mediation she conducts, this dilemma will recur; she will be faced with the same tension between concentrating on the outcome with the possibility of silencing the parties' authentic emotional expressions or accept and perhaps support authentic expression of strong emotions that may put a successful outcome at risk. Acknowledging that each conflict situation is unique and will require her to make this choice anew, Niamh affirms that her anxiety about having the skills and strategies for effectively responding to the parties' emotional conversations is at the heart of her dilemma.

In Niamh's example and my own, we have been considering reflective practice as a self-activated and private process. In the next chapter, we will examine the use of reflective practice methods in group settings—reflective practice groups. Before turning to those shared experiences, I want to mention guides in the appendices that I created to assist in reflection-before-action and reflection-on-action.

The Guides for Reflection

There are three principal means of acquiring knowledge . . . observation of nature, reflection, and experimentation. Observation collects facts; reflection combines them; experimentation verifies the result of that combination. Denis Diderot

Clinical faculty in the early 1980s family therapy training program I attended emphasized the central importance of knowing, at each moment in a therapeutic intervention, why we would choose a certain strategy or tactic (a form of reflection-in-action). Being resourceful, creative, and proficient in applying the strategies and techniques we were learning was insufficient without the knowledge of why we made these clinical choices. Our teachers drummed into us that choices must be based on an action plan, created prior to the outset of a session and tested throughout the therapy session. Conceived, supported by, and consistent with a meticulous assessment of the clients and their circumstances, each of our activities was an element in an ongoing process of hypothesis development, experimentation, and perceptive reflection on the results of our actions. We were required to complete a questionnaire both prior to and following each client meeting to ensure thoughtful preparation before meeting with clients and critical assessment following a session.

For the presession questionnaire, we were asked to set out the following:

Data—what we knew about the clients: personal information as well as the history, characteristics, and consequences of the issues they presented.
Theory—the initial theory we would rely on and the reasons for choosing this theory: why it was appropriate and pertinent.
Hypothesis—a preliminary explanation for the presenting issues: why the clients were behaving as they were. Initial interventions would be based on these suppositions.
Action—the strategies and techniques we might employ, including the reasons for our choices and the likely outcome of or reactions to our actions.
Assessment—client behaviors that could signal whether our actions were being helpful or were off the mark: confirming our hypothesis or pointing to the need for revision.

Subsequent to each client meeting, we answered a similar set of questions:

Observation—We described what had occurred, the techniques and strategies we employed, and how the clients responded to our interventions. We offered possible explanations for their reactions.
Hypothesis—Was our hypothesis confirmed, needed to be altered, or off base? We explained the reasons for our analysis.
Theory—Was the theory we decided on appropriate to the client's situation or unhelpful, and what is the basis for our conclusions?
Plan of action—A plan was devised for the next meeting, noting specifically whether and in what ways we would retain or revise our hypothesis and the resulting strategy and tactics.

I hadn't intended to become a family therapist; I had enrolled because I was fascinated by and wanted to learn how to apply systems theory to family conflicts and to sharpen my practice skills. As a result of routinely using the questionnaires, my practice became more deliberate, responsive, and focused. I learned to rely on reflection and analysis, not merely reaction and habit. I learned the importance of theory in shaping practice decisions, and as a result, I found a solid footing for my practice. I was more poised and self-assured. Choosing a strategy or technique based on a thoughtfully crafted hypothesis not only made good sense "in theory" but also worked brilliantly. Even more, I gained the confidence and humility to be flexible and responsive as I continually assessed and altered my hypothesis and interventions.

Coincidence or something more? Shortly before enrolling in family therapy training, I had been introduced to and read *The Reflective Practitioner* (Schön 1983). Shockingly and delightedly, Schön's description of reflection-in-action and reflection-on-action dovetailed with the family therapy program's process of hypothesis, leading to experimentation followed by analysis. I saw how I could bring together Schön's reflective methods and the discipline of completing the questionnaires. Over the next couple of years, I reworked the family therapy questionnaires. I created what I refer to as "guides" to improve conflict practitioners' capacity for self-reflection. I was aware that Schön hadn't proposed reflection-before-action. However, I had already learned (and experienced) the indispensable value of the pre-session questionnaire to prepare for client engagement. I created a guide for pre-session reflection as well as an instrument to facilitate reflection following a client session. In the decades since, as I used the guides in my practice and received feedback from colleagues and students, I continually modified them, incorporating the elements of Reflective Debrief®. Versions of the Guide for Reflection before Action and Guide for Reflection following Action are included in the appendices and available for download on the publisher's website.

Always desire to learn something useful.
Sophocles

Use the guides regularly. I know you will discover what I experienced during those family therapy sessions and later as I continued the reflective routines in my mediation practice. These guides promote the systematic practice of reflection, and their consistent use will have a noticeable and positive impact on your practice. They are not intended as inflexible templates to be applied mechanically. Using them, you will discover that not every question is pertinent to every puzzling moment in every practice situation. Answer those questions that seem relevant to your approach to practice, pertinent to the context, and likely to be helpful. Write your responses. Like keeping a learning journal (I will discuss journals later in this chapter), a record of your reflections has these benefits:

1. You begin to see patterns—questions or situations that keep recurring—from which you can evaluate strategies and tactics that have been helpful or ineffective.
2. The process and discipline of writing sharpens your reflections and analysis.
3. Writing slows the process of thinking and analysis, and as a result, reflections are more considered, conscious, and comprehensive.
4. Writing your thoughts, reactions, confusions and insights markedly increases the likelihood that you will use what you have learned.

Structured Reflective Instrument®

Writing in a journal reminds you of your goals and of your learning in life. It offers a place where you can hold a deliberate and thoughtful conversation with yourself. Robin S. Sharma

In earlier chapters, I referred to the work of my colleague Tzofnat Peleg-Baker, who has developed a remarkable and effective tool for reflection—the Structured Reflective Instrument® (SRI). This instrument is constructed, in significant respects, on the principles of reflective practice and provides practitioners with an additional method for learning from and through their experience. A sample from the SRI is included in the appendices.

ON A REFLECTIVE PATH FOR BUILDING PROFESSIONAL MASTERY IN THIRD-PARTY INTERVENTIONS

The SRI—A Pragmatic 4×4×4×4 Reflective Tool

Tzofnat Peleg-Baker, PhD

"One cannot see what they haven't noticed yet and cannot notice what they did not see."

Why?

The Structured Reflective Instrument® (SRI) is a behavioral research–based reflective framework I designed to help conflict interveners address the invisible—implicit emotional issues parties always struggle with across cases but have difficulty identifying or talking about. Interveners tend to address tangible issues parties easily speak about relating to the content—the explicit instrumental matters that brought them to the mediator. This typical inclination to attend to substantive issues often results in a cyclical movement—a stubborn attachment to positions, repetitive argumentative bargaining, and a premature search for solutions before exploring needs, aspirations, and goals, leaving significant elements unrevealed in the shadow.

For many years, I have observed that this traditional model of practice fails to capture the complexity and fluidity accompanying conflictual situations. The essential issues shaping parties' behaviors and determining whether they make progress and are satisfied with the process and the outcome remain untouched.

My purpose in designing this reflective framework is to help professionals reconsider taken-for-granted, habitual ways of thinking and practicing. By incorporating the hidden aspects of the SRI in their practice, I hope interveners develop better capabilities to provide a more holistic service that addresses parties' fuller range of concerns beyond the typical transactional exchange.

WHAT DOMINATES CONFLICT INTERVENTIONS?

Negotiation and conflict studies show the profound significance of addressing emotional issues within conflictual situations. Parties, negotiators, and mediators wish to address emotional and invisible concerns (Charkoudian et al. 2009; Curhan et al. 2006, 2010; Peleg-Baker 2012b). They aspire to pursue a broad spectrum of social-psychological outcomes related to identity, relationships, and the process of decision making. While the nature of these issues is implicit and intangible, they play a pivotal role in shaping behaviors. Failing to address them can impede meaningful and constructive engagement and result in an impasse (Curhan et al. 2006, 2010; Peleg-Baker 2012b; Schweinsberg, Thau, and Pillutla 2022). Heightening awareness of these concerns becomes imperative for fostering constructive dialogue, effectively addressing them along with the explicit substantive issues, and ultimately reaching satisfactory agreements.

However, the intervention process often leans toward rationalist and transactional approaches. Interveners tend to focus primarily on substantive matters explicitly communicated by the parties and on the pursuit of agreements, typically overlooking emotionally charged, subtle, and fluctuating social-psychological undercurrents inherent in conflictual situations. This oversight may leave parties feeling frustrated and ill-prepared to navigate their emotional, psychological, and relational challenges constructively, thus hindering progress toward an agreement or settlement. Recognizing and addressing these hidden issues is not only instrumental in achieving tangible goals but also a crucial end.

In the past three decades, scholars in negotiation and mediation have increasingly criticized the neglect of intangible, implicit factors (e.g., Bush and Folger 1994; Charkoudian et al. 2009; Peleg-Baker 2012a, 2012b; Picard 2002; Winslade and Monk 2000).

HOW DECISIONS ARE BEING MADE DURING CONFLICT INTERVENTIONS

After presenting what interveners attend to and setting the stage for discussing how to improve interventions' quality and decisions, I'll examine how interveners typically make decisions, which can shed more light on potential barriers to effective engagement and best outcomes.

Decisions are automatic and unconscious. In mediation's dynamic and fast-paced context, judgments tend to be predominantly intuitive and automatically executed. Decisions are inherently automatic and unconscious, a phenomenon extensively supported by growing research on cognitive processing, decision making, implicit social cognition, and expertise (Bargh and Chartrand 1999; Battaglio et al. 2019; Kahneman 2011). Numerous underlying mental subprocesses play a role in most behaviors, often without individuals being consciously aware of them. Implicit attitudes, beliefs, and stereotypes can significantly influence behaviors, sometimes even contradicting one's explicit intentions and goals (Deutsch and Strack 2010; Kahneman 2011; Wilson 2011; Wilson, Lindsey, and Schooler 2000). Observational studies on mediators' work affirm the prevalence of automated, intuitive decisions, with a clear emphasis on overt substantive issues (Peleg-Baker 2012a).

These decisions primarily fall under system 1 processing, characterized by automatic, unconscious, and intuitive reactions based on pattern recognition stored in memory (Bodenhausen and Todd 2010; Deutsch and Strack 2010). The automaticity of these decisions directs interveners' attention toward more overt goals, what is salient. Consequently, settlements or agreements take precedence, often at the expense of critical underlying social-psychological determinants that are likely to be relatively overlooked. Importantly, interveners may not be aware of the origin of their practice decisions, and distinguishing between flawed and skilled judgments becomes challenging unless decision makers engage in a thorough self-examination (Kahneman and Klein 2009).

Overconfidence. Despite the tendency to focus on visible aspects while overlooking crucial underlying factors driving conflict, professionals often display high confidence in their abilities to navigate emotional, relational, and psychological situations. This confidence is frequently rooted in their extensive experience and intuition. As described by Kahneman and Klein (2009), the concept of pseudo-experts best illustrates professionals who have acquired expertise in one domain and assert proficiency in a related one, even when they may lack capabilities in the latter. For example, in our laboratory studies (Kressel et al. 2012; Peleg-Baker 2012a), a few lawyer-mediators committed before the intervention to address emotional implicit goals during the intervention and expressed high confidence in their ability to do so. However, during the intervention, they exhibited relatively weak skills in managing latent psychological and relational subtleties that appeared to stand in the way of making progress or creating an agreement. Despite considerable familiarity with legal aspects, they demonstrated limited proficiency in recognizing implicit social-psychological subtleties and an ability to address them effectively. Still, they were confident in their ability to tackle these intangible issues. When invited to reflect with the researchers on their work after the intervention by watching and discussing their video, most did not take the opportunity to reflect. Claiming knowledge while lacking the capabilities to deal with certain aspects risks complacency and failing to recognize the need for deep inspection or reflection.

The automatic nature of decisions, especially in rapid, tense, or uncertain circumstances such as third-party interventions, coupled with overconfidence, poses the risk of stagnation and impasse and can impede professionals from continuous improvement. An overconfidence mindset inhibits learning and can discourage reflective practices (Peleg-Baker 2012b; Peleg-Baker and Lang 2022). When professionals are excessively confident in their abilities, they may lack the incentive to seek further growth. However, without profound self-examination, interveners are susceptible to repetitive flaws that may even counter their original intentions and goals. The absence of critical self-examination and continuous learning can hinder progress and perpetuate ineffective approaches in conflict circumstances. Professionals accumulate many years of experience but miss opportunities to build expertise in their field.

HOW CAN THIRD-PARTY INTERVENERS GET BETTER IN WHAT THEY DO?

There are two approaches to professionalism. Traditionally, individuals pursue training or formal education, attaining a certain level of proficiency. With accumulated experience, professionals often settle into a stable, average performance. Working independently, as typical for most conflict professionals, they reach their limits and may habitually practice without clearly understanding what went well and why. When something goes awry, there might not be anyone available to help identify and rectify the issue.

While the traditional path allows professionals to reach a certain point, it is not without its limitations. It can lead to stagnation. Professionals may inadvertently repeat the same errors and cease to improve. This path, characterized by fixed routines, as stressed throughout this book, can hinder the identification of obstacles and the development of effective solutions.

This approach characterizes the field of conflict and mediation. Basic mediation programs usually consist of thirty to forty hours of skills-based training, with minimal reflective opportunities, if any (Hedeen, Raines, and Barton 2010; Lang 2019). While some mediators may undergo apprenticeship programs and advanced training courses, the traditional focus remains on acquiring and refining techniques and skills, primarily to facilitate settlements. There is often limited attention to continuous learning and improvement and especially to the development of capabilities to address the implicit nuances shaping parties' behaviors. Furthermore, most third-party interveners, especially mediators, typically work alone in isolation. This isolation can further limit the exchange of insights and hinder the development of professionals in the field.

The alternative approach to professionalism is a continuous journey of learning and improvement. By committing to this path, professionals can expand their professional growth and evolution. This approach also highlights the importance of external perspectives and shared learning to heighten awareness, provide a more comprehensive understanding of reality, facilitate behavior analysis, and encourage the adoption of new practices. While it may be challenging to have others observe our actions, this process ensures critical reconsideration and empowers us to progress and enhance our capabilities.

Documenting little details of your everyday life becomes a celebration of who you are. Carolyn V. Hamilton

A "future orientation" is at the heart of the alternative approach to professionalism. This means focusing on not only how good we are at present but, more important, how excellent we can become. Professionals who embrace this philosophy consistently learn from their experiences, persistently strive for improvement, and can ultimately attain the highest levels of professional mastery.

WHY REFLECTIVE PRACTICE?

Reflective practice and structured frameworks like the SRI align with the principles of the second approach, fostering continuous learning and improvement among professionals. This philosophy is grounded in the belief that to enhance our skills, we must consistently engage in inquiry and reflection, an ongoing learning process of evolution, becoming, and getting better.

Structured reflection, a proven learning method, has practical applications in diverse fields, such as expertise, business, education, and medicine. When applied purposefully—in the context of goals—and structurally, it has been shown to enhance overall performance, improve learning outcomes, refine unconscious intuitive judgments, and boost diagnostic accuracy and clinical reasoning in the medical field. For example, in studies involving medical students and physicians, a reflective condition was compared to an immediate diagnosis condition—participants offered immediate diagnoses after reading the case and writing the most likely diagnosis—and a differential diagnosis condition—participants considered alternative diagnoses if the initial hypothesis was to prove incorrect. In the reflective condition, participants gave a first diagnosis and then listed findings supporting the diagnosis and against it and the findings expected to be present if the diagnosis was correct but were absent if incorrect. Additionally, they listed alternative diagnoses if the initial diagnosis proved incorrect and followed the same procedure for each alternative diagnosis. The reflective condition, where participants engaged in structured reflection, led to improved clinical problem solving, diagnoses, and diagnostic learning; reduced errors; and helped overcome salient distractive features, disruptions, and availability bias. Reflection also facilitated understanding new information about the disease (Mamede and Schmidt 2023; Peleg-Baker and Lang 2022). These findings in many studies demonstrate the tangible benefits of structured reflection in real-world professional scenarios.

Structured reflection, a process that involves a deep examination of actions or hypotheses within the context of intentions, is critical for continuous learning. Intentional and active engagement with one's actions and intentions is crucial for identifying gaps between intentions and reality and areas for improvement. Such intense cognitive processing involved in structured reflection is likely to contribute to the formation of a complex schema and mental representations, resulting in better performance.

Simply executing a behavior without the intention to improve may not lead to significant performance enhancements. Improvements depend on deliberate efforts to change particular aspects of performance. As highlighted by Kahneman and Klein (2009), complex understanding can potentially supersede the inclination toward flawed automatic intuitive judgments. Therefore, structured reflection, driven by intention, is a powerful tool for continuous learning and improvement. Professionals who keep improving for decades engage in purposeful practice in a safe training environment where they practice specific aspects with supervision or guidance; build on opportunities for reflection, problem solving, and repetition; and receive feedback.

The power of structured reflection is amplified within a group setting. This shared experience, as in RPGs, is instrumental in enhancing experts' mental representations, memory skills, problem-solving capabilities, decision-making effectiveness, and proficiency in making skilled intuitive decisions. Moreover, this process aids in narrowing the gap between actions and intentions, fostering a more aligned and intentional professional practice. Structured reflection in a group setting benefits individual professionals and contributes to the collective learning and improvement of the entire group.

WHY THE SRI?

The SRI is a purposeful, goal-oriented reflective tool designed to assist third-party interveners in enhancing the quality of service they provide parties by addressing a broad range of explicit and implicit social-psychological concerns and goals.

Through intentional, structured cognitive processing, the SRI results in heightened awareness of automatic judgments, particularly concerning implicit drivers of their behaviors. Grounded in behavioral science research, the SRI comprises four dimensions, each with specific questions tailored to address explicit and implicit social-psychological goals. One dimension pertains to explicit substantive issues directly expressed by the parties. In contrast, the other three dimensions focus on implicit concerns, which often underlie conflicts: parties' sense of identity, relationships, and process concerns.

The SRI emphasizes acquiring new insights and skills through practical application in alignment with adult learning principles. By systematically and deliberately attending to specific aspects of practice, the SRI can support restructuring mental representations, foster deeper and richer cognitive frameworks, and enhance the practitioner's competence in making rapid and effective decisions during the uncertain and dynamic circumstances of interventions.

The interplay between system 1 and system 2 is crucial. System 1, the fast, automatic, and unconscious judgment, may seem uncontrolled. However, its quality strongly depends on the deliberate processing of system 2 (Bodenhausen and Todd 2010). System 1 intuitive reactions, rooted in past experiences, can be enhanced through methodical and purposeful system 2 cognitive processing. This interplay is crucial for decisions made in fast, uncertain circumstances, highlighting the need for conscious reflection on specific dimensions of the SRI.

Furthermore, reflecting on experiences with colleagues can be a unique and valuable learning process. It exposes professionals to new and different perspectives and, by so doing, can broaden their understanding. However, expanding the mind with new perspectives relies on humility and our ability to recognize the limited lens through which we view the world. Reassessing our actions and recognizing our incompleteness benefits our ability to notice more and to truly appreciate others' perspectives. This interchangeable inner and outer dialogue encourages questioning our attitudes, values, assumptions, biases, and habitual behaviors and reassessing our actions considering the new perspectives we meet externally. It is an active, reflective engagement that stimulates the development and improvement of decision-making skills. As we consider different views, we become more open to reconsidering our actions, trying out alternative approaches, and continuing the cycle of growth and improvement.

An expanded mind eases the way to flexibly navigating interventions, continually working toward excellent performance, and becoming the best professionals we can be. It is a process that keeps our eyes wide open to increasingly complex understanding and practice. The more skillful practitioners become, the less flawed their intuitive decisions are (Kahneman and Klein, 2009).

The SRI is not just a theoretical tool but a practical instrument that can be applied to situations in various stages of the conflict intervention. It is not limited to comparing intentions versus actual behaviors but also serves as a lens for critical reflection on both failed and successful decisions within each of the four dimensions. The instrument provides specific questions and instructions to scrutinize behaviors that either facilitated or hindered each goal. It guides interveners to consider prospective behaviors that can effectively address each goal in the future. Whether used individually or within a group, in preparation for an intervention, during the intervention itself, or in the post-intervention phase, the SRI is a versatile tool that can enhance the effectiveness of mediation interventions.

The SRI reduces interveners' reluctance to address "messy" emotional issues by making implicit factors explicit. In turn, it lays the groundwork for genuine conversations and propels parties toward discussing the core of the conflict. Mediators attested that systematically engaging with the SRI dimensions alongside colleagues helped them reconsider crucial questions, such as what they should prioritize or when to address identity or relational concerns. Mediators reported a redefinition of the level of their responsibility and a refinement in how they perceive their role as interveners. One mediator expressed, "Attending to implicit needs does not mean becoming psychotherapists. We can support psychological and relational needs without having parties lying on the couch."

The SRI distinguishes itself from standard mediation debriefing, which typically centers on agreement or solution by posing general questions such as what you thought you did well, whether the parties were satisfied with the process, or what was challenging about the case. These general questions might be too vague to elicit effective learning or induce a shift in habitual behaviors. In contrast, the SRI offers a goal-oriented reflection. The Process dimension, one of the four reflective dimensions, is provided in the appendices. The SRI promotes deliberation, effective learning, and behavior change with its structure and specific questions.

Mediation, a complex process, operates within a low-validity environment. This is primarily due to the high variability of disputes, which differ in participants, situations, and goals, making each case unique. However, parties involved in these disputes share similar motivations, emotions, and reactive behaviors. They commonly experience an increased need for recognition, react defensively, engage in power struggles, and become anxious when confronted with emotional and painful challenges. (For further discussion, refer to "The Conditions for the Quality of Intuitive Judgments" and "Implications for Mediation" in Peleg-Baker and Lang 2022.) These unique challenges underscore the need for practical tools like SRI.

The SRI, a practical tool, guides interveners, steering them toward a wide range of goals, mainly the implicit social-psychological aspects that fuel conflict. It plays a crucial role in increasing the validity of the intervention environment by focusing on the emotional, underlying motivators that characterize all human interactions despite the differences across cases. Additionally, the SRI allows professionals to discern repetitive cues in the conflict environment. When systematically practiced, its structured approach, specific questions, and detailed instructions can significantly help interveners consider implicit issues and make better decisions about what to pay attention to and when, thereby improving the overall effectiveness of the mediation process.

Learning Journal

The purpose of a learning journal "is to enhance your learning through the process of writing and thinking about your learning experiences" (University of Worcester 2016). A learning journal is a written collection of observations, questions, recollections, and reflections. Jennifer Moon (1999) notes that reflective writing is a valued aspect of professional development. Objectives of a learning journal include the following:

To develop learning in ways that enhances other learning
To deepen the quality of learning in the form of critical thinking or developing a questioning attitude
To facilitate learning from experience
To increase active involvement in learning and personal ownership of learning
To enhance professional practice or the professional self in practice
To enhance creativity by making better use of intuitive understanding
To foster reflective and creative interaction in a group (188–93)

Learning journals may be used for general or broad-spectrum learning, that is, identifying and reflecting on learning activities such as webinars, conference presentations, reading books, articles, blogs, reflective practice group case presentations, and conversations with colleagues. Learning journals may also function as the source for critical self-reflection, especially when used in conjunction with the guides to reflection.

A learning journal differs from case summaries, logs, or process notes, which are a record of the activities, behaviors, and exchanges between the participants and involving the practitioner. The perspective of these observations and recollections is objective, outward looking, and descriptive—considering who, what, where, when, and how—and the goal is often to create a record of events or to plan future interactions.

A learning journal, though, is a reflective tool for learning—a means of systematically recording your thoughts, impressions, concerns, questions, and reflections as well as significant incidents and actions. Informal in structure yet intentional in action, the learning journal is a record of whatever comes to mind as you engage in practice, read, join in discussions, and take part in other learning activities.

Barbara Bassot has written articles and books, produced instructional videos, and lectured extensively about reflective learning journals. To learn much more about learning journals and their nature, purposes, and benefits, I encourage you to look for her books, articles, and recordings.

Bassot (2016, 31) identifies some of the significant differences between reflective journal writing and writing that is not reflective.

Reflective writing is:	Reflective writing is not:
Written in the first person (I, me, we, us)	Written in the third person (he, she, it, they)
Critical in the sense of offering a critique	Critical in the sense of only focusing on the negative
Analytical	Descriptive
Spontaneous	Calculated
Free flowing	"Doctored," what I think I should write
Honest	"Kidding myself"
Subjective	Objective
About engaging with my feelings and processing them	A means of ignoring my feelings and burying them
A tool for helping me to challenge my assumptions	An excuse to ignore my assumptions and allow them to influence my work in a negative way
An investment of time	A waste of time

As is readily apparent from these contrasting lists, reflective journaling is distinct in format and emphasis, as we saw in the comparison between reflective practice and reflection in chapter 2. More important, the underlying objectives are markedly different. A learning journal is introspective, examining incidents in practice to uncover explanations for what occurred. The process involves reflection and self-assessment. The goal is "to generate both a new understanding of the phenomenon and a change in the situation" (Schön 1983, 68).

Reasons to Make Use of a Learning Journal

1. By keeping an ongoing record of your observations and reflections, you begin to see patterns—unsettled questions or perplexing situations—that recur. From these patterns, you can evaluate when certain actions have proved helpful and when they have been less useful. With this analysis, you can decide to adjust your thinking and your strategies and tactics.
2. Taking time to identify and then think about an unusual practice situation improves your understanding of what occurred and helps explain why it occurred. This information will help you figure out how to respond when the situation arises again.
3. The simple act of recording an idea or strategy anchors the information in your memory and improves the likelihood that you will use that approach in your practice.
4. Stopping to think about your experiences and then making notes about them are parts of ongoing learning. New ideas and fresh perspectives will strengthen your skills, sharpen your insights, and make your actions more effective.

Guidelines for beginning and maintaining a learning journal are set out in the appendices.

Harry Potter:	What is it?
Albus Dumbledore:	This? It is called a Pensieve. I sometimes find, and I am sure you know the feeling, that I simply have too many thoughts and memories crammed into my mind.

—J. K. Rowling, *Harry Potter and the Goblet of Fire*

The elements in this chapter point to one simple truth and the reason for this book—to learn from and through our experiences in order to become more capable, responsive, and effective, a ceaseless spiral of learning unfurling outward and upward in a process of professional evolution and growth. We make use of reflection (reflection-before-action, reflection-in-action, and reflection-on-action), the SRI, and a learning journal because reflective practitioners seek to deepen their knowledge, increase their insights, and sharpen their skills.

Each method described in this chapter is subjective, inward looking, and contemplative, carried out individually and in private. In the next chapter, I will describe the use of Reflective Debrief® in a group setting or in a focused conversation with a coach, supervisor, or mentor in an interactive and outward-facing process.

Exercises

Exercise 6.1

Think of a skill you learned that initially required concentration and intention but now you do it without having to be deliberate and methodical. What was your learning process?

Exercise 6.2

How do you respond when you experience a surprising or puzzling moment in practice? What method has worked best for you, and why? Have you tried other methods that weren't helpful?

Exercise 6.3

Can you imagine using one or more of the reflective methods? Which of them are you most likely to use? What would encourage you to try using them? What is the impediment?

Exercise 6.4

Consider Tzofnat Peleg-Baker's section. Can you recall a situation where you were aware of and responded to a party's implicit need? How did you become aware of the need? How did you respond? What was the effect of addressing this implicit goal?

Exercise 6.5

As part of your professional work, do you keep a journal, case notes, or other written records? In what ways do you find these writings helpful?

CHAPTER 7

Reflective Practice Groups

Time is the continuous loop, the snakeskin with scales endlessly overlapping without beginning or end, or time is an ascending spiral if you will, like a child's toy Slinky. —Annie Dillard

In chapter 6, I offered examples of self-reflection and presented guides to structure individual, private reflection. Reflective practice can also be a shared experience through participation in a reflective practice group (RPG), an opportunity to learn with others using the same methods and following the same principles we use in individual reflections:

> I began my path toward mediation over the past several years. When I was invited to participate in an RPG with Susanne Terry and Michael Lang, I didn't hesitate to join, though I really had no idea what I was getting myself into. I ended up in a group of experienced mediators and experienced reflective practitioners.

> *What I learned and learned to love about reflective practice is its fundamental underlying nonjudgmental philosophy. No advice given. No praise or negative critique allowed. The group, mostly through the person leading the reflection and asking the questions, gives the practitioner space to work through whatever is troubling or confusing to them.*
>
> *The practice is valuable for mediation itself in that by refusing to give judgment or provide an opinion, the client is given the opportunity to work the questions. The person with the question can figure out what makes sense—in reflective practice and in mediation—how to approach the underlying question or problem.* —Fritz Langrock

My first experiences with reflective practice were individual in nature, and I continue private reflection as a routine aspect of professional practice. Happily, reflective practice came relatively easy to me because I am naturally disposed to introspection and thoughtful self-analysis and (modesty aside) am curious and an eager learner. I offered several examples of and methods for self-reflection and presented guides that structure individual, private reflection in chapter 6.

> *I am not a teacher, but an awakener.* Robert Frost

This chapter is devoted to group reflection, through RPGs, relying on the same basic principles and methods (Reflective Debrief®) used in individual self-reflection. As I noted earlier in the book, other professions have adopted and now routinely use reflective practice concepts and methods. Further, these professions, including nursing, social work, and education, commonly use group debrief to reflect on and learn from their experiences. Other than RPGs that I and Susanne Terry have organized and led, there are few (possibly none) opportunities for dispute resolution practitioners to participate in group reflection. There are other forms of group learning, of course, but none provides the shared learning experience possible in an RPG.

There are a number of reasons why practitioners participate in RPGs. The following are among the most frequently cited incentives. Comments from members of RPGs are interspersed throughout this chapter.

- Not all of us have the discipline and resolve required for systematic and sustained use of individual reflective methods. We may be committed to the principles and goals of reflective practice and welcome the practical benefits of reflection—deepened knowledge and strengthened skills—but find it difficult to sustain a consistent and routine process of reflection:

    > *The longer I mediate, the more aware I am of the gap between the theory of mediation and the realities of my practice. On top of this, it seems as though my experience can sometimes get in the way of the growth mindset that I try to apply to each new mediation. So I may end up choosing interventions and strategies based on my own knowledge and previous experiences rather than on what may more likely match the parties' own needs. I have found regular reflective practice to be an essential part of my internal traffic light system; not only does it help me try to ensure that my practice remains actively conscious rather than routine, but I value the infinite loop of insight and personal development that, to me, are vital to a rewarding and sustainable mediation practice.* —Phyllida Middlemiss

- Setting aside time for reflection while maintaining a demanding professional practice may seem nearly impossible at times. Like any habit we want to develop, maintaining the discipline of reflecting on our experiences requires attention, consistency, and practice. RPGs are an indispensable, structured, and systematic supplement to our individual practice of reflection:

> *We always say that the advantage of mediation is that the solution is in the hands of the parties. If we try to lead the parties to a solution, they may agree, albeit reluctantly, but feel less than satisfied. Learning to adopt reflective practice should have been obvious but was, in fact, a revelation to me. It's not easy to make the change, but with a good deal of practice, I learned that by asking the right questions instead of trying to steer the parties to a solution that the mediator thinks is the right one, I draw the solution from the parties themselves. If they have identified the solution, they are much more likely to feel satisfied with the outcome. The difference is profound and has affected my approach to many areas of my own problem solving.* —Colin Bourne

- Some of us are naturally drawn to communal experiences. We seek out and enjoy opportunities to talk with colleagues, finding the solitary nature of reflection less valuable, engaging, and constructive:

  > *Being part of an RPG has helped me to process difficult issues that I have subconsciously internalized. As a self-employed mediator, I don't have colleagues to download on, and being an extrovert, I process my thoughts by talking to people. Reflective practice has helped me to process and release challenging experiences in a healthy way and enabled me to come to my own realizations and conclusions about how I can improve the way I mediate. Often, it can access deeper areas within me that need more personal work, which I find invaluable as I strive to always learn about myself.* —Julia Burns

As one naturally driven to reflection—an attribute that instantly and naturally attracted me to reflective practice nearly forty years ago—I am familiar with a singular drawback. It is possible to become enmeshed in a circular process of self-referential introspection—going over the same incident from the same perspective repeatedly and without insight or progress in solving the dilemma that prompted the reflection. Talking with others—voicing our questions—in the presence of others who offer encouragement, support, and guidance often reveals what our internal musings have concealed:

> *I am a recent convert to reflective practice. The concept immediately resonated with me, and now that I have learned a little about it, my appreciation has grown. Why am I so enthusiastic about spending time this way—especially when I really don't have time to take on extra activities? In common with many mediators, I have a passion for mediation, and this disposes me to keep wanting to learn more about it. The main driver, however, is that reflective practice enables me to see and understand why I do what I do when I am mediating and to learn about what I do at a number of different levels and from the perspective of other mediators. I also get to go through this process with a number of like-minded mediators from various different sectors who are all happy to reveal their actions and thoughts in a collegiate environment. It is a rich, rewarding experience wrapped around with an enormous spirit of trust and generosity. I wish I had started down this path sooner, but it is one I shall follow from now on. It will, I am certain, enable me to be a better mediator.* —Tim Willis

Joining with others to learn from our experiences helps overcome our isolation and provides encouragement to use reflective methods. In RPGs, we develop a community of learners as we share stories, finding commonality in our experiences and the dilemmas we confront. The support and guidance of learning groups allow us to make use of the reflective practice principles in a collegial environment:

> As with similar skills found in other fields, like therapy or social work, no amount of telling can fully convey how to do something. We must try it for ourselves, and very

often we must also rely on ourselves to know how well we performed. Practitioners who are able to reflect-on-action . . . are better equipped to advance beyond the stage of "good enough" to become real experts in their practice. Reflective practice groups . . . are composed of mediators who support one another in non-judgmentally exploring the assumptions and motivations that underlie their interventions. (Lang and Arms Almengor 2017)

Research studies offer a further rationale for participation in an RPG, supporting the notion that group reflection—the shared experience—provides a rich, enduring, and indispensable method for learning from our experiences (Peleg-Baker and Lang 2022).

> I like a teacher who gives you something to take home to think about besides homework. Lily Tomlin

Why Practitioners Need RPGs

There is no tradition of or organized process for supervision or mentoring in conflict resolution practice, unlike professions such as teaching, nursing, and social work, in which licensing requires extensive supervision and mentoring following formal education. Moreover, in these and other professions, supervision or mentoring for ongoing professional development is an accepted and common practice (for some, even a requirement for continued licensure or certification). For conflict practitioners, there is no universally recognized process for professional development through mentoring—no standards or guidance list of objectives to advise mentors or to guide practitioners who may seek advice from colleagues, senior practitioners, or other professionals. Opportunities for practitioners to experience learning through coaching or mentoring are limited to feedback or coaching following role-play activities in training courses and continuing education programs. In some states, mediator certification systems require applicants to shadow an experienced mediator or act as co-mediator in one or more conflict situations. Even in situations where mentoring or coaching is prescribed, there are no standards or criteria for offering feedback, only a specified number of hours of mentoring. As a consequence, the mentor determines the nature of and method for feedback, which too often is limited in time and spare in content and very likely prescriptive. Thoughtfully and meticulously crafted requirements for mentoring mediators established by the Supreme Court of Virginia (2022) are welcome and notable exceptions.

In our professional development courses, seminars, and other learning sessions, we learn to apply strategies and techniques, but the only opportunities to practice these skills are in relation to "canned" scenarios—not actual practice situations. Experiential learning relies on exercises and role-plays created by the trainer in which participants practice techniques and strategies in response to learning goals established by the trainer. Moreover, role-play opportunities are few in number, the experiences are time limited, and the activity focuses on an isolated portion of a more wide-ranging intervention. As a consequence, much of the learning in these training programs is passive, coming from observation or lectures. As a result, whatever we learn is not easily transferred to our real-life experiences:

> With many years of experience supporting novice and experienced mediators, seldom is a practice so valuable regardless of experience level. More experienced mediators welcome the opportunity to reflect on their choices and assumptions in an intentional way—keeping themselves out of the practice "ruts" created over time. New mediators can be supported in building a practice where they critically consider their interventions and are provided tools to

reflect before, during, and after sessions. As a supervisor, this removes me from the position of "telling" someone how to change and allows me instead to sit alongside as they explore their practice options. —Karen Carroll

Of course, there is value in every learning experience. Training courses and similar education programs are a crucial part of a practitioner's professional development. However, they do not provide personalized learning. When educating a group of practitioners, the trainer cannot create individualized learning opportunities. Nor is it feasible to expect these courses to meet the distinct learning needs of each participant. Still, it is a serious shortcoming.

Mentoring and individualized supervision, except within group practices such as community mediation centers (as Karen Carroll notes above) and some court-related programs, is seldom sought and more rarely offered. Our profession has no tradition or custom of supervision. As a result, the practice of mentoring or supervision is not widely available or often sought.

The path isn't a straight line; it's a spiral. You continually come back to things you thought you understood and see deeper truths. Barry H. Gillespie

The requirement for and acceptance of supervision in Australia, as Jodie Grant describes in her section on reflective practice and supervision, is a welcome exception. Even when groups or agencies certifying practitioners require supervision or mentoring or co-mediation with an experienced mediator, requirements vary, and obligation for supervision pertains only to the process of becoming approved or certified. In my own experience, becoming a Florida Supreme Court Certified Family Mediator in Florida required "supervision," involving ten hours of observation and co-mediation. There was no requirement for feedback or mentoring from the "mentor." And I received none. Without belaboring the point, our profession lacks meaningful and commonly available opportunities for mentoring or supervision.

It's also true that, generally, we practice alone. We aren't likely to discuss our work with colleagues in any level of detail that would support learning from experience. Our work is observed only by participants, and even if they agreed to discuss their experience, they are unlikely to have the knowledge or objectivity to provide useful feedback. Nevertheless, some practitioners provide feedback forms seeking comments from their clients. Our commitment to confidentiality and privacy necessarily excludes outsiders who might observe our work. That same obligation limits opportunities to discuss practice questions with our colleagues.

Consequently, we have few if any methods for assessing the effectiveness of our efforts or learning from practice experiences. More important, none of the methods commonly used, such as client surveys and conversations with colleagues, are designed to help us understand why an intervention succeeds or fails—a prerequisite for living "through the initial shocks of confusion and mystery, unlearn initial expectations, and begin to master the practice" (Schön 1987, 311). Instead, we are more likely to use settlement rates and number of interventions conducted as measures of our competence and effectiveness. However, experience alone does not guarantee high-quality practice.

Many practitioners believe that if their cases settle, they must be competent. They confidently assume that failure, meaning lack of an agreed outcome, likely results from parties' lack of motivation or other circumstance unrelated to their competence. As a result, they might believe they are in the groove (or the zone) when in fact they are more likely operating on autopilot. Strategies and tactics become the ordinary routines of practice, relying on prior experience as a guide to future action. The result can be complacency. We may be competent, but we are not achieving the level of excellence of which we are capable.

Practice does not make perfect. Only perfect practice makes perfect. —Vince Lombardi

In summary, this is the nature of the problem within our profession that limits the expanding spiral of professional growth and evolution:

1. Conflict intervention practice is necessarily a private and confidential endeavor, unobserved by others who might offer feedback or comment. Generally, "we are solitary beasts, prowling the savannahs of conflict, not part of a herd (or practice group)" (Lang and Arms Almengor 2017). We lack an independent method for assessing whether our efforts were responsive and effective or clumsy and ineffectual, and we can't learn why certain interventions were on the mark or fell flat. Settlement rates, often cited as a measure of competence, are inadequate and unreliable.
2. Learning opportunities are based on goals, methods, and activities devised by the trainer. So what's the problem? There are two. First, learning in these programs and courses is largely passive (lectures, slide shows, and demonstrations). Second, these events involve limited opportunities for experiential learning—the hands-on application of knowledge and skills, with individualized attention, coaching, or feedback. Crucially, none of these courses and programs allow us to learn from our day-to-day practice experiences.
3. We encounter surprising and sometimes puzzling situations for which prior experience does not provide a ready answer. Over time, we develop practice habits; we rely on favorite stories, techniques, and strategies. With success as our guide and trial and error as our method of analysis, we weed out less helpful behaviors, focusing on a repertoire of interventions that has produced good results. When interventions become routine, not purposeful, based largely on prior experience and not the unique circumstances of the parties and their interactions, we are not at our best. Ironically, our reliance—even dependence—on predictability and routine can impair our efforts when we dismiss surprising and unexpected behaviors that don't readily fit within the domain constraints of our model.
4. We want to address the unexpected as well as to become more adept at our practices and seek opportunities to learn—to advance along the spiral of our professional development:

First off, without reflection on one's practice, skilled practice will likely not develop. Almost by definition, learning requires reflection. Presumably, every practitioner reflects, to one degree or another and in one way or another, on their engagement with each new case. I try to pay attention to two areas. One is my behavior in the mediation case at hand. The other is my understanding and beliefs about my role generally. Thoughts on the latter help me consider the former, provide a framework for considering the former. My challenge is setting aside dedicated time for this part of practice. The work itself is demanding enough. There is much to be said about the how of skilled reflective practice, but regular participation in an RPG, even if that is a group of only two, will help with both setting aside dedicated time and the how. —Tim Hicks

Reflective Debrief® as experienced in an RPG is an effective method for addressing these challenges. Consider the young girl and her father as well as my experience in the supervision seminar. What do they have in common? In each story, we see that surprise and puzzlement lead to inquiry, a coach is engaged who does not reveal the answer but instead encourages exploration and discovery, and the result of that nondirective process is that both the young girl and I resolved our respective dilemmas and became more proficient at solving problems generally:

> I'm in two RPGs, which have aided my development as a mediator, a coach, and a restorative practitioner in many ways.
>
> One occasion where I was discussing a case which went badly, the questions asked by the group led me to realise how I had neglected to empathise properly with a very angry character that I had classified internally as a "bit of a bully." I failed to recognise properly the extent of the injury he felt, and this may have contributed to him keeping his defenses up. My bias toward the underdog was what kept me out of connection with him, and I don't think I'd have realised this without my reflective practice session.
>
> Other occasions, either one-on-one or in a reflective practice session, enabled me and sometimes myself and a co-facilitator/co-mediator to figure out the best course of action to take when mediating or facilitating. —Catherine O'Connell

The way isn't a circle and never can't be a circle unless you repeat the same after the same. Is it possible to find something new?... The way is spiral, and I will keep believing in this!
Deyth Banger

Now, having presented the nature of a problem in our profession, let's consider the solution. The title to this chapter and the many quotations from participants in RPGs are more than hints at the answer. RPGs are an indispensable, structured, and systematic supplement to our individual practice of reflection.

What Is an RPG?

Simply put, an RPG is a purposeful and structured learning group, guided by the principles, values, and theories of reflective practice. Members present and describe puzzling practice situations, and making use of Reflective Debrief®, facilitators and group members help the presenter reflect on an experience or puzzling moment, clarify the problem, understand its origin and its impact on the intervention and the practitioner, and, as a result, gain insight into and solutions for their practice dilemmas. The principal objective of an RPG is to improve the quality and effectiveness of practitioner interventions by finding practical solutions to puzzling practice dilemmas and in that process strengthen our existing skills and develop our knowledge. The key objective of an RPG is to help us become more adept, resourceful, confident, and effective mediators by means of self-exploration, self-assessment, and self-discovery. The repeated use of "self" in the preceding sentence is purposeful and reflects a unique learning approach that relies on the notion that lifelong learning occurs when the learner identifies a surprising practice situation, struggles with the problem, and discovers a solution uniquely suited to that learner.

A central quality of RPGs is the emphasis on individualized learning grounded in consideration of actual practice situations—an effective remedy for the shocking inadequacy of hands-on practice opportunities in mediator training in general and professional development in particular. In RPGs, practitioners grapple with real-life dilemmas, not simulations. They discover solutions to troubling incidents and practice dilemmas. Insights gained and lessons learned are practical, relevant, and responsive to the unique needs and concerns of the practitioner. Moreover, reflections lead to knowledge the practitioner is likely to make use of in future practice situations. A unique and crucial feature of RPGs is that the "debrief" offers a level of personal attention unavailable in any other professional development activity. At the same time, every group member benefits from an individual debrief, discovering knowledge and insights for themselves.

A key attribute of an RPG is that group members assist one another to investigate and reflect on their experiences, even when self-examination may be unsettling and confusing. For example, group members help the presenter resist the unconscious urge to focus on the details of the story rather than the nature of and likely reason for the surprising incident. That tug is familiar to most practitioners because our profession is grounded in people's compelling stories, the unfolding drama, difficult interactions, confusing events, and the human toll. Not surprisingly, many of us are more comfortable talking about what happened, telling a story about the intervention, than reflecting on the experience and its impact on us as practitioners.

As I mentioned previously, a key distinction between reflective practice and other modes of case consultation is the emphasis on exploring why something occurred rather than discussing and evaluating what took place. Other methods consider the situation as an observer almost clinically studying the situation. Reflective practice is a subjective process, placing us within the story of the events, seeking explanations for the events, and examining our responses—what we thought, what we felt, and how we could respond:

> *Reflective practice has given me an opportunity to consider my practice (and others' examples) in a compassionate and nonjudgmental environment. I think that has been the most important aspect to allow me to feel comfortable contemplating the behaviors and motivations of parties and myself. The opportunity for the nonjudgmental query is unique, in my experience, and offers a space that is quite different to the other mediator discussions, such as supervision sessions. In those, I can often find myself seeking to justify the choices I made in the moment of mediation, which can get in the way of noticing what happened and thinking through why that might have been the case. I have noticed a sense of spaciousness in reflective practice and appreciate the opportunity that space gives me to reflect, to learn, and to grow as a mediator.* —Phillipa Brown

It can at times be unsettling and demanding to dig into the confounding circumstances of our dilemmas, to examine our experiences and explore answers to our dilemmas. Instead, we may be tempted to turn to others for solutions. Asking for advice or recommendations is less complicated and demanding than engaging in a process of self-examination. In addition, offering advice to ease the presenting person's discomfort and confusion is tempting for group members.

I think the most important quality of a mentor is that they are open to following students where they want to go. Not always pushing their own agenda. Cordelia Jensen

Within an RPG, group members hold tightly to a principle, parallel to the notion of self-determination commonly acknowledged in conflict practice, that the most useful, meaningful, relevant, and durable solutions are ones discovered by those facing the dilemma. Participants in an RPG know that with encouragement and assistance through helpful questions, practitioners can discover why a situation was puzzling, how to respond effectively, and how to apply lessons learned from self-exploration to similar practice challenges.

Differences between an RPG and Other Practice Development Groups

In chapter 2, we examined the distinctions between reflective practice and forms of self-examination and self-improvement, such as conversations with colleagues. In a similar manner,

I want to differentiate RPGs from other types of professional development groups. I discussed a number of these distinctions in chapter 1.

In an RPG, the focus is analytical. Of course, we first consider the context in which the dilemma arose in order to examine what occurred. Describing the context, retelling events, and describing behaviors provide a basis for critical analysis—for understanding why a surprising event or behavior occurred, why it was notable, and why it was puzzling. Relating the story of the intervention is not, as is true for other methods, an opening for and invitation to receive offers of advice or practice recommendations from group members or the facilitator. In an RPG, an essential objective for which the context is an essential foundation is discovering an "aha" moment when the presenter recognizes, for herself, both how the situation arose and how to resolve her dilemma:

> *When something puzzles me, especially where self-doubt arises, it's like a tangle of threads. As it goes round in my brain, it becomes more knotted. The advice of others, however wise or well intentioned, adds more threads to the tangle and more tension.*
>
> *This kind of facilitated reflective practice eases the tension, reassures me that with time, persistence, reflective questions, and insight, I will be able to untangle the golden thread of meaning. —Nancy Radford*

Within an RPG, the debrief conversation is structured and organized—a systematic process that begins with a question—what the presenter wants to learn from the debrief. My colleague Susanne Terry and I developed a guide to help RPG members prepare a practice dilemma for presentation. The guide, Case Presentation Instructions for a Reflective Debrief®, is included in the appendices. The clarity of the presenter's question is crucial to the success of the debrief. It becomes the framework for the reflective conversation. The ensuing reflective process is organized, focused, and methodical, though being systematic does not mean the process is fixed and inflexible. Within the debrief, as with most conflict interventions, the process is elastic, stretching and contracting as required to meet the goals of the while holding tightly to the fundamental principles of reflective practice: that self-exploration leads to self-discovery.

You might ask, "If I know the answer to this dilemma and my approach has worked well in similar situations, then what's wrong with offering advice?" Advice has a place in professional development but a strategic and limited one. To be meaningful, relevant, and useful, advice needs to be offered only after the presenter has grappled with the dilemma on her own and as a result more clearly understands the surprising practice situation. Here's the thinking that supports the reflective approach—why we do things this way. There are three justifications for resisting the often compelling urge to offer advice. First, we weren't there—I know that's an obvious statement, but it's an essential piece of the reason for our approach. We know very little of what occurred. We have only a snapshot of the events and circumstances, a few key facts at most, and certainly not enough to understand what occurred. Second, our perception of the participants is sketchy, a patchwork of moments that don't readily give us a clear understanding. We did not see and hear the participants—their tone of voice, whether one dominated the conversation, the manner in which they engaged—or we were distant. Finally and most significant, each of us has a unique style, model of practice, and set of beliefs that shape our work. No two of us will see a situation the same way. No two of us will respond to in the same manner. Consequently, one person's advice—no matter how well considered and thoughtful—cannot adequately address the problem. Imagine asking someone who knows little about you to select your meal at a restaurant, decide what film you should see, or choose your clothing. These ideas and recommendations might be brilliant, but do they suit you? Advice may be spot on, but those moments are rare and cannot be the basis of or substitute for helping a colleague find her own answer. We have created guides to help RPG members effectively engage in the reflective process. In the appendices, we have included several guides for RPG participants. "RPG Basics" sets out the foundational guidelines. "What to Ask/Not Ask" provides examples of questions that encourage reflection and those more likely to stifle the reflective conversation.

> True mentors don't make their mentees a clone of themselves. Bernard Kelvin Clive

How Do We Benefit from Participation in an RPG?

First and as a preface, I want to acknowledge the theoretical underpinnings of reflective practice. Since I first read *The Reflective Practitioner* (Schön 1983) in the mid-1980s, I hungrily devoured books and articles exploring theories about the process of learning and the development of mastery. Schön's notion that reflection leads to improved effectiveness was the first and remains the most significant inspiration for achieving artistry in my practice. As I read Schön and others cited in this book, I ceaselessly wondered, how will these theories and methods make a difference in my practice, and how will they help me become a more resourceful, resilient, and effective practitioner?

Earlier in the book, I described a confusing and puzzling experience at a professional conference. I had volunteered to serve as mediator in a demonstration. The session presenters, the two role players, and later others at the conference warmly and enthusiastically commented on my approach—actions I could neither explain the basis for nor likely repeat. Mentally replaying the events, it seemed I had merely done what seemed right and helpful in the moment. That naive—and simplistic—answer was inadequate. I wanted to learn from the experience, to understand my actions, with the ultimate goal of improving the quality of my work. But I had no tools for the sort of self-assessment that would have yielded helpful answers. By chance, a friend encouraged me to read *The Reflective Practitioner*, and now almost forty years later, I help others use the methods of reflective practice to learn from their experiences. Why? Because I know the practical benefits of self-reflection.

I have interposed comments from members of RPGs in India, Ireland, South Africa, the United Kingdom, and the United States within my own thoughts throughout this chapter. Early in the book, I referred to these comments and noted I had invited participants in RPGs to add their voices, their personal experiences, to the narrative of the book. These practitioners speak powerfully and persuasively, from their own experiences, about the value of being a member of an RPG and the shifts in their practices as a result.

Let me add my own observations from the perspective of a group leader. The benefits of an RPG and the methods of reflective practice are both intrinsic (having its own inherent worth) and extrinsic (having value acknowledged by others—specifically, the participants).

Two words sum up the benefits of being a member of an RPG: "confidence" and "competence." As professionals, we all have known the satisfaction (even exhilaration) when we have responded to a particularly challenging situation and used our knowledge and skills with confidence and competence to help our clients engage in productive discussions about thorny and troublesome conflicts. In those moments, our competence shines. At the same time, our confidence rises. We know we have been resourceful and capable; we know we have served our clients with the highest level of professionalism. That's why we participate in RPGs: to improve our capabilities and increase our effectiveness.

You'll notice that the benefits of RPG participation are both the sense that we have capably and skillfully used our knowledge and experience to our clients' benefit (competence) and the heightened sense of self-satisfaction and self-regard (confidence):

> *Participating in the RPG sessions offered me a fresh perspective of myself as a person and how that translated into my behaviours as a professional mediator. I didn't realise how self-conscious I was until I began reflecting on some of my behaviours in a professional setting and some of the feedback from Michael and Susanne made me reflect on bringing my true self to my professional space. As a mediator, I want to be as relatable and identifiable to the parties at the table, and being my authentic self, free and comfortable to share my imperfect human side, would help break the ice in a genuine way.* —Jonathan Rodrigues

I developed the table below to reflect these intertwined advantages of RPG participation—the internal (self-regard) and the external (the practical gains for the professional and the clients).

Intrinsic	Extrinsic
Feeling self-respect	Acquiring knowledge
Enhancing self-confidence	Enhancing skill competence
Attaining a measure of wisdom	Experiencing self-discovery
Increasing self-esteem	Gaining a measure of mastery
Having a sense of progress	Experiencing validation

A reflective debrief begins when a group member who is searching for an answer to a question prompted by a surprising and puzzling situation presents a practice dilemma—a question shaped by reflecting on and responding to the questions in the case presentation guide. In the process of self-exploration and self-discovery, stimulated by questions from the group facilitator and group members, the presenter gains competence and knowledge and thereby improves the quality and effectiveness of his practice—practical benefits that are immediately applicable. Additionally, through the debrief conversation, the presenter becomes aware of his own capacity for learning, and as a result, his self-confidence is boosted, and he experiences progress in his professional development:

> *In addition to finding a group of trusted colleagues, the largest benefit I have found in being a reflective practitioner is thinking through the commonalities of practice situations and finding solutions that help across my conflict work. It is usually during the presentation of a practice dilemma where the group elicits thoughts about similar situations and possible solutions. I am then better able to handle a certain personality or situation.*
>
> *Often as mediators, we are isolated in our own work. Taking the time to debrief and think through the mediations together allows a practitioner to determine why he/she did or said something during the intervention and what resulted from*

Instead of being like a circus where the trainer uses his stick to make animals do stunts . . . the system of education should be like an orchestra where the conductor waives his stick to orchestrate the music already within the musicians' heart in the most beautiful manner. The teacher should be like the conductor in the orchestra, not the trainer in the circus. Abhijit Naskar

that action or statement. It allows us to think through other options and outcomes or determine that what we did worked for a reason. That process makes us better at what we do. —Andi Paus

Practice Guidelines for RPGs

In RPGs, we use the process of and guidelines for Reflective Debrief®. To recap, the guiding principles are the following:

> Trust the presenter to learn what she needs.
> The presenter sets the scope of the debrief.
> Never use a statement when a question will do.
> Support self-exploration and self-discovery.
> Not our job to "get" the presenter to do anything or think in a particular way.
> No need for reassurance.

To encourage candid reflection and constrain the tendency to offer opinions or advice or to second-guess the presenter, we establish the following agreements or ground rules:

> We value *self-exploration* that leads to *self-discovery*. The most pertinent, individually relevant, and long-lasting solutions are those we discover for ourselves.
> We respect the privacy and risk-taking that self-exploration requires, and therefore we promise to maintain confidentiality.
> We seek to make evident the often-unacknowledged connection between theory and practice.
> We ask questions that invite reflection rather than make statements.
> We do not judge, criticize, or second-guess one another, overtly or subtly.
> We do not offer opinions, advice, or recommendations.
> We focus on and attend to the problem as presented to the group, not as we might interpret it.
> We respect each other's airtime in order to learn together and hopefully even have fun in the process.

> *What on earth would I do without colleagues to ponder with? They hold questions with patience, provide spaciousness amid my rushing thoughts, and renew a sense of curiosity and compassion where I may have stalled. What a gift, to reset and refresh in this way! Reflective practice is an essential vitamin for rigorous work, fortifying our ability to greet challenges and adjust to the unique and original needs of every case. It makes impartiality possible.*
> *—Jennifer Knauer*

Organizing and Creating an RPG

For almost forty years, I have participated in peer mentoring groups as a member or leader/facilitator. Through these groups, I have become a more resourceful and effective practitioner. Although I learned occasionally by example and sometimes as a result of prescriptive feedback (advice or instruction), more often, I learned through a rigorous process of self-discovery—the process of Reflective Debrief®.

In their organization, configuration, and method, RPGs systematically follow the process of Reflective Debrief®. However, the organization and management of RPGs varies widely. For example, the American Bar Association Section of Dispute Resolution group meets monthly for an hour and does not require preregistration or consistent attendance, although there are "regular" participants. Other RPGs have a fixed membership. The availability of reliable videoconferencing applications has eliminated geography as a consideration. I live in Florida and regularly meet with people from Ireland, England, Poland, Nigeria, Trinidad, India, and Israel as well as the United States. Routinely, group members span as many as ten time zones. Some RPGs have been organized and are sponsored by professional associations (see below for examples). Some groups are organized around an area of practice, though most draw an eclectic collection of practitioners. It's common for a group to include conflict practitioners from diverse areas of practice, such as mediators, conflict coaches, and facilitators. Many groups are made up of practitioners in diverse fields (in one group, there are members who focus on small claims and community disputes, construction and other commercial matters, and divorce and other family conflicts). In a single group, we may have folks who adhere to different models of practice (e.g., facilitative, narrative, transformative, or directive). I will say more below about group membership. No matter the format, structure, meeting frequency, or membership, all RPGs share a fundamental concern for improving the quality of practice through the reflective process of learning through experience.

Creating an RPG involves a range of issues, such as questions of logistics and membership. A detailed list of the questions and factors, including recommendations for optimal group formation, are set out in "Guidelines for Starting an RPG" in the appendices.

One pivotal factor to a group's success is effective leadership. Reliable, knowledgeable, and effective group facilitation is indispensable. Group membership can be eclectic or homogeneous, it can be fixed or floating, and it can meet in person or virtually—none of those aspects is as central as leadership.

Before explaining the critical role of a facilitator, I want to acknowledge that any time we gather with colleagues and commiserate, celebrate, or just tell stories about cases, we are better for the experience. Talking in the hallways at conferences, meeting over coffee at a café or a late-afternoon glass of wine or beer, or at a more structured get-together—each is an opportunity to strengthen collegial connections, collect fresh ideas, or simply enjoy the company of people who understand what you do at the most gut level. In my own experience, nearly forty years ago (before I learned about reflective practice), I was one of ten mediators who met monthly for a year. We shared advice and information about mediation practice, talked about our successes, and complained about our failures in free-ranging conversations with no agendas. As a relative novice and as one of two or three divorce mediators in Maine, I eagerly drove two hours to meet with these colleagues and was grateful for the opportunity to meet with and learn from them.

I am familiar with groups led by an enthusiastic and visionary person who initially gathered colleagues to discuss cases. And I know of groups that rely on a rotating form of leadership among members. These tend to be informal and unstructured opportunities for group members to share interesting or troubling case examples, and advice giving is a main feature.

A loose, informal leadership structure invites a loosely guided (if at all) discussion of professional issues. As a result, these groups are organized around information sharing and not the learning characteristic of the process in an RPG:

As a mediator, I am familiar with continuing professional development courses and regular supervision as a means of developing my knowledge of the mediation process and my mediation skills. Reflective practice has added a new dimension to my learning and helped me better understand and analyse my methods and approach to a mediation. It has challenged my assumptions and enabled me to draw on my own individual experience of my mediations and identify how I can more effectively meet the needs of the parties and respond to the unexpected dilemmas that can arise within a session. Reflective practice liberates me from a strict "rules" approach, and through the focused questioning of reflective practice, I am encouraged to discover my own insights and responses. —David Kendrew

Learning that takes place in an RPG requires a focused process managed by a skilled, versatile, and experienced leader who understands the principles and objectives of reflective practice and who is a capable and reliable facilitator.

In RPGs, the leader has three principal responsibilities:

Organizer—The leader as keeper of the process and of the group's goals must have a solid grasp of the principles of reflective practice and Reflective Debrief®. The leader also sustains interest in group interactions by at times describing or explaining what is occurring—monitoring whether everyone is engaged and ensuring that each has an opportunity to present a practice concern and to participate in the debrief. With regard to logistics, the leader usually organizes the meeting space (virtual or in person) and communicates with members (providing information as well as meeting reminders).

Facilitator—The leader is the manager of the group process. Among the facilitator's tasks are deciding when and how to include others in the debrief; reminding members to use questions when they fall back on statements; interrupting when someone proposes advice or makes a judgment about the presenter's dilemma; refocusing when the conversation drifts into a discussion of interesting but unrelated matters, such as training opportunities or journal articles; and overall keeping the focus on the group's purpose.

Debriefer—This role requires focus, attentive listening, and thoughtful questions, all of which help the presenter to identify the question to be answered and explain why a particular incident was puzzling or surprising. The debriefer initiates the reflective conversation, asking questions to frame the debrief. The leader, knowing that the purpose of the debrief is to help resolve the uncertain situation in a process of self-discovery, asks questions to encourage the presenter to examine the situation, its origins, and its impact and to engage in constructive self-assessment. Importantly, the debriefer knows when to invite group members to contribute to the debrief.

Successful RPGs rely on a skilled leader to manage these roles. In RPGs that have a consistent membership and have carried on for several years, members often develop the knowledge and skills of the group leader. In those situations, groups have flourished under the shared leadership on a rotating basis among members. You will find additional information on the three roles in the appendices.

My final words about RPGs. Participation yields obvious practical benefits. The debrief process works to build confidence and competence as we learn from surprising and puzzling practice situations. And it takes only ninety minutes per month—usually online. In your office or home, you can become a more resourceful and resilient practitioner. Invest the time.

Examples of RPGs

Federal Courts

Herman and Twomey (2005) describe RPGs—called advanced mediation practice groups—operating in the U.S. District Court for the Northern District of California since 2004. The program is active as of the date of publication. Small groups of mediators (six to twelve) meet monthly with a facilitator to discuss case situations and learn from one another. Participants address a practice challenge or a predetermined topic. There is a commitment to regular attendance. The goals for this program are

> providing a deeper learning experience than "one shot" continuing education training programs can provide; combating isolation; promoting collegiality among mediators; developing enhanced mediation skills; applying negotiation and mediation theory to the issues confronted; and promoting a reflective approach to mediation practice. (Herman and Twomey 2005, 15)

Knowledge you may get from books but wisdom is trapped within you, release it. Ismat Ahmet Shaikh

One of the paper's coauthors, Howard Herman, then director of the ADR Program, confirmed in a personal interview that at least as of the spring of 2020, all mediators who receive referrals from the court participate in monthly RPGs.

Mediators in other court settings, such as in the Seventh Circuit Court of Appeals and the D.C. Circuit Court of Appeals, have been relying on reflective practice methods for years. Similar peer learning groups are active in other federal court jurisdictions.

RPGs Sponsored by Professional Organizations

American Bar Association

The Mediation Committee of the Section of Dispute Resolution has promoted an RPG as a committee-supported activity. In the fall of 2016, Ava Abramowitz, on behalf of the Section's Mediation Committee, initiated an RPG for mediators and other conflict practitioners. Established as a "drop-in" group, participants joined a monthly one-hour teleconference discussion of unique or puzzling practice situations guided by a facilitator (videoconference meetings would come two years later). In November 2016, I was invited to join the group, and the following month, Ava invited me to be the coordinator/facilitator. This RPG continues to meet monthly more than seven years later, currently under the principal leadership of Laurie Amaya (also a member of the Academy of Professional Family Mediators RPG) and co-facilitated by Barbara Wilson (see the description of the Mediator Experience Live Interview in chapter 9).

Participants are attracted to this format for the following reasons:

- The drop-in nature means that preregistration is not required, and practitioners can join whenever they are able.
- Confidentiality is honored and protected.
- They gain valuable practice insights and tips.
- The puzzling practice situations presented by the participants are relevant, practical, and useful to all.

The number of participants varies from month to month, averaging eight to twelve mediators. Participants have included mediators (commercial, family, community, construction, workplace), organizational conflict and congregational conflict intervenors, academics, and ombuds. We have welcomed participants from dozens of states, Puerto Rico, the District of Columbia, and ten countries. Meetings have included participants who stretched across many time zones:

One of the many tools and benefits I have gained from reflective practice is a better ability to think or "respond" usefully in the moment. In mediation, very often you must quickly process what to say or do next, so developing this skill is critical but also difficult to achieve. Through reflective practice, I have learned to examine and understand the whys and whats of my thought processes, and the more I do this, I am increasingly able to think better and faster. Improving my processing skills means that I can better work in the moment to assist my mediation clients. While reading and studying reflective practice has supported my learning, being part of a monthly RPG has been the critical factor in development of these skills. In particular, these are skills that improve with continual practice. Meeting monthly in an RPG has given me the opportunity for practice and the ability to learn from that practice in a nonjudgmental and respectful environment that supports the growth and development of all the participants. As a mediator, my experience with reflective practice has been invaluable, has improved my mediation skills, and become an integral part of how I think and work as a mediator. —Laurie Amaya

Association for Conflict Resolution

The Association for Conflict Resolution (ACR) supports activities for its members that build on the principles and methods of reflective practice. In the late summer of 2017, my colleague Susanne Terry invited me to join her in designing and presenting a webinar on reflective practice sponsored by ACR. Assisted by Giuseppe Leone of the Virtual Mediation Lab in Hawaii, we developed, promoted, and delivered a two-hour webinar, "Why Do We Do the Things We Do? Reflective Practice—The Artful Mastery of Mediation." Approximately ninety mediators participated. Many but not all were members of ACR. The webinar objectives were described as follows:

> For experienced mediators and other practitioners, our actions can become repetitive, almost habitual, and we can become complacent. For novices, there is a tendency to adhere unfailingly to a prescriptive format learned in their training courses. Participation in reflective practice groups allows more experienced practitioners to challenge their working assumptions. Novices can receive feedback from their colleagues allowing them to develop their own approaches as they also gain the ability to learn through and from their experiences. (Lang and Terry 2017)

Shortly after this presentation, ACR announced the formation of an RPG for its members that would meet monthly in a videoconference format with Susanne and me as facilitators. Nine practitioners originally registered for the group, and over time, the group has included as many as fifteen members, practicing in a wide array of conflict settings (private, court, community, government).

Academy of Professional Family Mediators

Cultivate an appreciation and passion for books. I'm using passion in the fullest sense of the word: a deep, fervent emotion, a state of intense desire; an enthusiastic ardor for something. Cassandra King

Almost from its inception, the Academy of Professional Family Mediators (APFM) offered a case consultation program of advice and recommendations delivered by experienced practitioners. Because the organization's commitment to professional development was well established, there was immediate interest when members were offered the opportunity to participate in an online RPG. APFM invited me to lead the group, and in the summer of 2017, the case consultation/RPG began. Ten mediators registered for this experimental program, which met monthly via videoconference. At the end of the six-month pilot program, the participants agreed to remain available to one another on an ad hoc basis to provide support and advice. They had grown to know and trust one another and to learn from each other. The success of that first program led to the formation of a successor RPG that has been meeting regularly for close to seven years. Together, we have written and published articles on mediation and reflective practice, delivered conference presentations and webinars, and helped one of the members organize and manage an RPG for mediators in South Africa (see below for further information about the group).

Association of Northern Mediators

Having learned about reflective practice at a webinar I presented, Nancy Radford, executive director of the Association of Northern Mediators, organized and recruited members for a monthly RPG in 2021. My colleague Ava Abramowitz and I continue to co-facilitate the group. Word of the group's success prompted interest from others, and a second group was launched in 2023, with Nancy Radford joining Ava and me as facilitators.

Mediators Institute of Ireland

For years, the Mediators Institute of Ireland, a prominent organization of professional mediators in Ireland, has endorsed sharing and learning groups as an essential means of promoting continued learning and professional development. Recently, the organization renamed these RPGs, embracing reflective practice as a vital and effective method for building mediator competence. Several years ago, I was invited to facilitate one of the sharing and learning groups, utilizing the reflective practice model and the process of Reflective Debrief®. Group members practice in the areas of workplace, family, and community mediation, and membership includes highly experienced practitioners and novices. Recently, the group welcomed a new member from Ecuador.

Nebraska Mediators Association

Members of the Nebraska Mediators Association, having attended a presentation on reflective practice that I delivered at the association's 2019 annual conference, invited me to help them organize and then facilitate an RPG. We have been meeting monthly for nearly five years. Two years ago, with the group members' consent, I invited Tzofnat Peleg-Baker to act as co-facilitator and to introduce the Structured Reflective Instrument® (SRI) to the group (see chapter 6 for information about the SRI).

KwaZulu-Natal Society of Mediators

Having been a member of APFM group and realizing the benefits of reflective practice, Tracey-Leigh Wessels, a mediator from South Africa, organized a preliminary training session to introduce reflective practice and subsequently developed an RPG for South African mediators facilitated by members of the long-running APFM RPG. The success of the South African group, which included the president of the KwaZulu-Natal Society of Mediators, has led to the formation of a successor group sponsored by the local professional organization.

There is no certainty; there is only adventure.
Roberto Assagioli

League of Mediators of Ukraine

Even amid the storms and tragedies of war, family conflicts requiring mediation continue. In fact, a number of domestic disputes leading to separation and divorce have been exacerbated by war conditions, including spouses on deployment in the military and families separated as women and children fled as refugees to other European countries. Tatyana Bilyk, on behalf of the League of Mediators of Ukraine, an association of family mediators, invited Susanne Terry and me to present a webinar explaining and demonstrating the methods and principles of reflective practice. That session led to a request for us to facilitate an RPG for members of the League. The RPG began in April 2024 with seventeen Ukrainian family mediators. It was my first experience facilitating a group where we relied on simultaneous translation. Funding for simultaneous translation was provided by the American Arbitration Association through the AAA-ICDR Foundation's Diversity Scholarship program.

In my years of practice as a teacher and author and as a leader of many RPGs, I know the hunger for learning that exists among practitioners. In addition, there is a desire to share our experiences with our colleagues. RPGs provide both—an exceptional learning experience and the chance to share that experience with fellow practitioners. I will end this chapter with another comment, this one from a practitioner trained to facilitate RPGs and who is now leading one of her own:

> *Since being part of an RPG, I've developed a keener eye for reviewing mediations and determining what could have been done better, or just differently. I find that using the questions for before, during, and after helps me understand what I plan on doing or did and also think about other possibilities—especially with those mediations that appear to be more challenging from the outset.*
>
> *We just started our own RPG with volunteer mediators. Although there was initial trepidation on the process ("What, you aren't going to tell us what we need to do?" or "We can't tell others how we would have done it?" both answered by "Let's do it through the RP process first"), we had great discussions on the principles of mediation and what they mean to us. We look forward to becoming skilled at using reflective practice principles. —Lew Blanchard*

Exercises

Exercise 7.1

In the course of your professional training and in your practice, were you ever mentored or coached—not including feedback received following role-play activities? If you were mentored or coached, recall a mentoring experience that was memorable, one where you learned something of lasting value about your approach to practice. What did you experience that was memorable? What did the mentor say or ask that you found helpful? If you were not mentored or coached, imagine an ideal mentoring situation. What would happen? How would you be treated? What would be positive and helpful about the interaction between you and the coach?

Exercise 7.2

Recall an experience in a training course, seminar, or other learning activity in which you either observed or participated in a role-play. What was the nature of the feedback from the instructor or coach? Was it prescriptive or elicitive? How did the role-play practitioner respond to the feedback? Did you learn something (technique or strategy) that you could apply in your practice?

CHAPTER 8

Reflective Debrief®

A self-reinforcing upward spiral: performance stimulating pride stimulating performance.
—Rosabeth Moss Kanter

Previously, we explored several reflective practice methods, all of which are notably self-directed. That makes sense because we practice mostly alone, without observers to comment on our actions or to provide supportive and corrective feedback. In *Educating the Reflective Practitioner* (1987) and *The Reflective Practitioner* (1983), Schön describes and offers extensive examples of the application of reflective practice in what he terms the "reflective practicum." Advocating that the reflective practicum is essential to professional development (he uses the term "artistry"), Schön asserts,

> Indeed, nothing is so indicative of progress in the acquisition of artistry as the student's discovery of the time it takes—time to live through the initial shocks of confusion and mystery, unlearn initial expectations, and begin to master the practice of the practicum; time to live through the learning cycles involved in any designlike task;

and time to shift repeatedly back and forth between reflection on and in action. It is a mark of progress in a reflective practicum that students learn to see the learning process as, in John Dewey's terms, "the practical work . . . of modification, of changing, of reconstruction continued without end." (1983, 311; 1987, 7)

This chapter deals with interactive reflective practice methods carried out through conversation with a coach, mentor, supervisor, or peers. These conversations, like self-reflection, are guided by the principles of reflective practice and utilize the process of Reflective Debrief® as a basic guide or structure for learning from puzzling, surprising, and mysterious moments in professional practice. In her essay below, Jodie Grant, a supervisor of mediators in Melbourne, Australia, described the application of reflective practice concepts and methods in her supervision practice. Whether learning through the reflective method of debrief or the process of reflective supervision, practitioners swell the ever-expanding spiral of our professional growth and evolution.

I first presented the Cycle of Reflection in *The Making of a Mediator* and in the first edition of this book. Patterned on the work of Schön (1983), Kolb (1984), Gibbs (1988), and Johns (2000), I created a model of reflection that would suit conflict resolution practitioners and that fit my understanding of the reflective process:

> I must emphasise that all models of reflection are merely devices to help the practitioner access reflection. (Johns 2004, 19)

The current version, Reflective Debrief®, which shares common elements and a common purpose with every model I have examined, was developed over years of use and testing with students and colleagues and in cooperation with my colleague Susanne Terry, who gave the process its name. Each model begins with an experience in professional practice. In the debrief process, the practitioner describes the notable incident, engages in an examination of and reflection about the situation, analyzes what went wrong and identifies what could have been done instead, and, finally, decides on a different set of behaviors for the future.

> We cannot teach people anything, we can only help them discover it within themselves.
> Galileo

Reflective Debrief® diverges somewhat from the other models. First, unlike many models I studied, we do not include an evaluation component or stage. Asking what went well or wrong or what could have been done better tends to produce incomplete assessments, defensive reactions, or justifications, limiting opportunities for learning. In contrast, deeper and lasting professional development results from exploring why the incident was confusing, unsettling, or puzzling. In Reflective Debrief®, the sole criterion we apply is that something occurred that was surprising and puzzling to the practitioner and not whether the practitioner may have erred. As with my role-play conference experience, I was unsettled and confused because the experience had been surprisingly successful.

Second, I believe that the overarching goal is to encourage learning that has lasting implications as well as to find answers to practice dilemmas. Reflective Debrief® is intended "to open up perspectives and access ways of thinking about clinical challenges and dilemmas" (Kurtz 2020, 4). We tend to ask the following:

What did you find puzzling about this incident?
What are your thoughts about why the incident occurred?
What did you notice about your reactions and those of the parties?

What assumptions influenced your approach?

From answers to these questions, practitioners discover solutions to the immediate dilemma and build their capacity to respond effectively to similar situations.

Before describing and sharing examples of the six stages of Reflective Debrief®, I want to offer a few preliminary comments about the overall process of reflective practice that are embodied in the model illustrated below.

REFLECTIVE DEBRIEF
A MODEL DEVELOPED BY MICHAEL LAND & SUSANNE TERRY

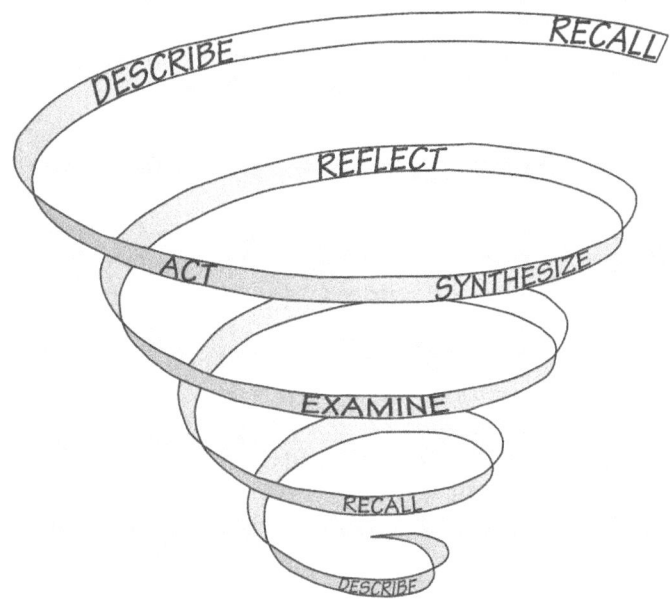

I was unsettled by the apparent one-off nature of the reflective cycles proposed by Schön and others, including my own original design. I puzzled over what seemed a troubling contradiction between the goal of reflective practice—iterative and thriving process of learning from and through experience—and a circular process of reflection with defined beginning and ending points. I was troubled that other models of the reflective process imply but do not fully explore the connection between the outcome achieved in the debrief (action) and the practitioner's overall professional development. It seemed more reasonable to think that each answer to a puzzling practice question is also integrated into the practitioner's knowledge, available to her in a variety of practice circumstances, in this way building capacity, strengthening skills, and developing confidence. I envisioned a process that could have a wide-ranging, comprehensive, and ingrained effect on professional practice. I believe (and more than two decades of experience with this process confirms) that the reflective practice process repeats unceasingly. With each iteration, new lessons become integrated with existing knowledge in an ever-expanding continuum of professional development—in essence, a spiral of growth and evolution:

In reflective experimentation, the idea is to build upon existing knowledge by drawing from experiences and learning to make educated selections based on the relevant information. (Farres 2004, 3)

The model of Reflective Debrief® epitomizes the essential aim of reflective practice—voracious curiosity that nourishes a ceaseless process of learning from experience:

> Both ordinary people and professional practitioners often think about what they are doing, sometimes even when doing it. Stimulated by surprise, they turn their backs on action and on the knowing which is implicit in action. They may ask themselves, for example, "What features do I notice when I recognize this thing? What are the criteria by which I make this judgment? What procedures am I enacting when I perform this skill? How am I framing the problem that I am trying to solve?" . . . There is some puzzling, or troubling, or interesting phenomenon with which the individual is trying to deal. As he tries to make sense of it, he also reflects on the understandings which have been implicit in his action, understandings which he surfaces, criticizes, restructures, and embodies in further action. (Schön 1983, 50)

Applying Reflective Debrief®

Success is not arriving at the summit of a mountain as a final destination. It is a continuing upward spiral of progress. It is perpetual growth. Wilfred Peterson

I want to take you through the six stages of Reflective Debrief® with reference to a workplace mediation. As the model on the previous page shows, those elements or stages are Describe, Recall, Examine, Reflect, Synthesize, and Act.

In the example that follows, I include reflections during the mediation session—reflection-in-action (in square brackets) and reflection-on-action (those from several days later).

Reflections begin with a surprising incident or puzzling moment. Reflection isn't necessarily spurred by a dramatic or game-changing incident. The practitioner's curiosity is awakened by something notable, an extraordinary or surprising action or exchange where practice routines do not suggest a ready response (Lang and Taylor 2000):

> When intuitive, spontaneous performance yields nothing more than the results expected for it, then we tend not to think about it. But when intuitive performance leads to surprises, pleasing and promising or unwanted, we may respond by reflecting-in-action. (Schön 1983, 56)

Frequently, it is the overall experience and not an individual moment that is unsettling or puzzling—as occurred for me with the workplace mediation I describe here.

Describe:
A twenty-five-year veteran of a company claimed that his dismissal was unwarranted. He agreed to participate in mediation with a company official from human resources. We met at a chain hotel near the airport in a typical large, drab meeting room where we were seated at one end of a table that could accommodate twenty. My sole contact with the participants had been individual pre-mediation telephone conversations, each lasting less than fifteen minutes, during which the former employee complained

that he didn't understand why he was fired. "They won't give me an explanation. I just know it was wrong." The company representative assured me that there were adequate reasons. "We did our due diligence and are satisfied with the basis for termination."

After a brief introduction, I encouraged them to describe the basis for the complaint and the reasons for the firing. The discussion bogged down almost immediately. The complainant spoke about his long tenure with the company. He pointed to a series of performance-based promotions, the last to a supervisory position. He contended that his firing was unjustified. When I prompted him to explain why he objected to the company's decision, he declined my request. [This was the first puzzling moment.]

Next, the company representative confirmed that there had been an extensive and thorough investigation leading to the decision to terminate the complainant's employment. He offered nothing more specific. Even when asked directly by the complainant, the representative refused to offer details of the investigation. "You already know everything we discovered and the reasons you were fired." He too declined my request for further details. [My puzzlement intensified.]

Recall:
[Their reticence to talk is surprising and confusing. Why are they holding back? Each seems to be waiting for the other to reveal some bit of information they can pounce on and either rebut or argue over. I am feeling irritated with them and by their behavior. Why schedule a mediation to which we all traveled and then behave like bad-tempered eight-year-olds?]

> Growth is a spiral process, doubling back on itself, reassessing and regrouping. Julia Margaret Cameron

I wondered why they were unwilling to provide a reason for their refusal to offer anything substantive. What could explain the behavior of not just one (which I have experienced previously) but both? I encouraged each to speak, reminding them that success depended on a frank exchange of information and ideas. The complainant robotically repeated, "I did everything right. The company had no cause to fire me." In similar fashion, the company representative repeated, "The investigation was thorough and unbiased, and the violations of company policies were fully substantiated."

[Strategically, the next move is to meet with each of them privately where perhaps I can temporarily interrupt their poker-faced silence, learn why they are so resistant to speaking, and decide how best to assist them.]

Examine:
Meeting separately, I asked each participant: "Are you finding this process helpful?" "Do you think there is a chance of settling this claim through mediation?" "Are you interested in finding a solution today?" What each revealed was as irritating and disappointing as it was unexpected and instructive. The complainant had recently consulted an employment lawyer who had advised him to (1) say as little as possible and (2) let the company make the first move. The lawyer was confident that any offer would be inadequate, and then they would file suit.

The company's lawyer had instructed the representative to withhold an initial offer, insist that the complainant make the first move, and make a lowball counteroffer. The representative was further advised, "Do not offer details of the investigation. If he doesn't like that, let him sue."

After each party confirmed that the dispute could be resolved only in court and explaining the basis for my decision, I ended the mediation.

Why is it that I remain unsettled by this frustrating and disappointing experience? Over a long career, I have experienced numerous instances when parties were unwilling to communicate and, as a result, the mediations concluded without a successful outcome. What is it about this situation that still irritates me? I think it was their appearance—bored, disengaged, smug, lacking accountability for their behavior, and unashamed at the wasted time and effort.

Reflect: (The following comments are in the nature of reflection-on-action.)
Puzzling moments prompt curiosity. This stage of the reflective process is characterized by more intensive self-exploration and critical self-examination.

Having identified the principal source of the uneasiness that remained long after the mediation concluded, I wondered why I was annoyed by behaviors that were unapologetically and shamelessly unhelpful. I had experienced similar behavior in other mediations without a gut feeling of annoyance. I wondered what could have motivated their smug attitude—not just their decision to withhold information? What could explain their apparent disdain for the process? On reflection, I became aware of an assumption that might have sparked my reaction. I had conducted several mediations involving this company and its employees, and in those sessions, participants frankly and freely exchanged ideas, information, and even accusations. No matter how contentious they may have been, the parties in these mediations genuinely wanted to find a reasonable solution. I expected these two to behave similarly. Is it possible that I became annoyed because their behavior and attitudes were inconsistent with my past experience? Had I become cynical and even intolerant? And, if that's true, did it show? Could they—did they—pick up on my attitude, and did it influence their behavior? And could my attitude have affected the nature and tone of my questions and comments? I wondered whether my reaction to their diffidence might have become a barrier to thinking clearly.

> It's possible that one of the reasons you got on the path of mastery was to look good. But to learn something new of any significance, you have to be willing to look foolish.
> George Leonard

They weren't rude or disrespectful to me. They were merely disengaged from the process, unwilling to share ideas and information, and they had concluded before arriving that the mediation would almost certainly fail.

Synthesize:
Recalling the events of that afternoon, I had arrived already annoyed by (1) the schedule (I had requested a morning session to avoid late-afternoon traffic for my return journey); (2) my reliance on GPS to navigate an unfamiliar route (I had nevertheless encountered unexpected and frustrating construction-related delays and detours); (3) my delayed arrival, meaning that lunch was a tasteless, prepackaged sandwich from the hotel's snack bar; and (4) a cold, unwelcoming, and cavernous room. In decades of mediation practice, I have dealt with all sorts of adverse circumstances yet managed to retain my focus, equilibrium, and professionalism. What was it about these circumstances that put me on edge?

In pre-mediation phone calls, each participant indicated he was eager to meet and exchange proposals and was hopeful a "deal" could be achieved. Consequently, I envisioned an intense and argumentative but hopefully constructive conversation in which my experience, knowledge, and skills would be put to the test. Instead of a lively and productive conversation that might push aside my frustrations, it was a numbing, tiresome, and unproductive experience.

As I weigh the most probable reasons that this experience persistently irritates me, the answer will not be found in the parties' attitudes or behavior but instead in my own prickliness. There were so many indicators, all of which I either minimized or dismissed, warning me to decline the engagement, yet I persisted. Factors that clouded my vision included (1) believing I could be helpful because I had successfully mediated employee dismissal claims involving this company and (2) wanting to retain a positive client relationship. As a result, from the moment I entered the bleak, chilly conference room, I was off-balance. I wasn't able to be at my best—to be calm, focused, resilient, and responsive.

Act:
I became aware of two simple and common lessons from this unsatisfying experience. First, be mindful of why I say yes and when I should consider declining an offer of work. Don't allow enthusiasm to obscure possible drawbacks. Second, take a moment before beginning a session and ensure that I am able to give my full attention to the parties and their goals.

The parties were on a trip to nowhere, and I was merely an invited witness to this leg of their journey—most definitely a journey to Abilene (see Harvey 1988). I was the only one in the room who thought this journey was worth taking. No matter what I did, the outcome was predetermined—by agreement of the parties. That would be annoying and exasperating for any mediator. But the reasons this situation remained an irritant was because I was upset with myself for having ignored the warning signs of a potentially ill-fated experience and because I felt manipulated, duped even, by the parties.

This example relies on self-reflection (reflection-in-action and reflection-on-action) to illustrate the six stages or elements of Reflective Debrief®. Now let's consider the application of the debrief process as a structured conversation between a practitioner and a mentor in which the mentor (debriefer) guides the practitioner in a process of self-exploration and self-discovery (Lang and Terry 2013).

Guided Reflective Debrief®

The Reflective Debrief® conversation is based on the following principles:

- With guidance and encouragement, practitioners can explore, make sense of, and discover their own answers to puzzling situations.
- Self-discovery resulting from self-exploration produces learning that is both practical and enduring.

Debriefers are guides; they are not authorities. Like the father in the "tic-tac-toe" story and the supervisor in the family therapy training course, the person facilitating the debrief does not offer advice, direction, or recommendations. Through questions and observations, the debriefer encourages exploration, self-reflection, and self-discovery:

A circle is the reflection of eternity. It has no beginning and it has no end—and if you put several circles over each other, then you get a spiral. Maynard James Keenan

I freely admit my default response to just about anyone's request for assistance is to share my advice, asked for or not. As a mediator, I have worked hard to not share my opinions and advice, and the use of reflective practice has supported that growth.

However, when working with new mediators, I find myself still wanting to share my advice. Using reflective debriefing with novices as well as expert mediators has been a shift for me. Acting as a debriefing partner in this way puts me alongside the mediator I am listening to, not above them. I know that when others sit alongside me, I can find my way by engaging my curiosity and self-awareness. I am now able to do that for others, and in doing so, I find myself more deeply connected to them. And I hope they are more deeply connected to me. Reflective practice has allowed me to foster more trusting, respectful relationships with other mediators as well as the clients I serve. —Kim Reisch

The following explanation is based on the idea of a one-on-one conversation between the presenter (practitioner) and mentor (debriefer) using the process and principles of Reflective Debrief®. For this illustration, I am using comments—in italics—taken from the family therapy supervision example and, in a couple of instances, from the story of the young girl and her father.

Describe:
The debriefer begins the Reflective Debrief® by inviting the presenter to offer a brief, focused description of the incidents, behaviors, or interactions that were unanticipated and surprising. Next, the debriefer asks the presenter, "What is the question you want to answer?" The presenter's response to this question establishes the initial focus for the debrief:

> *The pragmatist in me was concerned about "progress" in completing the settlement. In addition, I wondered whether the couple's behavior resulted from my lack of skills to help them redirect their attention to the substantive issues. I was puzzled at how deftly they could sidetrack substantive discussions.*

Occasionally, it's necessary to ask the practitioner for more detail on the surprising incident or behavior. Having a reasonably clear "statement of the problem" is essential; otherwise, the conversation can dissolve into a lengthy description of the case, the parties, and their behaviors or simply become a litany of complaints. The result can become a case review without a clear sense of direction and purpose.

In the appendices and available as a download on the publisher's website is a guide, "Case Presentation Instructions for Reflective Debrief®," used by participants in reflective practice groups to organize their thoughts and focus their practice questions for a Reflective Debrief® conversation. We also use this guide for one-on-one (mentoring) debriefs.

Above all, and guiding the path of the debrief, is the question asked by the person presenting the puzzling practice situation—not what the debriefer might think relevant or significant. This is key. As debriefers, we can't simply ignore or stop ourselves from having our own sense of the problem. Acknowledging that, we nevertheless focus on the question posed by the presenter.

The debriefer may ask questions to understand the context of the dilemma and in particular, if necessary, to clarify the question posed by the practitioner. Such questions include the nature of the practice situation, the type of conflict being addressed, and the attitudes and behaviors of the participants. During this initial part of the reflective conversation, the debriefer continually balances the relevance and usefulness of this information against the risk that the conversation could become fixated on and bogged down by unnecessary details of the practice situation:

How did these clients explain their reasons for choosing mediation?
So, describe why you are frustrated with the behavior of this couple.

Recall:
The debriefer invites the practitioner to recall the puzzling moment—what occurred, what may have preceded or precipitated the incident—and reflect on her experience, particularly what she was thinking and feeling and strategizing as the situation unfolded:

> *What was the moment of surprise for you? What was the nature of the puzzling moment?*
> *As you observed the unexpected and unsettling situation, what were you thinking? Were you aware of how you felt? Did you experience an emotional reaction? How did you respond to this unexpected incident? And what was your goal?*

In Reflective Debrief®, questions are used to elicit reflection and self-assessment. They never seek a justification for the puzzlement or the practitioner's response. For that reason, debriefers do not ask, "Why did you decide to meet separately with the parties?" Questions of this nature put the practitioner on the defensive. If that occurs, the need to explain oneself interrupts the process of self-reflection and may cause the practitioner to close down, effectively ending the debrief.

Examine:
Comments and responses from the practitioner become the basis for the debriefer's questions, helping the practitioner identify the particular source of her uncertainty:

If you hear hoof beats, think horses, not zebras—unless, of course, you happen to live in zebra territory.

> *In what ways does this situation stand out for you? What in particular do you find puzzling? On reflection, what is the question you want to answer?*

With such questions, the debriefer sharpens the focus of the practitioner's reflection. Finding the source of the puzzlement is crucial to finding helpful and relevant answers.

Reflect:
Questions also encourage the practitioner to identify possible explanations for the incident:

> *What do you make of their behavior? What's behind their actions? Think of as many possible explanations as you can. Once you have a list, you can evaluate them and decide which is pertinent and useful. What were your assumptions, for example, about the pace of the mediation or about the attitude of people who seek mediation? How did those assumptions affect your actions?*

The emphasis on self-discovery relies on the inherent (and trusted) capacity of the presenter to discover answers to their practice dilemma. Answers derived from self-exploration and self-discovery are likely to be pertinent to the situation, relevant to the practitioner's beliefs (Constellation of Theories), and satisfying. In this respect, the underlying principle of Reflective Debrief® mirrors the central idea in conflict practice of self-determination.

Synthesize:
Based on the presenter's question and goals, the debriefer will invite the presenter to create a plan to address the uncertainty and confusion regarding the puzzling moment:

> *How will you test this hypothesis?*
> *I understand your challenge. You want to act decisively in keeping with your professional role and be sure that you are carefully and respectfully testing this new hypothesis.*
>
> Sometimes, solutions to the puzzling moment lead to a new strategy or technique to be used in a subsequent meeting. In other debrief conversations, the presenter may be seeking to understand her reactions (or inability to respond) to a puzzling moment because the result of that exploration is likely to affect their practice generally. For example, the debrief may help the practitioner recognize, as was the situation for Niahm Lahane in the preceding chapter, why she was troubled when an exchange between participants quickly became loud and aggressive. In the family therapy supervision example, the supervisor's questions helped uncover my unconscious assumption—parties in mediation should be focused on problem solving.

Act:
In the concluding stage of a debrief conversation, the presenter mulls over and decides how to use insights and strategies generated as a result of the reflective process. If the puzzling moment concerns an ongoing intervention, the debriefer's questions encourage the practitioner to identify and describe specific actions and strategies she will undertake. Here, as well as throughout the conversation, she does not offer solutions or comment on the presenter's proposed plan of action. The puzzling moment may have occurred in a previous intervention; therefore, questions about action focus on how lessons from the debrief will affect the practitioner's responses to similar puzzling moments in the future.

The conversation with my family therapy supervisor concluded with these questions and my responses:

> Q: *What do you think might happen if, instead of working to change their approach, you accepted who they are?*
> *What would happen if you mirrored their sociability?*
> R: *Maybe I could treat the session informally the way they do rather than having any kind of structure. Maybe that's how I can join their resistance, feel more relaxed, and stop trying to persuade them to be serious about making some decisions.*

There's a similar exchange between the young girl and her father when she decides to try a new strategy for the game.

The Guiding Principles for Reflective Debrief®: An Introduction

Having described the unfolding of a reflective conversation, let's investigate the underlying principles that shape the general structure, quality and character, and primary method (elicitive questions) of Reflective Debrief®.

Reflective Debrief® may be used in various settings, including a one-on-one conversation between colleagues, in the context of supervision, in a training course as an element of role-play coaching, or within a reflective practice group. Later in this chapter, my colleague Jodie Grant will describe the use of Reflective Debrief® in the context of mediator supervision. In each instance, the following basic principles shape the debrief and guide the actions of the debriefer. You will find an extended list of these guidelines in the appendices:

Trust the person presenting the puzzling practice situation (the *practitioner*) to describe the situation, state the question they want to discuss, and learn what they need.
The focus of the debrief is determined by the *practitioner*.
Never make a statement when a question will do.
It is your job to support the *practitioner*'s reflection and not to substitute your own ideas about the problem situation.
It is never your job to "get" the *practitioner* to do or understand anything.
There is no need to reassure the *practitioner*. Instead, remain focused on your task, which is to help the *practitioner* discover the answer to their question.

Let's consider each of the guidelines.

Trust the Practitioner to Learn What She Needs

Debriefers, like conflict practitioners, base their actions on the fundamental principle of self-determination. Although widely discussed and commonly accepted as a founding principle of our profession, we have difficulty agreeing on what this represents in actual practice situations. For those of us who follow the principles of reflective practice and regularly use the method Reflective Debrief®, honoring self-determination is essential. Let me explain how I and my colleagues understand and apply the principle of self-determination to a Reflective Debrief®—what we actually do in a Reflective Debrief® (see also "The Ten Attributes of a Reflective Practitioner" in chapter 3). In the appendices a worksheet, "Comparison of Roles," points to the similarities in attitude and action of the reflective debriefer and a coach/mediator/facilitator. You will see how closely the two roles match up.

Consider the mindset (the attitude) of the debriefer. We believe the presenter knows the answer but is unaware of it. We believe the presenter is able to discover and will ultimately find answers to a surprising and puzzling practice incident that are appropriate to the circumstance, that are practical in their application and effect, and that match the practitioner's beliefs and mode of practice. In that respect, the debriefer relies on the presenter to identify the source of the puzzlement and to define the question for the debrief. Debriefers do not attempt to revise or reshape the question or substitute their own ideas about answers to this confusing experience. It's not about us. What the presenter finds puzzling and unsettling the debriefer might not have noticed or, having noticed the situation, may have dismissed the incident as inconsequential. The debriefer's perception will only get in the way of assisting the presenter's exploration and discovery.

> I'm not afraid of storms, for I'm learning how to sail my ship. Louisa May Alcott

The Mediator (Presenter) Limits the Scope of the Debrief

We acknowledge that the presenter is the expert in this situation. Not only is he aware of what occurred and why the incident was unsettling, but he is also best positioned to discover answers that are relevant, useful, suitable, and acceptable.

Debriefers do not hold on to expectations about a specific outcome—or whether there will be an outcome—that is, whether the practitioner will gain insights into and answers about the puzzling moment or learn new ways of responding either to that incident or similar situations. Of course, debriefers hope that every reflective conversation yields results that are helpful and satisfying to the practitioner. Debriefers also understand that answers to the presenter's questions may not immediately emerge, often because the presenter needs more time for reflection. As Rilke advises us,

> Have patience with everything that remains unsolved in your heart. Try to love the questions themselves like locked rooms and books written in a foreign language. Do not now look for the answers. They cannot now be given to you because you could not live them. At the present you need to live the question.

Debriefers encourage practitioners to adopt a curious mindset, to approach the reflective conversation with a voracious desire to learn and a resolute commitment to rigorous and candid self-examination.

Never Use a Statement When a Question Will Do

With self-determination, the cornerstone of the debrief, questions—especially elicitive questions—are unparalleled in their capacity to invite self-reflection, encourage exploration, support self-examination, and nurture self-discovery. Thoughtful and critical self-examination will be interrupted and almost certainly compromised by offers of advice or recommendations or judgments about the practitioner's response to the puzzling moment. Any opinion, whether favorable or critical, distracts the presenter and shifts attention from reflection. Instead, the presenter's concentration is disrupted and refocused on addressing the comments or suggestions or defending himself from what may be subtle (or overt) criticism concealed within the shell of a "helpful suggestion."

Even well-intended suggestions are counterproductive and tend to produce defensiveness and lack of trust. Without the ability to trust the debriefer (or others in the group), the practitioner will be more guarded and less candid. Debriefers (and group members) must become adept in the use of open-ended or elicitive questions and able to self-correct when about to offer an opinion or advice.

The appendices include a guide for debriefers and members of a reflective practice group, "What *Not* to Ask or Say—What to Ask or Say." Below are examples that help explain the distinction between troublesome and off-putting comments from helpful questions that address the same topic. Counterproductive comments appear in italics, followed by constructive alternatives.

> *Why did you decide to . . . ?*
>   When you chose to act, what influenced your decision?
>   At that moment, what thoughts occurred to you?
> *Did you consider . . . ?*
>   When that situation occurred, were there other choices you considered?
>   What were those options? How did you come to your decision?

The two questions "Why did you decide . . . ?" and "Did you consider . . . ?" are subtle ways to introduce an opinion about how the practitioner could—or should—have addressed the surprising and puzzling incident. Questions (concealing comments or judgments) such as these express the values, opinions, and perspectives of the person asking the question; they are inconsistent with the central goal—assist the practitioner to explore the puzzling moment and discover their own answers. Questions of the nature of "woulda, shoulda, coulda" serve only to distract the practitioner, pulling his attention away from their own reflection. Debriefers are mindful that they don't think or act in the same way as the presenter. As Susanne Terry succinctly observed, "They have their own brain."

> *Every nuance, every inflection in a voice, the quality of air, even—they all get mixed up in this soup of the story developing in our minds.*
> Susan Vreeland

Support the Presenter's Reflection and Exploration

Debriefers believe that if the presenter can identify the thinking that led to the decision, then it's possible to determine the basis for the unsettling situation. And with that knowledge, the presenter will find the answer to his practice dilemma. The debriefer asks questions that prompt self-examination and support the presenter's intention to learn from experience. In turn, this supports self-discovery. Relying on questions that help the practitioner uncover the answers for himself results in lessons that are firmly anchored in the mediator's experience and are not merely some tips, tools, advice, or additional rules of mediation practice to be remembered.

> Knowledge is an unending adventure at the edge of uncertainty. —Jacob Bronowski

The debrief relies as well on the practitioner's steadfast commitment to engage in critical self-examination, a rigorous and meticulous process of reviewing the circumstances of the puzzling moment in order to discover why the events occurred. The practitioner is not engaged in self-deprecating judgment; rather, conscientious self-examination leads first to insights about the source of the puzzlement and then to lessons applicable either to the current practice situation or to future similar incidents.

Exploration does not follow a straight line from question to answer. There is no blueprint or road map for Reflective Debrief®. Instead, like every conflict engagement, the pathway of Reflective Debrief® that leads from uncertainty to insight is unique to the circumstances and the practitioner. In addition, exploration is an iterative process; the debriefer's questions invite the practitioner to pursue an idea, gain knowledge from mulling over each question, make necessary adjustments, and eventually discover the answer she seeks. The debrief process unfolds like the inexorably expanding spiral of professional growth and evolution.

> One's destination is never a place, but a new way of seeing things. —Henry Miller

Don't Get the Practitioner to Do Anything or Think in a Particular Way

Throughout the reflective conversation, the practitioner is in charge. The practitioner decides what events, circumstances, or behaviors to address; what outcome is acceptable; and when to stop the debrief. Debriefers are agents, or facilitators, actively and thoughtfully assisting the practitioner during the reflective process of self-exploration and self-discovery. We follow the line of thought initiated by the practitioner.

Of course, as we ask questions, as we encourage and support the practitioner's process of self-examination, it's impossible to avoid generating our own explanations (hypotheses) for and answers to the puzzling moment. When that happens, we face a seductive pull to lead the conversation in a certain way in order to test our hypothesis. We may be tempted to nudge the debrief in a certain direction because we genuinely believe the practitioner will appreciate and benefit from that subtle redirection. That would be a mistake. What matters in the debrief are how the practitioner has experienced the puzzling moment; what explains why the incident was surprising and puzzling; the nature of their cognitive, emotional, and strategic responses; and what they seek to learn from the experience. Substituting our assessment of the puzzling moment, inserting our perspectives, leading the practitioner toward an answer that we find satisfying and responsive—all this is self-serving and contrary to the fundamental principle of self-determination that underpins Reflective Debrief®. Don't do it.

That said, we aren't merely trailing after the practitioner, following their direction without independent agency and thought. Mindful of our role and the goal of the reflective conversation, we may nevertheless identify moments when we can invite the presenter to consider alternative perspectives. Timing is crucial; debriefers don't interfere with the practitioner's reflections prematurely. Noting a moment when progress has come to a standstill, we want to be certain the practitioner is prepared to listen to and respond thoughtfully. Proper phrasing is also essential, reminding ourselves to ask genuinely curious and inviting questions.

Do exactly as you're told without variation of adjustment. Do it their way until you're wise enough and experienced enough to do it your way. Be happy and ready to fail. Expect to take it on the chin and do this with a passionate mentality. Joyfully leap toward the sword, the opportunity to learn and embrace what happens in order to grow. Kagekuma

For example, conducting a debrief during a reflective practice group that felt labored, I wondered whether we seemed to be covering the same ground because the practitioner hadn't identified the right question to address the puzzling situation. I broached the problem in this manner:

Me: Are we heading in a direction that's helpful to you?
P: I thought so, but I'm not any clearer about the answer to my question.
Me: Any idea why that might be happening?
P: I'm not sure. I feel like I'm going in circles trying to find an explanation for what happened.
Me: What if you looked at the situation from a different perspective. Would you be willing to try that?

From this exchange, you might wonder whether I am subtly and cautiously leading the practitioner to accept my views, and it could certainly appear that way. What restrains my impulse to lead and redirect is this mindset: I am prepared to accept the practitioner's choice—to listen to my perspective, remain focused on the current train of thought, or propose something I hadn't considered. I am purposefully subtle—not sneaky—but intentionally careful to leave open all possibilities. I do not want the practitioner to say yes because they feel pressured or because they respect my role as the debriefer.

No Need for Reassurance

Consistent with the guidelines of Reflective Debrief® and in support of the practitioner's attention to the examination of their experience, debriefers do not offer reassurance to the practitioner about the circumstances and how the practitioner handles the puzzling incident. The debriefer is not responsible for lifting the presenters or protecting their ego. No matter how earnest and compassionate they may be, offers of reassurance compromise the process of self-discovery, shifting the focus from the debriefer's reflections to the offer of support and encouragement. Debriefers avoid phrases such as the following:

> Wow, that was a really difficult situation they put you into.
> You handled that disruption as well as anyone could.
> I understand what it's like to deal with people like that.

Instead, the debriefer, sensing the practitioner's irritation or distress and seeking to explore how the experience affected the practitioner, relies on questions such as the following:

What was your reaction? How were you feeling when that surprising disruption occurred? When you are faced with situations that are irritating, how do you generally respond? What was it you found particularly challenging in that moment?

The description and examples reflect the role of the debriefer, the person guiding the reflective conversation. The appendices include a guide for presenters, "Guidelines for Your Debriefing."

Now What?

Through Reflective Debrief®, the presenter gains insight into the puzzling or frustrating situation and learns new ways of responding to that situation and to similar incidents. This result is achieved when the debriefer's commitment to the principles and goals of the reflective process is joined with the presenter's curiosity and commitment to exploration and discovery. In some instances, Reflective Debrief® yields stunning and illuminating insights; in others, knowledge is revealed slowly—a gradually and perceptively emerging awareness, stunning to witness. Reflective practice and Reflective Debrief® have the essential aim of "bringing intuitive and emotional understanding" to our professional practice (Kurtz 2020). Because reflective practitioners are concerned with the practical implications of these insights, the debriefer asks, "What will you do with what you've just learned? How will you integrate the knowledge you've gained into your practice? What will be different about your work?" The nature of learning is immediate—solving the puzzling practice dilemma—and it can reverberate for years, another step in an unfolding process of learning from experience—part of the spiral of professional development, expanding upward and outward, growing and evolving.

> Knowledge you may get from books, but wisdom is trapped within you. Release it.
> —Ismat Ahmet Shaikh

In the following essay, Jodie Grant describes the use of reflective practice methods in her supervision practice, working with mediators and social workers. In the example, you can see clearly how she incorporates the basic principles of reflective practice and the process of Reflective Debrief®.

The capacity to learn is a gift. The ability to learn is a skill. The willingness to learn is a choice. Brian Herbert

SUPERVISION AND REFLECTIVE PRACTICE

Jodie Grant, Director
Shifting Sands
Family Dispute Resolution & Mediation | Professional Education & Training | Supervision
Melbourne, Australia

THE CONTEXT OF SUPERVISION

I began work in Australia in Family Mediation/Family Dispute Resolution[1] following a primary career as a social worker. While social work and mediation practice are distinct professions, in Australia both embrace supervision and reflective practice as a crucial means of improving the quality and effectiveness of practice for students and novices as well as more experienced practitioners. Supervision and reflective practice have proved to be vital to developing skills and knowledge, enhancing learning and practice, in working toward "excellence in practice" (Lang and Taylor 2000, xi).

For social workers in Australia, there is a long history of supervision and reflective practice that more recently has been adopted, embraced, and applied to mediation practice for students, beginners, and experienced practitioners. The following observations reflect my experiences in both professions and illustrate key connections between supervision and reflective practice.

The supervision element in social work education utilizes theories of critical thinking, adult learning, and experiential learning in support of the development of professional practice. Supervision

- encourages the use of critical reflection to challenge underlying beliefs and values in assumptions and behaviors;
- highlights the importance of collaborative mutual goal setting and encourages each student to participate in developing and reaching their learning goals;
- emphasizes experiential learning, underscoring the role of reflection in experience-based learning (Kolb 1984; Schön 1983);
- focuses on the individual's resources and expertise (person- or client-centered therapy; Rogers 1951); and
- utilizes self-directed learning and learner-centered education (i.e., drawing on practice wisdom, knowledge, and skills of participants).

Initially intended as a supportive and reflective space, supervision developed therapeutic elements and later incorporated educational processes.

Educational theories related to critical thinking, adult learning, and experiential learning are also applied in teaching conflict resolution in Australia, especially family mediation (or family dispute resolution). Supervision, including the use of reflective practice principles and methods, plays a valuable role in developing knowledge, skills, and competence of conflict resolution practitioners. As it had in social work education and professional development, supervision of conflict resolution practitioners has become an accepted and widely adopted element of ongoing professional development.

GOALS OF SUPERVISION

Our goals as practitioners are to be competent and resourceful, learn from our experiences, and persistently develop our practice. Practitioners must be mindful, curious, and purposeful. Supervision provides a framework that continues the link between cognitive and experiential learning first developed in initial education and training programs.

My goals as a supervisor of mediators are to

- build knowledge and skills,
- monitor and maintain ethical standards and responsibilities, and
- provide professional support (Milne 2009).

Goal or Function	Example of Action
Evaluating	Providing critical feedback and assessing the mediator's competency and effectiveness.
Supporting	Acknowledging and affirming the mediator's actions.
Instructing	Providing information on organizational expectations, norms, and mediation standards, ethics, and practice elements.
Providing feedback	Giving helpful advice—affirming or critical feedback to improve the quality of practice.
Debriefing/coaching or reflective practice	Assisting the mediator to explore a puzzling practice situation in order to discover an answer for themselves.

Providing an ongoing learning environment (with reflective practice elements) allows supervisors to

- ensure competence and ethical performance;
- promote development of appropriate skills, knowledge, and professionalism;
- assist mediators to address clients' interests and enhance outcomes;
- enable monitoring and regulation of ethical practice;
- utilize reflective practice to advance professional growth and evolution;
- support and mentor; and
- work toward developing best practice and artistry.

MODELS OF SUPERVISION

In my supervision practice (and in Australia generally), supervision serves a number of purposes and utilizes a variety of approaches to identify and respond to the unique learning needs of each practitioner while also fulfilling other supervision goals. These methods extend across a continuum of styles from facilitative to directive and include reflective practice, case review, education, coaching, teaching, instructing, guiding, and mentoring. A supervisor's functions vary, depending on the supervisor's preferred style, organizational need (if the practitioner works within an agency or similar setting), or the supervisee's circumstances. Essential to effective supervision in any setting is an explicit agreement between supervisor and supervisee, establishing the relationship and setting goals and expectations and defining roles and responsibilities.

My supervision approach is shaped by the theories of Kadushin and Harkness (1976), Proctor (1997, 2008), Inskipp and Proctor (2001), and Hawkins and Shohet (2000, 2006):

- According to Kadushin and Harkness (1976), the three main functions of supervision are to educate (fostering professional competence, skills, knowledge, and attitudes), to support (evolving the professional self), and to administer or manage (supporting accountability, ethics, and responsibility).
- Proctor (1997, 2008) and Inskipp and Proctor (2001) highlight the importance of experiential learning and development through self-reflection, the supervisory relationship, professional accountability and standards, and the need to address challenges and improve practice.
- Hawkins and Shohet (2000, 2006) emphasize the supervisory relationship as crucial to the development of and improvement to (the supervisee's) practice.

These theories support my focus on the tasks of educating, guiding, and supporting the practitioner and ensuring ethical practice. I concentrate on creating a working alliance as the foundation for a trusting, responsive, and effective relationship.

In my supervision practice, I feature reflective practice as a mechanism to build self-insight and self-awareness that contribute to the practitioner's professional development and growth. In bringing together reflective practice and supervision, I rely on the principles and practices articulated by Lang (2019), Hewson and Carroll (2016a, 2016b), Schön (1983), and Finlay (2008).

My style of supervision is eclectic. Remaining consistent to the foundations I've noted, I tailor my approach to the unique needs and interests of the supervisee, considering the context of their work, learning goals as stated by the supervisee and identified in my assessment, and organizational interests, including relevant standards of practice, ethical requirements, and legislative frameworks.

HOW SUPERVISORS CAN USE REFLECTIVE PRACTICE WITHIN THE CONTEXT OF THEIR SUPERVISORY ROLE

Reflective practice as used in supervision provides the opportunity to improve the quality of practice, to learn from and through practice—to deepen knowledge and sharpen skills. As a mediator supervisor, I understand that learning achieved through reflective practice requires a strong commitment to the principle of self-determination, meaning that I act as a guide, encouraging practitioners to find their own answers. This opportunity for learning can be lost with a more directive, instructional approach. Instead of drawing out reflections through elicitive questions, the supervisor may be *inclined* to instruct or tell the supervisee what to do, to give the supervisee the answer to the practice dilemma. The risk of lapsing into an instructional mode can be greater if there is a history of a teacher–student relationship.

The following are areas of inquiry I explore with mediators in supervision that involve reflection and self-discovery:

- Uncover their underlying assumptions.
- Identify the impact of biases, assumptions, and personal reactions to the participants.
- Explore the congruence between what they say about their practice and what they do or did.
- Search for links among their thoughts, feelings, and actions.
- Understand why they chose certain techniques and interventions, assess their effectiveness, and identify other opportunities.
- Examine the effectiveness of verbal and nonverbal behavior and actions—the parties' and their own.
- Consider whether power imbalances may have affected the course of the intervention and how those dynamics were managed.
- Articulate the theoretical underpinning of their approach and strategies.
- Investigate how the practitioner influenced the process, participants, and outcome.
- Examine the extent to which their perceptions of conflict—their theories, values, and beliefs—impacted their understanding of the situation and how they responded.

Success is not final, failure is not fatal: it is the courage to continue that counts. Winston Churchill

AN EXCHANGE BETWEEN A SUPERVISOR AND SUPERVISEE USING REFLECTIVE PRACTICE METHODS

As in other settings, the supervisor using a reflective practice approach asks elicitive questions and maintains curiosity, allowing the practitioner to find their own answers and insights. The supervisor, who may also see her role as an instructor or adviser, must resist the temptation to tell the practitioner what to do by offering answers or solutions. (However, there may be times when the supervisor assumes an educative role, especially if ethical concerns are raised.) The following exchange, edited for this essay, is based on an actual supervision session in which I used the reflective practice method to support and guide the supervisee's exploration of her dilemma:

Supervisor: What's the problem that you are addressing? What's the question you want to answer? What is it that you would like to learn from our conversation?

Supervisee: The question that I'm puzzling about is how hard I should work to engage a party who seems resistant but says she wants to participate in mediation. She says the right things, but her behavior tells me something else.

Supervisor: Can you give a case example where you experienced this?

Supervisee: The mother initiated mediation and has been active in getting the process in motion but has not shown up to an appointment. The father kept his appointment. The mother is being evasive, and the father is now anxious to proceed. I'm worried about becoming an agent for the father, and so I am managing the dynamic with the mother carefully.

Supervisor: What is the mother saying to you about the timing and scheduling of the mediation?

Supervisee: She tells me she wants to participate; she suggests appointments, and when I schedule the appointment, she says she can't attend. So she tells me she wants to do it, but I'm left wondering whether she does.

Supervisor: What's your guess? What's your hypothesis about her behavior?

Supervisee: My hypothesis is that she doesn't want to engage in this process—there are a couple of factors impacting that, and part of that is the cost—my fee. That could be a problem for her.

Supervisor: So one possible explanation for her behavior is her concern about money.

Supervisee: Yes.

Supervisor: Has she expressed that directly to you?

Supervisee: No, not directly. I have asked her if she can manage the costs, and she's danced around it a bit.

Supervisor: Have you considered other possible explanations apart from money?

Supervisee: At the moment, the parenting arrangements suit her. So she may want to maintain the status quo. In the meantime, the children are not spending much time with their father.

Supervisor: So are you saying that it's possible that she is comfortable and change means something different and uncertain?

Supervisee: Well, she has experienced a huge amount of change in a short period of time, including stress around the end of their relationship as well as uncertain financial circumstances. It's possible that anything that causes her to focus on something other than survival could be difficult.

Supervisor: I'm not assuming there are any more explanations, I'm just wondering whether you see additional reasons why she is behaving this way.

Supervisee: She has said she'd like to have this conversation directly with the father, so she might want to do that. She just might not be ready for mediation.

Supervisor: Given these possible explanations for her behavior, have you done anything to test out those hypotheses or explanations?

Supervisee: I have. I've been conscious of not shaming her but asking questions to give her the opportunity to think about it. I asked whether a different timeline might work better. I asked about a different financial arrangement. We talked about a counselor that could help support her to build her capacity and readiness for mediation. So I've tried to address some of these ideas. I'm also mindful that she hasn't engaged in the process yet. That's also a tension . . .

Supervisor: How do you decide how much time and energy to invest before you say this is someone who is not ready or willing to proceed? Is there a point where you say, I can't invest more of my time unless I'm being respected and compensated?

Supervisee: I don't feel disrespected. I feel she's doing the best she can, and her capacity is reduced because of the circumstances she is in.

Supervisor: Is there a way for her to be respectful and to honor your time for her to make a decision—to move forward with mediation or not? And if the decision is to move forward, then to meet with you, engage you properly and with appropriate compensation. I'm not suggesting this is just about money. Money can signal commitment.

Supervisee: I agree that paying for a service, even token payment, shows a commitment, an investment. It's about honoring the other person.

Supervisor: Does that same principle apply to you in relationship to her?

Supervisee: Yes.

Supervisor: You've tried to help her make a choice about proceeding with mediation, but she hasn't been willing to meet with you. So, back to your original question, how much more time and effort are you prepared to expend?

Supervisee: Just last night she made an appointment. I'm not sure she will proceed, but she has made an appointment, which is a step forward.

Supervisor: What would you need from her to continue making the effort?
Supervisee: My response is there's a trickiness in this. . . . The trickiness is that we only ever see the tip of the iceberg and people bring their best to their engagements with us. They share the version of themselves they want us to see. If she is delaying things because the current arrangements suit her, that is something she may not be ready to admit to herself or me. There's an element of face-saving here. I can ask the question; I'm not sure her answer will reveal what's underneath the surface.
Supervisor: Would it be important to you to ask the question?
Supervisee: Yes. And if we are going to continue, I can ask her, What do I need to know in order to provide you with a service that is helpful and constructive? Then she has the opportunity to talk about timing and delays.
Supervisor: Is it challenging to confront behavior in a way that doesn't convey judgment? . . .
Supervisee: Yes.
Supervisor: Is it possible for you to be curious but in a nonjudgmental and open way, inviting her to tell you what has affected her choices? What would you think of that?
Supervisee: I like it. As you are saying it, I find that popping into my head is that whether mediation is a parallel to what she's going through with her ex-partner . . . and whether that's playing out with me. So that capacity to be curious and wonder and have that conversation might have multiple layers of benefit.
Supervisor: And when would you have that conversation?
Supervisee: When I see her, which I'm hoping is this week.
Supervisor: We have our fingers crossed . . .
Supervisee: If not, I'll probably have to rethink that.
Supervisor: Rethink in what way?
Supervisee: Decide whether I pull back and tell her I'm available but stop reaching out to her.
Supervisor: Can you do that? Have you reached a point where you've answered your question about how much time and effort to expend?
Supervisee: Definitely, I can and will.
Supervisor: Are you okay to stop here?
Supervisee: Yes . . .

REFLECTIVE PRACTICE ASPECTS OF THE CONVERSATION

The supervisor demonstrates presence and thoughtful attention, asking questions, generally being encouraging, but not offering solutions. It would have been simple for the supervisor, relying on her own experience, to say, for example, "You've done enough. Remind her of your contact information and let her come to you when she's ready." However, offering advice would interrupt the supervisee's reflections and as a result would limit exploration of the question presented and likely prevent the discovery of her own solution.

The supervisor's questions encouraged curiosity and nurtured self-examination with the goal of inviting the supervisee to develop insight and self-awareness. The supervisor moved deliberately and thoughtfully, which allowed time for the supervisee to pursue her thoughts and as a consequence enabled them to engage in her own analysis.

Throughout the exchange, the supervisor avoided offering answers—asking questions rather than being guided by instruction. The supervisor challenged the supervisee to think for herself, to examine a range of options and take responsibility for discovering the answer to her practice dilemma by encouraging curiosity, deeper thinking, and further insights. At the conclusion of the reflective conversation, when the supervisee had answered her question, the supervisor asked the supervisee to create a practical plan to address the original question.

REFLECTIVE PRACTICE IN SUPERVISION

This reflective practice exchange demonstrates how within a supervisory working alliance (or relationship), reflective practice offers the supervisee opportunities for self-reflection and self-assessment, promoting self-examination and self-discovery. The supervisor nurtured the supervisee's learning and the development of her practice by remaining curious, posing open-ended questions, and generally encouraging the supervisee to follow her own train of thought, to develop her own hypotheses and engage in her own analysis. This exchange supported the supervisee to reflect on her experiences and articulate her thinking and to consider how she made various choices. Using reflective practice in supervision in this way allowed the supervisee to take responsibility for her learning, to notice what was happening, to analyze it, to critically examine her underlying assumptions, and to consolidate what she learned into her practice. The supervisee was able to identify the puzzling practice situation, assess the circumstances, and answer her question.

This reflective conversation met the supervision objectives of education, developing competence, supporting the practitioner in her practice, and promoting her sense of agency and accountability and responsibility. Fundamentally, it enabled the supervisee, identifying a single puzzling practice experience, to resolve her dilemma about that client relationship and develop a new and broadly applicable approach to the question of "when have I done enough?"

Return to the Beginning

Just as the spiral inexorably and continuously opens out, the learning process of the Reflective Debrief® and reflective supervision does not end with the debriefer's or supervisor's final questions. The reflective practitioner is curious about and looks forward to the next puzzling moment (because it will inevitably occur) as an opportunity to extend and build on the lessons learned.

> For last year's words belong to last year's language
> And next year's words await another voice.
> And to make an end is to make a beginning. —T. S. Eliot, "Little Gidding"

Note

1. Since 2006 in Australia, under changes to the Family Law Act (1975) and Family Law (Family Dispute Resolution Practitioners) Regulations 2008, family mediation is referred to as family dispute resolution (FDR), and family mediators are referred to as family dispute resolution practitioners. This practice sits underneath legislated requirements and obligations.

CHAPTER 9

Reflective Practice in Training and Education

Moving along the upward spiral requires us to learn, commit, and do on increasingly higher planes. We deceive ourselves if we think that any one of these is sufficient. To keep progressing, we must learn, commit, and do—learn, commit, and do—and learn, commit, and do again.
—Stephen Covey

We've all had this experience. At a workshop or training course, the instructor sets up a role-play and asks for volunteers. Uneasy, you face your fears and potential embarrassment and raise your hand. You're handed a scenario and given five minutes to read the script, make notes, and plan your approach. You settle into the "mediator's chair" and, when instructed, begin the exercise. Role-play exercises are an established, time-honored, and traditional teaching process for developing skills, testing knowledge, and building competence. In fact, the use of experiential exercises as a required teaching method has been codified in legislation, court rules, and professional training standards. And for good reason.

> Knowledge is knowing a tomato is a fruit; wisdom is not putting it in a fruit salad. Miles Kington

Managed well, simulations are a compelling, dramatic, and effective learning technique. Given the shameful lack of internships and opportunities for supervision or mentoring commonly available to apprentice practitioners in other professions, role-play exercises and simulations are often the only available method for direct practice experience. It is deplorable then that, too often, they are managed ineptly. Too often, the simulation exercises are supervised by coaches who may be experienced and competent practitioners but who are insufficiently trained in managing role-play feedback. In other situations, there are simply too few coaches to provide timely and meaningful feedback. Consequently, intense and powerful learning opportunities from role-plays are handled clumsily and ineffectually. Let me offer a personal experience to illustrate this point.

Instructors and role-play coaches rely primarily on a generally prescriptive approach to provide guidance, acknowledge proper technique, point out errors, and offer corrective instruction. We are all familiar with the mantra-like language, either in question form and asked of the role player or offered as cortical commentary by the coach:

What the role player did well
What the role player did poorly
Skills that need work or need to be learned
What could have been done differently

Instead of being like a circus where the trainer uses his stick to make animals do stunts . . . the system of education should be like an orchestra where the conductor waves his stick to orchestrate the music already within the musicians' heart in the most beautiful manner. The teacher should be like the conductor in the orchestra, not the trainer in the circus. —Abhijit Naskar

I attended an introductory forty-hour family mediation training course in partial fulfillment of the requirements to become a certified family mediator. By this time, I had already designed and presented similar courses, created and taught in two graduate programs in conflict resolution, and been in mediation practice for thirty years. Yet local rules did not credit such experience; everyone seeking certification was to complete a basic training course.

> A mind once stretched by a new idea never regains its original dimension. Oliver Wendell Holmes

We participated in several role-play exercises, as observers, as parties or attorneys, and, at least once, as mediator. At the conclusion of each role-play simulation, a coach offered feedback—orally and then afterward with written critique. The "Mediation Role Play Critique" was based on a preset list of topics and format as prescribed by rules governing mediator certification. The following is a portion of the written feedback I received—essentially the same as the coach's comments immediately following the role-play. Despite years of experience, I looked forward to receiving thoughtful and useful feedback. My hopes for a meaningful learning experience were dashed. As you read further, consider that trainees with no prior training in or experience with mediation received the same type of feedback.

Topic Area	Coach's Comments
Opening statement	Detailed explanation of confidentiality Length?
Accumulating information	Excellent reframing of parties' positions and developing an agenda
Developing issues	Very nonthreatening
Problem solving and negotiation	Addressed attorney's interruptions Focused on strengths of each party Caught yourself using "we"
Closing the session	Good closure

The coach used the same approach in three other role-play exercises in which I was an observer or disputant, and I learned from others that all coaches in the course adopted this method of feedback.

At the outset, our coach explained that the objectives of the critique were to inform and instruct, but I couldn't work out (not in that moment or years later) how this approach offered either information or instruction:

- The coach opined that my opening statement was too long? What does that mean? How could I have reduced the length of my comments? What would be the ideal length, and what are the criteria?
- Why point out "excellent reframing" without explaining in what way my actions were helpful to the parties and to the progress of the mediation? What was it about the way I managed the reframing that was excellent? Also, is it always good to reframe the parties' statements?

I don't want to suggest that the prescriptive nature of the comments was the problem. Prescriptive feedback can be helpful, even essential, when offered mindfully and at an appropriate moment, such as when demonstrating proper technique; correcting behavior that is clumsy, ill-timed, or potentially damaging; affirming correct use of a skill or strategy; or providing information about a particular element of the process. For example, the following form of prescriptive feedback comments would have been responsive, constructive, and useful:

- In your introductory statement, you repeated yourself in several instances, extending the length of your comments. Were you aware of this? Were you aware of whether the parties were paying attention to you?
- Similarly, when you reframed what each party had said, you helped them listen and understand one another. As a result, they seemed to focus on the issues rather than disparaging one another.

No matter how helpful, the notable downside of this approach is the failure to account for the student/trainee's perceptions—the meaning they give to events and the reasons they chose to act in certain ways.

Let's imagine that if instead of a prescriptive approach, the coach had relied on the guidelines, principles, and methods of reflective practice. Imagine if she had asked the following:

- When you reframed the wife's statement, what was your goal?
- Is this your normal style, or did you adopt a nonthreatening behavior for a particular reason? How do you think your approach benefited the parties?

- You asked the parents for the children's names and their interests and hobbies. What were you thinking in asking that question?
- Was there a moment during the role-play when you were puzzled? What occurred? How did you respond?

Proper preparation prevents poor performance. Author unknown

Any of these questions would prompt reflection and encourage a critical examination of my choices, particularly the reasons for my actions. Elicitive questions might encourage me to question why I had acted in a certain way and lead to lessons I could apply in other situations (e.g., thinking about the introduction, when I am anxious—and this context of the role-play certainly increased my nervousness—I ramble on, talking at the parties. At the beginning of the mediation, I was preachy). As Susanne Terry and I observed, use of reflective practice "helps develop the mediator's capacity for self-discovery and leads to learning that is personal, relevant and lasting" (Lang and Terry, 2013).

Two examples demonstrate the benefits of applying the principles and methods of reflective practice to provide role-play feedback that is individualized, relevant, and useful.

First, in the Masters' Program in Dispute Resolution at Antioch University, students participated in a three-stage reflective practice exercise developed and refined to achieve two goals: (1) provide faculty with an opportunity to observe the students and assess their knowledge, skills, and ability to apply theory thoughtfully and conscientiously and (2) provide an opportunity for students a chance to learn from practice experiences through the application of the principles and methods of reflective practice.

Students selected a scenario (family, construction, community, or commercial) and decided whether they would act as mediator, negotiator, or group facilitator. Fellow students served as parties for the simulations; the rest of the class were observers. Each exercise lasted approximately forty-five minutes. Immediately afterward, faculty conducted a Reflective Debrief®. Both the role-play and the debrief were recorded on video.

Student-practitioners were asked to identify an incident or interaction during the exercise when they were surprised and puzzled. Through questions like those used in Reflective Debrief®, instructors encouraged the student to reflect on the experience and explore their puzzlement. Students received a copy of the videotape and wrote an essay about their experience in which they used the process of a reflection-on-action.

Second, a federal department created an in-house workplace mediation program. I served as lead trainer for a weeklong basic mediation training course. I also mentored a number of in-house mediators who delivered some of the course presentations and served as role-play coaches. They would eventually become the lead trainers for the course.

Every participant acted as mediator in three of the five role-play exercises. Based on the principles and methods of reflective practice, the primary feedback method relied on questions to elicit the trainees' reflections and insights, guiding them to learn from their experiences. Of course, the trainees were novices; they had limited understanding of and experience with mediation practice. Consequently, there were occasions when coaches would offer prescriptive correction and instruction.

The coaches learned both the rationale for and the methods of elicitive coaching. For some, it was a steep learning curve. The coaches were lawyers and employment counselors accustomed to giving advice—that was the nature of their role and responsibilities in the department. They occasionally had difficulty restraining their impulse to inform, advise, or instruct or to ask questions, such as "Why did you . . . ?" "Why didn't you . . . ?" or "Weren't you aware that one party was . . . ?" Yet in time, they became accustomed to and successfully used the elicitive coaching method. That approach to coaching was universally adopted within the department. To train role-play coaches in the elicitive method, I wrote the script for and the department produced a thirty-minute video, *Coaching the Mediator Student*.

As we all became comfortable with the objectives and methods of elicitive questions, we found additional opportunities to use reflective questions. For example, we revised the course syllabus, especially the segment on communication skills, where we emphasized the importance of and practical value from the mediator asking open-ended, elicitive questions.

All motion is curved and all curvature is spiral. Walter Russell

Over the past twenty years, I have adapted and revised the elicitive coaching method (we now use the term Reflective Debrief®). I now use this approach for role-play exercises in every seminar and training course and, of course, in reflective practice groups—essentially any situation in which there is an opportunity to learn from and through experience.

> This seems to be the law of progress in everything we do; it moves along a spiral rather than a perpendicular; we seem to be actually going out of the way, and yet it turns out that we were really moving upward all the time. —Frances E. Willard

Three Examples—Reflective Practice in Training and Academic Programs

Having set the problem—ineffectual teaching methods for developing practice skills—let's consider three examples that demonstrate the potential for incorporating reflective practice into the design and delivery of professional education.

Susanne Terry and Ava Abramowitz have written essays for this edition, describing their approach to professional education and explaining the methods they use to incorporate reflective practice principles into their education programs—Susanne as a mediation trainer, Ava as a law professor. I will then explain a novel and creative training method, the Mediator Experience Live Interview (MELI), developed by a colleague, Barbara Wilson.

"I'M NOT SO SURE ABOUT THAT": THE ARTISTRY OF TEACHING REFLECTIVE PRACTICE WITH THE BEGINNING MEDIATION STUDENT
Susanne Terry

This year is my fiftieth year of actively practicing and teaching mediation. I entered the field of conflict work coming from backgrounds of journalism and social change activism. Each of those parts of my background gave me valuable experience that has shaped how I have practiced as a mediator, facilitator, teacher, and consultant. Journalism taught me that the first question I ask will not get me a thorough enough response. A better understanding of a situation lies many questions deeper, and no matter what, I will never understand the situation as well as those who have had firsthand involvement. As a social change activist, I quickly learned that it is not me that makes the change; it is the people most affected by the circumstance that make the change. I also learned that the problem can't be solved unless it is framed correctly.

I think my work is like a spiral: you keep coming back on yourself, but you're at a different place. Cornelia Parker

As I began to become interested in the work of helping others with conflicts, I relied heavily on the concepts and writings of Brazilian educator Paulo Freire, who developed the concept of "critical pedagogy," in which both teacher and student are learning while in dialogue. This, of course, meant that rather than just answering questions for people, I was training myself to ask what I came to think of as "engagement questions." It also meant that when I asked a student/trainee a question, its purpose was not to get an "answer" but instead to engage them about how they were thinking about the issue about which they were inquiring.

Twenty-five or so years ago, I had already established a method of engaging advanced students and professional colleagues in a reflective dialogue about their work. This process, which I was using to debrief mediations, was similar to the work being done by Michael Lang and, through our work together, has been refined, used hundreds of times, and is now called Reflective Debrief®. This was another step in our ability to carry out an elicitive case debriefing process with a mediator.

A few years ago in speaking with Michael about this work, I felt it necessary, though, to add a caveat and said, "But of course, this process is only for people further along in their training and practice—advanced learners." There was a short pause, and Michael said, "I'm not so sure about that." It caught my attention, but we didn't talk much more about it other than to say that we would keep thinking about it and see what evolved.

Subsequent thinking about our conversation highlighted for me that the purpose of the Reflective Debrief® is to support mediators in thinking about something that puzzles them and to assist them in discovering what they may already know but don't yet realize they know. But how might this apply to beginning mediators, just being introduced to the mediation process and still having so much to learn? This inquiry brought me to a place of realizing that while new mediators may be learning a great deal about the principles and practices of mediation, there is also a lot that they already know and that I could be more helpful to them in accessing this hidden knowledge.

What did they know, and how could I find out about it? That question formed the basis for how I began to develop the process of teaching mediation in a reflective practice mode. From their first role-play mediation, beginning mediators know what they observed/noticed, and they also usually know their own reaction to it. They also know what they are wondering about and what was a mystery to them. Those two questions—"What am I noticing?" and "What am I wondering about?"—came to be foundational questions for mediators in my trainings. Why not get the new mediators working with those questions as their first step when looking back at the work they just did? Rather than asking them, "What went well?" and "What would you like to improve?" why not, rather than asking them to evaluate their work, invite them to reflect on it?

Within a few weeks of this thinking, I was leading a basic mediation training and had converted the debriefs of each of the role-plays to those two simple questions: "What did you notice?" and "What are you wondering about?" All of my role-play coaches had been trained by me and so were already familiar with the Reflective Debrief® we had done in their advanced work, so their training for this simplified version was easy. Our goal was to help them move away from evaluating themselves and others and fretting about whether they had done a "good job." Instead, we were immediately helping them begin a reflection on their experience. The debriefs were not places for being assessed or getting a bunch of answers; rather, they were a time of discovery and exploration.

I realized something on the ride. I realized if I wait until I'm not scared to try new things, then I'll never get to try them at all.
Marie Sexton

Based on that and subsequent experiences, I began to look at what additional opportunities for learning reflective practice were present in the early training. After a bit, I realized that there was a pattern of six questions that I had been asking myself:

1. What do new mediation trainees bring with them that may either help or interfere with their being good mediators?
2. What are some key challenges I face as a trainer?
3. What are some of the misconceptions or assumptions of mediators in training that can be impediments?
4. What habits need to be unlearned by mediation trainees?
5. How can I help them build their reflective practice muscles?
6. What changes do I need to make in how I teach?

Here is a closer look at each of these.

WHAT DO NEW MEDIATION TRAINEES BRING WITH THEM THAT MAY EITHER HELP OR INTERFERE WITH THEIR BEING GOOD MEDIATORS?

My experience told me that they

- want to be helpful and have experience of being told that they have been helpful,
- are interested in problem solving and seeing resolution,
- enjoy being useful,
- are often good at spotting something that has been missed, and
- appreciate the ability to do their job and see positive results.

All of the above are positive traits and can make learning easier. However, the very traits that can help them be good mediators can also be impediments, particularly if the participant is wed to them to the extent that it makes their own needs more important than the needs of the parties. This is a key opportunity for inviting reflection on the importance of keeping the parties, not the mediator, as the central actors in the mediation process.

WHAT ARE SOME KEY CHALLENGES I FACE AS A TRAINER?

In my efforts to understand how I might do a better job in introducing new mediation trainees to reflective practice, it seemed to me that it would be wise to look carefully at pressures or challenges that I experience as a trainer. The key ones were the following:

Feeling pressure of a lot of material to cover. Mediation, even as it is first being introduced, is a complex process involving theory, concepts, principles, practices, and tools. We try to stage this in a manner that helps the new learners build on a simple framework, adding new material as we move along. We always feel it is not enough time.

Dealing with the complication of simplifying a process that becomes more complex as we learn more. The more we try to simplify our materials, the easier it is to see the exceptions and deviations to whatever we have stated. Participants in training seemingly have a never-ending capacity for creating interesting and sometimes bizarre scenarios and wanting to know how to handle them, even before they have learned and practiced the basics.

Facing the challenge of encouragement without sacrificing quality of learning. Trainers are always faced with a dilemma of not unnecessarily discouraging participants but simultaneously being responsible to those things that need to be corrected. A mediation trainer does not want to be so positive and supportive that people think that "anything goes." Quite the conundrum!

Finding time enough for skills practice so they begin to be more than a mental exercise. As a trainer, I place an extremely high value on practice so that participants can experience what it feels like to actually be putting the information into action rather than just storing it in their memory banks.

WHAT ARE SOME OF THE MISCONCEPTIONS OR ASSUMPTIONS OF MEDIATORS IN TRAINING THAT CAN BE IMPEDIMENTS?

- Misunderstanding our job description
- "Up to me" thinking
- Agreement being the only positive outcome

It is fairly common that new mediators may have the thinking that it is up to them to "get" the parties to reach agreement. This has been promoted in particular types of mediation and also occurs prominently in the legal community. This thinking is disempowering to the parties and keeps the mediator as the central player in the process. If the mediator also embraces the assumption that "getting an agreement" is the only thing that counts in a mediation, the likelihood is that the mediator will gradually use more and more directive techniques in order to bring about a settlement that helps the mediator feel satisfaction.

WHAT HABITS NEED TO BE UNLEARNED BY THE MEDIATOR IN TRAINING?

- *Evaluating* ideas, beliefs, and choices of parties. When we evaluate something, either positively or negatively, we put our stamp of approval on it or withhold our approval from it. Both positive and negative evaluations imply that it is our right to do so. Doing either can impede the continuing thinking process about why they made a particular choice due to the mediator approving or disapproving. Evaluations in the reflective process short-circuit the thinking process.
- *Thinking they understand* what parties are trying to tell them too quickly. Understanding how I might experience a situation because of my unique history and personality is different from understanding how someone else's history and personality cause them to experience a similar situation. I, as a person helping a mediator debrief, might know how I experience a particular situation, but do I know how they experienced it? It is the same as when we are acting as a mediator and hear a story from a party about a work situation in which they, in front of colleagues, were reprimanded by their manager. The party says, "I was really upset," and the mediator, relying on imagining themselves being furious if they were in that situation, says, "I understand" and moves on. However, had the mediator inquired further about what "upset" meant to the party, they could have been surprised to find that "upset" wasn't anger or embarrassment but rather distress at thinking that they had made an error that could have negatively affected coworkers and perhaps even the company.
- *Confusing what you observe* with a conclusion you might make. Learning to "figure out what is going on" is an important developmental task in life. There is also a point where we become so used to the process of quickly reaching a conclusion that we fail to ask ourselves whether there could be any other reasonable answer for what we have observed. We see a young child run into the street after a ball and is nearly hit by a car, and we observe their parent rush to them pick them up and begin loudly criticizing the child in an agitated manner. Do we conclude that they are angry, or do we also consider that they may be frightened or alarmed that the child didn't hear the loud honking and might have a hearing problem? Mediators must learn to focus on what they observe. Remember that there may be more than one conclusion that could be drawn, and inquire if it needs further exploration.

> When you seek advice from someone, it's certainly not because you want them to GIVE advice. You just want them to be there while you talk to yourself. Terry Pratchett, Jingo

- *Moving to solve the problem* without understanding what the problem is and what the various layers of information are that feed into the problem. The feeling of finding a fix for a problem is one that we all enjoy. However, when working with complex human interactions, looking at a level beneath the obvious is almost always likely to be helpful.

HOW CAN I HELP THEM BUILD THEIR REFLECTIVE PRACTICE MUSCLES?

After reflection and analysis, I then came to a point of asking, "Given all of this, how, then, do I introduce and instill the concept and habit of reflective practice into my teaching?" One thing I was pretty sure about was that it needed to be through the vehicle of "doing" rather than "talking about."

In designing the methodology, there were several things I believed were true about how people learn. My experience was that they learn by doing the following:

- *Seeing a model* that is demonstrated consistently and well
- *Being able to use information and experience they already have* and thus being able to contribute
- *Being invited to back up* from points of view, analyses, or solutions that are formulated prematurely
- *Having an environment that is "safe"*: no shaming, being good-natured, having no setups for right/wrong answers, and showing genuine appreciation for risk-taking and vulnerability
- *Being asked to explore* rather than give the "right" answer
- *Being asked to muse* about how they might have reached a particular conclusion

- *Being invited to respond to questions* that don't take them down a path of what is "right" or "wrong"
- *Being asked to consider a broader picture* than they may have previously thought about

WHAT CHANGES DO I NEED TO MAKE IN HOW I TEACH/DO TRAININGS?

The changes had to be in me as a trainer. My affect, training design, and feedback methods had to set the tone for making a switch to teaching in a reflective mode.

Where to start?

Having them identify their core beliefs. Even at an early stage in their training, mediators can begin identifying their core beliefs that will guide their work. What are they? Have them write them down. They will add to them and modify them, but eventually, they will have what Michael Lang refers to as their Constellation of Theories, which will guide their practice.

Eliminating evaluations in debriefing. For me, the first thing that had to be reconsidered was the way of ending the mediations with a feedback session of "What went well?" and "What needs to improve?" or even "What was challenging?" I felt that this method had two major flaws. First, they just finished their first (even second or third) mediation—do they really have enough expertise to critique themselves? Second, those questions had a set end point. You name several things in response to each question, and then you are done, hoping and expecting to do "better" next time. I substituted two new questions that have been proven to free people from second-guessing the first baby steps they have taken. Those questions are "What did you notice?" and "What are you wondering about?" If we don't want mediators evaluating the choices and the thinking of parties, let's not invite evaluation of ourselves or each other. The important questions at the end of each debrief usually are "What is something you learned?" and "Based on your experience, what will you keep thinking about?" These beginning steps in early mediation training lay the foundation on which we build all future reflective work—that of understanding why we make the choices that we do and why some situations are puzzling to us.

> *It ain't what you don't know that gets you into trouble. It's what you know for sure that just ain't so.* Mark Twain

Using the mediator as a source of information. In a debrief, when the mediator is asked, "What did you notice?" or "What are you wondering about?" it is followed by an invitation to explore their response more thoroughly. If an answer is "I noticed that they could be very cordial one minute, but then things would suddenly get very brittle and sarcastic," their coach might ask, "What did you make of that?" The mediator would also be prompted to think about a number of alternatives and then perhaps ask something like, "Looking at those alternatives, what's your guess about whether it is important to know what actually is going on at this point, and, if it is, how would you go about it?" We are helping them get into the habit of musing about many ways of thinking about a situation.

Assisting mediators to understand how they are reaching hasty conclusions. Any conclusion the mediator makes about what they think is going on with a party or between the parties can be followed with the question "What did you observe that told you that?" If a mediator says, "Well, the customer was so mad at the store owner—all she wanted to do was give her a hard time and ruin her reputation," it is the perfect time to ask, "What exactly did you see or hear that brought you to that conclusion?" Hearing the response about the customer's anger, choice of language, and facial expression, you can respond, "So you saw the behavior and concluded that a possible motivation might be retaliation—any other conclusion you might have also reached with the same information?"

Providing a "surround" coaching structure and process. Because new mediators have a default that will either cause them to evaluate themselves harshly or self-protect and not look at the more difficult aspects of doing the work of mediator, we need to see that all role-plays and debriefs are guided in a reflective mode. Trained and experienced coaches who have themselves had the experience of being in a Reflective Debrief® as well as assisting others in debriefing in a reflective mode are needed for a large part of the training. These coaches follow a simple structure for debriefing and engagement in reflection. They are teachers as well as guides and need to be in contact with the lead trainer about what they are seeing with participants and the particular needs they have. The coaches are there to help the participants live out the principles, use the structures, skillfully employ the tools, and constantly reflect on what is happening. Each debrief ends with "What will you be thinking about following this?"

Handling questions in a new way. In converting my training, one important and difficult area I had to address was how to deal with questions that participants asked. In using reflective methodologies, the first thing I had to learn was this: don't answer at first! By that, I mean that I don't want to think that what I have to give back to them is the all-important thing. Instead, I want to be engaged with them and let them know that I believe they are likely to have the capacity to provide some input into answering the question. Giving an immediate response is a habit. Break the habit. When it is important to answer the question, do so, but first try to engage the questioner's thinking. Here's a quick set of guidelines you can use as a starter in this practice:

- Try not to answer immediately—that's a habit.
- What's the blank they can fill in? What do they already know?
- Why are they asking? Why do they suspect it is important?
- What do they suspect is the answer? Why?
- How will knowing the answer make a difference?
- Create a dialogue to explore rather than simply answering. This helps the participant to step into a reflective mode.

Using story and example. Make sure your teaching includes examples/stories of situations where you got in trouble and learned from it. The goal is *not* "never make a mistake"—the goal is make sure everything is a positive learning experience.

Introduce early the idea that we all have our life experiences, fears/insecurities, and baggage that travel with us. These don't go away just because we are a mediator. Be pretty sure that if we have a difficult situation, it is made more difficult by something inside us. Reflective practice can mean keeping ourselves open to deeper exploration of our own inner landscape.

Introducing reflective practice into our early training can be as simple as changing one or two things about how we teach. It can also be a sophisticated and well-thought-out design and set of principles that specifically suits the particular type of mediation you are teaching. In addition to these possible adaptations I've covered here, we can also remember to remind our trainees about tools such as journaling or working with a reflective mentor and see that our written materials are not simply about the mechanics of the mediation process but also addressing the mindset of the reflective practitioner. An additional and important enrichment is regular participation in a practice group that works in a reflective mode. The Reflective Practice Institute International leads and sponsors such groups with members from around the world. All are dedicated to the deep work of reflective practice—a never-ending learning process. We experience, inquire and reflect, have new insights, and return to experience again. Every time we travel the path of the spiral of reflective learning, we reach deeper into ourselves and also strengthen our capacity to assist others who are dealing with their own difficult or puzzling situations.

Spoon feeding in the long run teaches us nothing but the shape of the spoon. E. M. Forster

As Susanne notes, the shifts required to embed reflective practice principles and methods are neither burdensome nor complicated. What's required are (1) curiosity about new methods and the underlying principles and (2) a mindset that we are training learners with the capacity to adapt and respond to novel and surprising situations, not merely practitioners capable of following a formula or recipe.

Ava Abramowitz describes how, in her law school class, she prepares students to become reflective practitioners.

NURTURING REFLECTIVE PRACTICE IN THE CLASSROOM
Ava J. Abramowitz

Academic colleagues who know of my friendship with Michael Lang often ask how I teach reflective practice in my negotiation and mediation courses. Telling my students about reflective practice is a good goal, I reply, but isn't preparing them to be reflective practitioners an even better one? Here is my road map for reaching that goal. By all means, play with it and make it you-ish.

There is no better place to teach reflective practice than in a law school negotiation or mediation class. Both dexterities require on-the-spot strategic decision making plus a plethora of skills taught nowhere else in law school. And if your students are like mine, they carry more baggage than an airport skycap—in no small part because of law school.

And, oh, is that baggage heavy. They competed to get into law school. They competed to get through law school. They are preparing to compete the second they get out of law school. And they take that "may the best person win, and it better be me" attitude into everything they do—even negotiation class.

For some, the baggage is heavier still. "Everyone is smarter than me." "Someday they are going to discover I don't belong here." "I don't even want to be a lawyer. My parents want me to be a lawyer." Oh, Philip Larkin, when you wrote "This Be the Verse," did you have my students in mind?

So the question is, how does one convince a totally certain but oft-frightened 3L to set aside all that baggage so they can learn? Twenty years of teaching negotiation two semesters a year, eighteen students to a class, has me fully persuaded that the writers of the song "A Spoonful of Sugar" had hard-earned, maybe even painfully acquired, wisdom and kindness that produced that song.

Accordingly, I tip law school upside down with a teaspoon of silliness, a cupful of humor, a quart of experimentation, and a total commitment to not judging performance. "Our classroom is the true Las Vegas," say I. "What goes on in this classroom stays in this classroom. I do not grade on performance. I grade on learning. If you want to negotiate trying on a style that is not you-ish, do it here. If you always cave and are sick of it and want to try out standing pat, do it here. You cannot fail for trying. If you apply the reading to what happened, if you explore its implications for you and how you negotiate, if you figure out your contribution to the experience and where you want to take your skill set next time, we call it learning. We do not agonize. We do not tap dance on our brains. (That only gives us a headache.) We analyze. This is not the real world. This class is a safe zone for you to prep for the day you leave school. Take full advantage of it. And if you fear losing your footing, simply say, 'Coffee,' and you and I will share a cup and talk—all to help you get your footing back."

They don't know what to make of it, so I start easy, within my students' ken. Early on that first day, I have them pair up and ask them to play the game they played when they were kids.

"You know this one," I say. "You face each other, put your elbows on the table, hold hands, and see what happens. I can't remember the name. Just shut your eyes and play."

The question comes quickly. "Do you mean arm wrestling?"

I appear not to hear the question.

The students sit down, clasp hands, shut their eyes, and arm wrestle, pinning down each other's wrists, from never to as many times as they can. (Maximum to date? After 20 years? Some 700 students? Three times but only once.)

After getting each pair to report its results and seeing the "no timers" burst with pride, the others with envy, I invite one student to play with me. "Don't be afraid," I stage whisper. "Relax. All will be okay." (It is the first class, after all.) As the student pushes my forearm down, I let it go limp and collapse onto the table. Once. Then again and again—until the student figures out what's going on and realizes that they can do the same, and we can go back and forth and back and forth, hitting the table as many as fifty times together!

I explain. "Interesting, the impact of life, of law school. Each of you assumed the game called for competition and demanded a winner. Not one of you thought for a minute that cooperation was allowed, even called for. That you all felt compelled to compete was the 'baggage'[1] you brought to the table—baggage so strong, so powerful, that not one of you considered that there was an alternative way, a more effective way, to play. Here's to the impact of law school."

I urge them to be mindful of the fact that everyone has baggage. That baggage might work for us in our families and maybe even with our friends, but it can become less useful, even self-defeating, in the work world and most certainly at the negotiation table, especially when we find it has encased our feet solidly in concrete.

I have my students submit weekly logs for the duration of the class, and I suggest they use the logs to open up their bags. That way, they can see for themselves exactly what they're carrying around—and decide what to keep and what to toss. I urge them to become reflective practitioners because people's baggage often affects their negotiation strategy, style, and choices, even when it doesn't serve their interests, often when they are completely unaware. Finally, I muse, if they think their bags are heavy now when they are in their twenties, can they imagine how much those bags will weigh in their thirties?

To bring home the point, I tell them about my last two years serving as an assistant U.S. attorney. I was handling mostly rape and child abuse cases as well as too-difficult-to-deal-with victims. And I share with them how I felt myself drowning in the pain of the people I was supposed to be serving. Therapy was what got me through and kept me serving. It was what taught me to separate people and their problems from me and my needs and allowed me to begin again to focus on being both an attorney and a person.

Net effect of the exercise? Students get introduced to the following:

- Baggage
- Competitiveness
- Collaboration
- Style
- Strategy
- Choice
- Therapy
- Mindfulness
- Reflective practice
- The role of the lawyer
- The fact that they are human beings, as is their teacher
- The fact that this class is safe—challenging but safe

With that, students start freeing themselves to learn.

Are they ready to be taught reflective practice with the new insights from their first class? Not a chance. Just as parties need the freedom to give themselves permission to move, students need the freedom to give themselves permission to risk. And reflective practice at its core is risky to the practitioner, especially when done in a group setting. So, no lecturing "these are the ABCs of reflective practice." Students need more evidence to convince themselves that it is safe to suspend their fears and begin to trust, to answer tough questions, no matter how softly broached, exploring the choices they made in the course of a negotiation. They need the chance to teach themselves that their negotiation class is not a threat to their future but a bona fide chance to try on new clothes and buy what fits.

I assure them they already know how to negotiate. Eighteen pairs of eyes make clear that the students have found common ground: not a soul believes it. They need proof. I get that, but I remain silent, purposely, as I also get that it is much easier for people to persuade themselves than it will ever be for another, including teachers, to persuade them. (Forty years of mediating has reinforced that insight.) So, I give my students the opportunity to persuade themselves: yes, they know how to negotiate. Here's the proof.

I ask them to divide up in pairs to plan a seven-day vacation together. "One of you," say I, "wants a vacation close to nature, sleeping under the stars, hiking, swimming—all to regain peace and equanimity and undo the stress of the last semester. The other of you wants a five-star vacation, to be treated as the prince or princess you know you are, with great food, luxurious sheets, top-notch nightly entertainment—all to regain peace and equanimity and undo the stress of the last semester. I don't care who is who. It's up to you. You have fifteen minutes. After ten minutes, I'll check in and see whether you want the extra five minutes."

The results are always fascinating and never predictable. They are also a great introduction to my students. Some decide on separate vacations. Some decide to split up the week—three and a half days here, three and a half days there. Some decide on staying at the same place for all seven days but also decide that one will spend the day, say, hiking, while the other will spend the day at the spa. Both will regroup but only for dinner. And some decide on seven days together in Hawaii, the beaches of the Riviera, a castle in England's Dales, enjoying the uncharted territory together. And all report that they are satisfied with their agreement. Yes, they agree they know how to negotiate. To prove it, each group proudly reports how they came to agreement.

What do I do with this information? With an addition here and an addition there, I reframe the original Thomas-Kilmann Conflict Mode Instrument away from style and give it a context that transforms it into a strategic negotiation planning tool. (After twenty years teaching, I no longer remember who seeded this idea.) I then ask the students to place their agreement in the appropriate box. The changes are shown here.

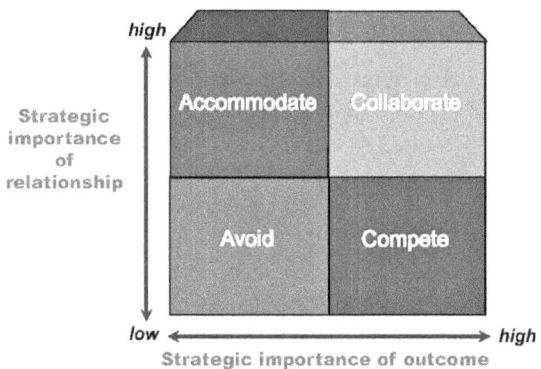

They assign their results as follows:

- AVOID—meet but only for dinner
- ACCOMMODATE—split up the week
- COMPETE—separate vacations
- COLLABORATE—Hawaii, here we come

What they learn is that strategy is a question of choice, not of default. With that realization, they can decide for themselves, "What is important to me—the relationship or the outcome?" And they can use the decision matrix to explore other issues: "What is important to me—reaching an agreement or successful implementation of the agreement I reach?" The teaching goals of each permutation are the same—to increase student choice, to decrease their sense that they are powerless, to empower them to recognize risk, to give them tools to manage it, and to learn that both "creativity" and "value" may lay outside of the settlement box—all with the recognition that exercising "choice" may mean they have to negotiate with themselves first.

So much to learn. Are they ready for reflective practice yet? One more set of tools, and then yes.

When you think about it, in any human interaction, be it negotiation, mediation, or asking for directions, the primary thing over which every person has control are the words that leave their mouths. Law students, trained in advocacy, learn in the first year how to get their point targeted and across. Unfortunately for them, while advocacy works in the courtroom, it is less successful in a room where someone can walk out. Hence, I teach the communication behaviors that first surfaced in Rackham and Carlisle (1978) and assign them the task of choosing one behavior that they have rarely used before. Most choose *seeking information*, not to get evidence they can use in a court of law but to develop clarity and a shared understanding.

Learning is not attained by chance, it must be sought for with ardor and attended to with diligence. Abigail Adams

The original research by Rackham, Honey, and Colbert (1971) that birthed Communication Behavior Analysis led to the determination that for a group to reach a decision, four things have to happen: (1) someone in the group has to put an idea on the table (*initiating*), (2) someone has to make sure that all are discussing the same idea (*clarifying*), (3) someone then agrees (or disagrees) for the idea to become actionable (*reacting*), and (4) someone has to make sure each player takes part in the process (*balancing*) so that buy-in is possible. (Someone means anyone, even everyone.)

Further research subdivided these four concepts into eleven communication behaviors, each of which is available to every player at the table. If your students are anything like my students, by the time they are a 3L, they think that only four of the eleven are available to them as attorneys: *proposing*, *giving information*, *disagreeing*, and *shutting out*. They are pleasantly surprised to hear that seven other behaviors are available and spend much of the semester figuring out which of the eleven work best for them in negotiations—and when and why.

Here, then, are the original eleven communication behaviors:

Initiating: Creating ideas and possibilities

- *Proposing*: Putting forward an actionable idea or suggestion
- *Building*: Putting forward an actionable suggestion that develops somebody else's idea

Clarifying: Ensuring shared clarity and a common understanding

- *Giving information*: Giving facts, opinions, feelings, or clarification to other people
- *Seeking information*: Seeking facts, opinions, feelings, or clarification from other people
- *Testing understanding*: Seeking to establish whether an earlier contribution or discussion has been understood
- *Summarizing*: Summarizing or otherwise restating the content of previous discussions or events

Reacting: Surfacing areas of agreement and disagreement

- *Supporting*: Expressing agreement or support for another person or for their contributions, concepts, and opinions
- *Disagreeing*: Raising objections and obstacles to another person's concepts or opinions
- *Defending/attacking*: Directly attacking or defensively blaming another person

Balancing: Evening out airtime

- *Bringing in*: Inviting in a person not currently involved in the discussion to speak
- *Shutting out*: Reducing another person's opportunity to participate, such as by interrupting

To many a student, hearing that there are eleven behaviors available to a speaker is eye-opening. All too often, they come to class thinking that their *proposing* routinely and invariably will be met with *disagreeing* (or, worse, *defending/attacking*) because they were out of line to propose anything.

Discovering that the Other had ten additional communication behaviors available to them offers an ancillary benefit. It frees many a student to understand that the reaction of the Other was the Other's choice (or baggage) and not the student's fault—a big first step toward being an effective negotiator. Better yet, they realize that they, too, have eleven choices. And with that knowledge, they can maximize the usefulness of their response.

And now the class is ready to hear about reflective practice.

In their logs, many of my students explain their own learning—and road maps—in words that tell me that they're starting to reflect with the best of us. Here's but one example:

> My biggest challenge was definitely learning not to think of the Other as another "me." When all is said and done this semester, I think my biggest success is moving past my initial inclination to think of the Other as an adversary [and] just thinking of them as an Other, working to advocate for his own client. Now, as I enter negotiations, I don't come in with assumptions as to how an attorney will negotiate. I come prepared with responses to any which way they could negotiate and focus on my client's key interests, *not* focusing solely on how and when the Other will trick *me*. . . . My main tip for me would be to approach every negotiation as a new slate. . . . Learn from each one but know that past negotiations are not necessarily indicative of this one.

And that is how I teach reflective practice. I ask questions, give students safe space to answer, and then? I get out of the way and let them learn at their own pace and in their own way.

To end this chapter, consider this brilliantly conceived and easy-to-manage technique for training mediators to understand the connection between belief and action, to use theory to understand a practice situation and then design an intervention.

MELI

MELI is a unique mediator training method developed by Barbara Wilson (2012). Defining expertise in conflict resolution practice is like trying to define art, beauty, or justice. We may agree on some elements of expertise, but because we are individuals with our own experiences, practice routines, and beliefs, we understandably hold multiple and frequently conflicting perspectives. Our profession is characterized by numerous and distinct methods, models, theories, and styles and encompasses remarkably and increasingly diverse disputes. Consequently, it is impossible to generate a single, commonly accepted notion of competent and effective practice. We may know excellence when we see it, but any effort to define its qualities and characteristics is an exhausting and ultimately futile exercise. Herrman and her colleagues (2001) conducted a research project to identify the specific skills and areas of knowledge required by mediators. They concluded that "the job analysis . . . provides a tool for enhancing our understanding of mediation . . . a tool capable of creating grounded definitions of knowledge areas and skills important to the job" (151). The study did not equate essential knowledge and skills with excellence. Ross (2000), examining the definition of success in mediation, proposed a "multi-dimensional framework, . . . utilizing a decision tree approach" (2). In a paper published in *Dispute Resolution Magazine* (a publication of the ABA Section of Dispute Resolution), Ava Abramowitz (2018) also grappled with the question of how to define success in mediation and acknowledged the difficulty of the task:

> Even if we could resolve the issues of definitions and metrics, mediation will remain too complex to be easily quantified. The reasons are well-known, . . . mediation involves people, often angry people. It also usually involves a disagreement or dispute that is daunting enough for the parties . . . to make them seek a neutral's help. It involves a process that is undefined and flexible. And it can take place at any moment in the lives of the parties and their dispute. (24)

As poor substitutes for a thoughtful and inclusive definition, we revert to and commonly rely on benchmarks, such as number of interventions completed, percentage of cases settled, or years of practice.

Wilson acknowledges that defining excellence or success is a daunting if not impossible task. Nevertheless, she tenaciously and thoughtfully persisted in creating a learning process for novice and experienced practitioners to benefit from the expertise of other mediators. Expertise in her view was not exemplified by mediators who share "war stories" of practice situations, recalling extraordinary and sensational incidents or cases. Instead, she developed MELI, an intensive interview with an "expert" in which the goal is to understand how the practitioner approaches practice challenges (thoughtfully assessing the circumstances) and the reasons for choosing particular intervention strategies or techniques:

> This mediator expertise live interview . . . is not proposed as a supervisory, nor as a corrective, nor as a form of coaching. Instead, its purpose is to bring forth the expert mediator's account of his or her practice for the benefit of those present. . . . MELIs are designed to facilitate the sharing of expertise . . . allowing mediators to access rich

data of practice and knowledge which might not be found in academic textbooks or training programmes. (Wilson 2012, 3)

How many of us have attended a professional presentation and listened to the presenter describe a challenging, controversial, or memorable practice situation, explaining breathlessly the brilliantly conceived strategy and creative tactic and the (always) astonishingly successful outcome. As Wilson notes, even though telling these "war stories" is an element common in most professional development programs, storytelling has limited value for these reasons:

1. What we may learn is limited to the specific model of mediation and the unique circumstances of the incident—matters such as the parties, context, nature of the conflict, and timing of the mediation. No effort is made to explore how we might apply any lessons from this extraordinary event to comparable situations in our own practices.
2. Lessons are confined to the presenter's interpretation and why she thinks the incident is significant. Her take on the situation is one possible explanation. There may be other similarly valid explanations for and interpretations of the interactions among the participants and the reasons they accepted the terms of a settlement.
3. The presenter's explanation and her response to the practice challenge are based on her unique set of beliefs—her core values. Seldom (if ever) does a presenter let us in on the theories that shape her understanding of and therefore shape her response to the situation.
4. We never learn why the incident mattered, how the presenter came up with her interpretation, how she generated a hypothesis, or why she selected the specific strategy and techniques she used.

As a result, the example is interesting but not instructive. It may be intriguing and captivating, but listening to the heroic deeds of the mediator doesn't help us become more capable practitioners—an inspiring sound and light show with little educational value.

MELI is intended to overcome the flaws and limitations of war stories as a teaching method by providing an elicitive learning opportunity. MELI involves an extended interview (up to ninety minutes) with a participant from the training course. The interviewer and interviewee discuss an unusual or puzzling practice situation in a structured conversation with the objective of "gaining access to the interviewee's cognitive processes, theoretical bases and rationale for the actions taken during a critical incident in their practice" (Wilson 2012, 15).

The difference in the objectives of MELI and the more typical method of storytelling is clear. MELI seeks to uncover the thinking that produced the action. The stories may be equally as compelling as those recounted in the more typical instructional setting, but a key distinction is that in the MELI process, the questioner helps pull back the curtain to reveal what the practitioner was thinking, not merely what she had done, in other words, connecting theory to practice.

To replicate as much as possible the spur-of-the-moment process that occurs in a mediation, participants invited to share their stories do not prepare for their conversation. Neither the interviewer nor the interviewee will be certain how the MELI will progress—a strategy that maximizes the potential for "unexpected insights":

> Other members of the learning group can benefit from these insights when they later encounter uncertainties and ambiguities in their own practices, to which they need to respond spontaneously. Other learning outcomes might be the affirmation of one's

own work, identification of more effective strategies, or insights into different theoretical constructs about practice. (Wilson 2012, 16)

MELI interviewees are selected from the cadre of training participants. They are experienced practitioners, capable of artful reflection, and able to engage in a conversation in front of their peers. This is an intentional strategy:

Interviewing someone who is already attending a training event as an audience member disturbs the notion that expert mediators must be charismatic authors, conference circuit speakers or other prominent people. (Wilson 2012, 13)

MELI begins as the interviewee is asked to identify a puzzling moment—an incident that was unusual or surprising, a tough case or unusual event they dealt with, and where their skills "made a difference" (Wilson 2012, 18).

What follows is a structured interview. Relying on elicitive questions and refraining from their own analysis or criticism, interviewers guide interviewees through a four-stage discussion of the incident:

1. to identify and hear a short version of the mediator's chosen story;
2. to rehear a fuller telling of the story;
3. to probe the mediator's thought processes regarding the incident; and,
4. where time permits, to facilitate a comparative discussion of each choice (decision-making) point, including asking the interviewee's opinion of how a novice practitioner might instead have acted at that juncture. (Wilson 2012, 17)

When I first learned of MELI, I immediately (and delightedly) noticed parallels between this process and Reflective Debrief®. Both methods involve the use of elicitive questions in a nonjudgmental discussion of critical practice moments; in addition, both aim to uncover the practitioner's perceptions and hypotheses and why the practitioner chooses to respond to the puzzling moment. To do that, the interviewer (MELI) or debriefer (Reflective Debrief®) asks the practitioner to describe their thought process and to consider the connection between belief and action.

In every teaching or training method proposed by Susanne Terry, Ava Abramowitz, and Barbara Wilson, we see the principles of reflective practice. Each approach shares the common goals of learning through experience, bringing theory and practice together. Adopting the mindset, the attitude, of reflective practice alters the method of teaching, not the content—the knowledge and skills of competent and resourceful professionals.

Unquestionably, competent practice requires basic tools, reasonable proficiency in their use, and a foundation in strategies, theories, and practices. As Wilson (2012) notes, "There are no shortcuts to achieving expertise. Simply put, you have to put in the hours" (11). But practice alone does not make perfect. Nor do skills and knowledge necessarily produce successful outcomes. As noted elsewhere in this book—and repeatedly—excellence results from our ability to use the right strategy or tactic in the right way and in the right moment and for the right reason. We acquire the ability to discern the "right reason" through reflective practice and Reflective Debrief®.

To end this chapter, take a moment and consider these two questions: Would you prefer to be taught by someone like the father in the tic-tac-toe story who nurtures learning without spoon-feeding you the answers? If you had a mentor or supervisor, would you want someone who uses reflective questions like the family therapy supervisor and who ignites your curiosity and encourages self-exploration and discovery?

I hope that, having given some attention to the learning techniques used by Susanne Terry, Ava Abramowitz, and Barbara Wilson, you would enthusiastically answer both questions with a fervent "yes."

Exercises

Exercise 9.1

Recall the experiential exercises in your mediation training courses. What was the nature and extent of the feedback? Was this helpful to you?

Exercise 9.2

Can you recall any lesson you learned through role-play exercises? Have you been able to apply that lesson to your practice?

Exercise 9.3

We all learn in different ways, so what form of feedback do you find most helpful?

Exercise 9.4

If you are an educator or trainer, how might you integrate ideas proposed in this chapter into your courses?

Note

1. Using the word "baggage" instead of any psychological term is intentional, as it allows the class to avoid labeling of any kind. We all have baggage. Our decision is whether to continue to carry it or let it go. ABA data on law students and mental health have made me a big believer in this approach. I am also a believer in therapy for students who are having severe problems treading law school. I have a list of therapists for them to consider, and I make it available to all who ask. As I tell all my students, "Only the strong seek out therapy. You are all strong enough to ask for help if ever, whenever, the time comes that you need it."

CHAPTER 10

Spiraling into the Future
Becoming Reflective Practitioners

One attribute of the human being is the potential to keep on growing, to keep on developing. And I think there's room in each of us. I hate to hear someone say, oh well, that man or that woman is sixty or seventy or eighty or ninety or a hundred, so he's finished. There's always something that can be transformed on the upward spiral. —William Segal

It's been nearly forty years since I followed the recommendation of my friend Robert Benjamin, who thought I would be interested in a book about professional learning and the crucial interrelationship between theory and practice. Reading *The Reflective Practitioner* (Schön 1983), I could not then have understood that one book would so profoundly influence the course of my professional work. It was a formative moment, a proverbial fork in the road. Now, reflecting on that early period of my career and my introduction to reflective practice, I am like the narrator in Robert Frost's poem "The Road Not Taken":

> I shall be telling this with a sigh
> Somewhere ages and ages hence:
> Two roads diverged in a wood, and I—
> I took the one less traveled by,
> And that has made all the difference.

I took the one less traveled, an unpredictable and unlikely path as a mediator and a reflective practitioner. As the poem's narrator concluded, finding and embracing reflective practice has made all the difference. Here I am ages hence, looking back on a nearly forty-year fascination with reflective practice, still curious, my spiral of learning continuing to expand. This is my third—and last—book about reflective practice for conflict resolution practitioners. I am not exiting the stage; instead, I am stepping out of the spotlight so that others may step in. As long as I am able, I want to be part of reflective practice groups, I want to teach and talk about reflective practice, and perhaps I will do a bit of writing. At the same time, I want to make room for and invite others to express their vision for reflective practice and to become leaders—in their own exceptional and unique way, speaking with their distinctive and remarkable voices. More than twenty practitioners have completed a certificate course in reflective practice group leadership I taught with my colleague Susanne Terry. This cadre of exceptionally skilled folks are poised to assume leadership of reflective practice groups and help shape the course of reflective practice in our profession.

> We judge ourselves by our intentions and others by their behaviour.
> Stephen M. R. Covey

I do not intend to fade away and disappear entirely; I won't be entirely silent, but I will be quiet enough so that other voices resound and can be heard.

> Silence is the root of everything. If you spiral into its void a hundred voices will thunder messages you long to hear. —Rumi

I did not imagine or create the principles of and rationale for reflective practice. Reflection-in-action and reflection-on action were not my invention. Rather, I have been part of the larger spiral of growth and evolution of reflective practice in our profession (and in others) that began for me with *The Reflective Practitioner*. Now I want others to extend and enlarge that spiral as I have been privileged to do for so many years—building on what we have learned, adding their own ideas, questions, and experiences. It's right, and it's time.

Following that stunning and career-altering initial association with Donald Schön and reflective practice, I have written articles and books and taught the theories and methods of reflective practice. I have organized and led reflective practice groups. Throughout the years since discovering *The Reflective Practitioner*, I have routinely made use of reflective practice to learn from my own professional activities. I have been an advocate, champion, and even cheerleader for reflective practice. At times, with a dollop of modesty and a knowing wink, I have referred to myself as the "Johnny Appleseed" of reflective practice, traveling the globe, promoting the practical benefits of reflective practice, working to increase awareness of reflective practice, and urging colleagues to adopt its principles and methods. For those unfamiliar with the legend, John Chapman was a pioneer who earned his nickname in the early 1800s as he traveled across parts of the United States and what is now the province of Ontario, introducing apple trees to farmers. I am hopeful that current interest in and enthusiasm for reflective practice and Reflective Debrief® will yield a bumper crop of reflective practitioners.

In that spirit of optimism, let me point to success stories where reflective practice has been embraced and flourishes, each example representing the potential for improving the quality of conflict resolution practice. I also want to identify questions for the future, areas for further study, opportunities to stretch the boundaries of reflective practice in our profession.

Reflective Practice Groups

Initially, I experienced reflective practice only as a personal and private process of seeking professional excellence (artistry) through individual self-reflection. The notion that it could be applied in group settings didn't occur to me for a number of years. I first understood the exceptional potential of reflection in group settings in the graduate conflict resolution program at Antioch (described previously). Since then and especially in the past five years, reflective practice groups are flourishing, and the number of groups and participants is mushrooming. I described a number of these initiatives in a previous chapter. Availability of reliable videoconferencing has profoundly affected the opportunity for practitioners to participate in reflective practice groups. Geography is no longer a consideration; now it's a matter of being mindful about time zones. I have led reflective practice groups with participants across thirteen time zones, from Hawaii to Israel. Recent increases in reflective practice group participation represent a response to the solitary nature of conflict practice; there is a need for contact with colleagues the opportunity to share stories, complain about difficult clients, and boast of successes. Beyond collegiality, there is a deep yearning among conflict professionals for a structured and safe setting where they can candidly discuss puzzling practice situations that reflective practice groups fulfill. Wondering what happens next, what we can learn from our experience with reflective practice groups sparks a few ideas and questions.

Sometimes the questions are complicated and the answers are simple. Dr. Seuss

Reflective Practice in Training and Education

In a preceding chapter, Susanne Terry and Ava Abramowitz described educational programs that creatively and successfully make use of reflective practice principles and practices. An additional example is the mentoring program for agency mediators that Judith Cohen designed and implemented in her role as ADR program manager. Cohen (2003) explains the rationale for the program and why she decided to build the program around the principles of reflective practice:

> A skilled mediator has had substantial training and experience, enough to have a "mediator tool kit" and to use the process techniques at his or her fingertips to decide on interventions. Counting on intuition and accrued skills, the skilled mediator normally can do a pretty good job guiding the parties through the process. Relying on a base set of techniques, however, may translate to a routine approach that causes the mediator to sometimes overlook what might be unique to a certain case, or be at a loss for how to address deviations from the norm. That is where reflective practice becomes essential to a mediator.

> She contends that solo practitioners, who lack opportunities for collegial support, can easily adopt this feedback process. In fact, she asserts that one of the benefits of the mentoring process is that mediators learn the method of self-reflection and are able to integrate it into their practices. "The layers of debriefing in the training program help novice mediators to develop the skills to 'mentor' themselves."

Adopting an elicitive approach to feedback and avoiding the familiar method of identifying what the trainee has done well or poorly, the trainer/mentor invites and encourages development of the skills and habits of self-examination—what Cohen refers to as "introspective thinking."

There are few training programs or university courses where reflective practice concepts and methods have been integrated into and become an accepted framework for professional education. Yet in these examples presented by Susanne Terry, Ava Abramowitz, and Judith Cohen, there is hope that the process of purposefully and thoughtfully learning from experience through reflective practice will become widespread. As Kenneth Boulding (1978) said optimistically and hopefully in *Stable Peace*, "anything that exists is possible."

> *Problems rarely exist at the level at which they are expressed. If you are arguing for more than ten minutes then you are probably not discussing the real conflict. Kare Anderson*

Reflective Practice and Professional Organizations

Two innovative projects drawing on reflective practice principles serve as inspiration for further creative approaches to learning and professional development. Each was developed to improve the quality of mediation by nurturing ongoing learning through experience. Each provides an opportunity for individualized learning. As affirmed in a guide for the Supreme Court of Virginia mentoring program for mediators, "Everyone will learn what he or she needs to learn, given the opportunity for reflection" (Twomey, Bissell, and Olchowski 2004, 2).

Wisconsin Association of Mediators

The Wisconsin Association of Mediators (WAM) supported the creation, publication, and wide distribution of a guide for mediator self-assessment and improvement, the Self-Assessment Tool for Mediators (Bronson et al. 1998). The objectives for this project are embodied in these three questions:

How do we continually improve the quality of our services as mediators?
How do we choose what information to focus on, when to intervene, and how?
As a group, how do we discuss differences among mediators and advocate for the provision of quality services? (1)

WAM promoted the use of the Self-Assessment Tool and made it available to mediators throughout Wisconsin. It is the first effort of its kind and is a remarkable instrument for improving the quality of mediation practice:

> Through regularly assessing their own conduct, mediators can explore and integrate their knowledge, skills, self-awareness, and ethical behavior to create a framework for choosing future interventions and to better serve their clients. Collectively, ongoing learning will build on and improve the competency of those providing mediation services. (Bronson 2000, 178)

The shortcoming of this guide is the feature that makes the Self-Assessment Tool so valuable. It is nearly always used in private. Its impact on the spiral growth and evolution of practice competence would be enhanced if practitioners shared their reflections with colleagues or mentors in a systematic, structured, and safe manner (Peleg-Baker and Lang 2022).

We cannot teach people anything; we can only help them discover it within themselves. —Galileo

Virginia Mediation Peer Consultation Project

Two statewide professional organizations developed a pilot mentorship program for mediators in Virginia in 2003. The Mediation Peer Consultation Project (MCP) is a welcoming forum where mediators can reflect on what happens in their cases and better understand the theories and techniques of their profession. The guidelines that follow emphasize nurturing and discovery, not evaluation (Twomey et al. 2004, 2).

The architects of the program relied on methods described in *The Making of a Mediator* (Lang and Taylor, 2000) and made use of elicitive coaching materials I had presented at mediation conferences in Virginia. The mentoring process is a nonjudgmental, reflective approach quite similar to Reflective Debrief®. Mentoring sessions involved "a small group discussion among peers (six to eight mediators and one facilitator) who reflect on critical moments from actual mediations. The purpose is to gain greater understanding of strategies, theories, outcomes, and alternative approaches" (Twomey et al. 2004, 6).

> Take advantage of the ambiguity in the world. Look at something and think what else it might be. Roger von Oech

Interviews with and surveys of MPC participants bear out the project's success. As one participant enthusiastically declared, "It really fills a niche. It has restored my enthusiasm for the practice" (Herman and Twomey 2005, 15). Encouraged by these results, the Supreme Court of Virginia formalized a mechanism for mediator mentoring.

Based on the MPC as well as the experience of mediators in the federal court in California that I described in chapter 7, Herman and Twomey (2005) conclude that

> participation in reflective practice groups looks like a sustainable method for advanced training that is readily available to court programs, state certification programs, community mediation centers and groups of private practitioners. It provides a way to guide mediators toward greater competence and self-awareness, and places substantial responsibility for quality control where it probably belongs—in the hands of practitioners. (16)

I am troubled and distressed by the widespread (and mindless) acceptance of the idea that learning involves giving students answers is the ideal or only way to teach. Prescriptive instruction invariably leads to situations where practitioners inflexibly adhere to practice routines that they were told (or taught) were the "right" way to mediate (e.g., always use private sessions at the beginning of a mediation or use private sessions only after an initial joint meeting).

Recall the tic-tac-toe story from earlier in the book. Now imagine that when his daughter complained that the games ended in a tie, rather than using questions to prompt her thinking, the dad had said, "If you want a different result you need to try something different. Place your pelican in the center position." Had that occurred, she would have undoubtedly learned a new strategy for the game. And what would have happened when that strategy failed, as it inevitably would have? How would she respond? Turn to her father for more advice?

> What is art but the life upon the larger scale, the higher. When, graduating up in a spiral line of still expanding and ascending gyres, it pushes toward the intense significance of all things, hungry for the infinite? Elizabeth Barrett Browning

If we apply the same analytical matrix to mentoring, what happens when a mentor advises a mentee in a situation to respond to miscommunication that was impeding progress in a mediation, "After each person speaks, you should summarize. That helps limit misunderstandings"? The prescriptive comment is more likely to ensure compliance rather than building an understanding of the purpose, timing, and effect of summarizing. By relying on the use of elicitive questions, the result is more likely to yield a deeper understanding and an enduring lesson—as well as a practical solution. As Judith Cohen (2003) affirms,

> Reflection can lead to the general discipline of more conscious decision making. Conscious practice gives mediators the ability to retrieve the lessons in future mediations, replicate what worked, and avoid what didn't.

On elicitive and prescriptive training models, John Paul Lederach (1995) noted, "The key is not choosing between one or the other, but rather the expansion of trainer repertoire to make both possible and therefore appropriate to the variety of settings and groups we trainers engage" (99).

These programs are representative of activities and efforts to make use of reflective practice principles and methods. They (and others noted in this book) confirm the widespread and diverse applications of reflective practice as part of professional development and education programs in a broad array of settings. In the bibliography, there are references to dozens of other ingenious uses of reflective practice methods and concepts in our own profession and others, including law, social work, accounting, education, community planning, nursing, and sports coaching.

Some questions for all of us who value and promote reflective practice to consider are the following:

- What can we take away from these two examples of organizational support for learning through experience?
- What would it take for our profession to embrace the notion and practice of mentorship?
- What prevents our profession from acknowledging the value of and creating opportunities for mentoring?
- Why are we willing to see ourselves as a distinct profession yet staunchly unwilling, like almost every profession, to create and promote learning opportunities such as mentoring?
- Is it possible to learn from the Virginia experience and create a mentoring process grounded in the principles and methods of reflective practice and the process of Reflective Debrief®?
- What are the barriers to developing new reflective practice groups? What have we learned about the successful creation of reflective practice groups and about the flaws in setting them up that will help us build new groups?
- How do we know whether participants in reflective practice groups or other reflective practice activities experience the long-term gains we believe result from reflective practice? How do we identify and track shifts in the mindset and activities of these practitioners?
- Is it possible to assess the relevance and fit of reflective practice across cultures? How would we examine whether the methods of practices, such as Reflective Debrief®, are universally suitable or need to be altered in consideration of unique cultural conditions and values?

Sometimes in life, your situation will keep repeating itself until you learn your lesson.
—Unknown

Additionally, reflecting on the lessons from the examples offered by Susanne Terry, Ava Abramowitz, and Judith Cohen, I wonder about the following:

- In what ways could reflective practice be incorporated into other university conflict resolution programs—undergraduate, graduate, and law school? What innovative course designs and methods would be required? And, most crucially, what shift in thinking about educating professionals would be required?
- Would it be feasible to introduce and utilize reflective practice methods, including Reflective Debrief®, within basic and advanced training courses in which the emphasis is teaching intervention skills and strategies and in which competency is measured in terms of ability to manifest those skills and strategies?
- What would be the impact on practitioners and our profession generally if professional organizations endorsed the value of and created opportunities for coaching, mentoring, and supervision and if these professional development activities made use of Reflective Debrief®?
- What would be required (and what would be the motivation) for government agencies, court programs, and professional organizations to endorse reflective practice methods and thereby increase opportunities for practitioners to learn about and draw on those methods?

All theories are legitimate, no matter. What matters is what you do with them. Jose Luis Borges

Conclusion

When I first wrote about reflective practice in 1998 (republished the following year on the website mediate.com), I knew of no one else in our profession—practitioners, trainers, or academics—who were thinking, discussing, or writing about reflective practice. Nor, to my knowledge, was anyone in our profession advocating its use as a means of developing artistry, that is, becoming competent and resourceful practitioners. Now, more than two decades later, there is widespread acknowledgment of reflective practice generally and a greater acceptance of the relevance and practical value of reflective practice principles and methods. With highly successful reflective practice initiatives, there is a growing confidence among practitioners and trainers in the benefits of this method of learning through experience. As a testament to its appeal among practitioners (though one I sometimes find irritating), peer groups that share the name reflective practice but rely on prescriptive forms of learning have become popular.

I never blame myself when I'm not hitting. I just blame the bat and if it keeps up, I change bats. After all, if I know it isn't my fault that I'm not hitting, how can I get mad at myself? Yogi Berra

To test the effectiveness of reflective practice for conflict resolution practitioners, we need additional research—carefully constructed, carried out, and assessed—that examines the application of the principles and methods of reflective practice, as I suggested in chapter 5.

After decades of using reflective practice, teaching the concepts and methods to others, writing (this is my third book on the topic) about its nature and application, and facilitating reflective practice groups, I don't need research studies to persuade me of the significant practical value of reflective practice. Comments from members of reflective practice groups embedded throughout the book are further testimony to the transformative potential and practical benefits of reflective practice. Yet I am endlessly curious and an insatiable learner, so I want to see what the research teaches us.

Now we are at the end of the book. As the King instructed the White Rabbit, I have begun at the beginning, and now that I have reached the end, I will stop.

I wrote the first edition of this book to provide a practical guide for practitioners who want to improve the quality and effectiveness of their practices (excellence) by using some commonsense and straightforward methods of self-reflection. In addition, I wanted to advocate the adoption and use of reflective practice techniques, such as Reflective Debrief®, in the training, professional development, and mentoring of practitioners.

> *Millions saw the apple fall, but Newton asked why. Bernard Baruch*

For this second edition, I wanted to incorporate what I have learned in the intervening years. That meant completely revising the book as well as adding new material. The spiral has taken another turn or two.

I wanted to provide more practice guides and worksheets—and make them available as downloadable documents—as a means of encouraging practitioners to take up and make use of reflective practice. I want this revised edition to serve as a how-to-do-it workbook as well as a comprehensive introduction to the concept and methods of reflective practice.

I wanted to add more "voices" to the story of reflective practice as well as to add information about innovative uses of reflective practice. To that end, there are four new sections by Ava Abramowitz, Tzofnat Peleg-Baker, Jodie Grant, and Susanne Terry.

In Greek drama, a group of performers—acting together as a chorus—comment on the circumstances and the characters in the play. Their voices describe, highlight, amplify, and explain the meaning of the dramatic events. Like a Greek chorus, members of reflective practice groups, describing their personal experiences with and the benefits they have derived from participation in the groups, give color and an added dimension to my description of these groups.

> *For in grief nothing "stays put." One keeps on emerging from a phase, but it always recurs. Round and round. Everything repeats. Am I going in circles, or dare I hope I am on a spiral? C. S. Lewis*

By nature, I am not good at endings. I am the one at the party who says good-bye and never leaves. This is the time to end, at least this chapter and this version of the book. For me—and I hope for you—the spiral of professional growth and evolution will continue.

We shall not cease from exploration
And the end of all our exploring
Will be to arrive where we started
And know the place for the first time. —T. S. Eliot

APPENDIX A

Guides for Reflection

Introductory comments regarding the Guide for Reflection before Action and the Guide for Reflection following Action:

The guides are prompts, intended to simulate your thoughts and inspire your reflections. You may find it helpful, as do many who regularly use these reflective questions, to write your answers in a learning journal or notebook. The discipline of writing tends to focus our minds and slow the reflective process, enhancing the quality and effectiveness of your reflection. In addition, you are creating a record of your reflections, a chronicle of your learning to which you can refer when a puzzling moment arrives that seems peculiarly and helpfully similar to an incident that provided practical lessons and useful insights.

These questions follow the sequence of the six-stage process, the Lang/Terry Reflective Cycle of Reflective Debrief®. You may find it useful to answer all the questions or respond only to those that seem especially relevant and useful for your reflection.

Guide for Reflection before Action

The following questions will help you

- prepare to learn from your practice experiences,
- generate a working hypothesis and evaluate its suitability and relevance,
- pay attention to surprising and perplexing situations that arise,
- remain open to new information,
- be curious about the likelihood of multiple perspectives,
- identify the parties' intrinsic and extrinsic goals, and
- assess the relevance and effectiveness of your "experiments," strategies, and interventions.

Describe

Given what I know about the client(s) and their situation,

What have I learned about the nature, context, history, impact, and sources of the conflict?
Who are the participants—principals and representatives—and what is their relation to one another in the context of the conflict situation?
What appear to be their likely issues—their conflicts—individually and together?

Am I aware of intrinsic goals of the parties?
  Relationship
  Identity
  Process
What have I learned about their outcome (extrinsic) goals?

Examine

What meaning do I attribute to this conflict—my explanation for the situation?
Is there a "theory" (or theories) that could help me understand this conflict and assist in generating an initial (working) hypothesis?
Am I able to form an initial (working) hypothesis?
As I envision the process ahead, what intervention may be useful, and what criteria will help me understand and assess their responses?
Is it possible at this early stage to identify potential barriers to and opportunities for achieving the parties' goals?

Reflect

What have I learned from similar conflict situations that may help me be effective, attentive, and responsive?
How do I avoid simply repeating an approach I used in similar situations?
Are there predictable areas of difficulty for me, such as bias, complacency, difficulty with listening, loss of focus, or automatic reliance on past experiences?
If any of these areas of difficulty arise, what will prompt me to recognize them, and how will I respond?
What do I hope or expect to accomplish through this work?

Guide for Reflection following Action

The following questions support self-exploration and self-discovery to two possible aspects of your practice. You may use the guide to reflect generally with respect to a particular conflict engagement or reflect on a particular surprising and puzzling moment in a conflict intervention. Answering the reflective questions will guide you to

- consider the overall engagement and discover lessons you might draw from that experience;
- pinpoint surprising, curious, or perplexing situations—puzzling moments;
- assess the effect of these puzzling moments on you and your work and discover the reasons they were unsettling;
- identify assumptions, biases, or mindsets that influenced your actions;
- consider whether you were open to novelty, alert to and then responsive to multiple perspectives, or followed routinized practice patterns;
- critically examine your working hypothesis and assess its relevance and fit; and
- by considering your thinking that led to these interventions, assess their relevance and effectiveness.

Before responding to the questions, consider the following:

Is your intention to reflect on the overall experience, or will you focus on a puzzling moment?
If more than one puzzling moment occurred, can you detect a pattern?
Is this puzzling situation similar to those you encountered previously? In what ways?
If you maintain a learning journal, are there entries in your journal that would guide and deepen your reflection?

Questions identified in *italics* are most useful for a broad, general reflection. Other questions may be pertinent to and helpful with either general reflection or reflecting on a puzzling moment.

Describe

In as much detail as you find helpful to your reflection, describe the context, such as the type of intervention, nature of the dispute, attitudes and behaviors of the participants (including representatives), and other elements of significance to you.

What is your goal for this reflection? What do you want to learn from the practice experience?
What was the moment of surprise, uncertainty, or puzzlement?
What occurred—the actions, behaviors, comments? Who was directly involved?
What occurred immediately preceding the moment—the circumstances, interactions, and behaviors? Describe the situation. At this stage, do not attempt to assign an explanation for what occurred or why you found the situation puzzling.

Recall

What was my overall strategy?
What interventions or techniques did I use to implement this strategy?
Did I invite and encourage and was I receptive to viewing the conflict situation and its possible solutions from multiple perspectives?
Did I invite and encourage the parties to create options and not simply choose from those that were readily at hand or were generally recognized?

As the puzzling moment occurred,

How was I affected emotionally, cognitively, and strategically?
What was I thinking? Did I have an idea why the incident had occurred—an explanation?
What strategies or responses did I consider?
What did I do to respond, and what were the results?
Was I aware of the parties' intrinsic goals (relationship, identity, and process) and the possible influence of these goals on the parties' attitudes and behaviors?
Is it possible that I missed, minimized, or ignored their intrinsic goals, and could my inattention to these goals explain why the puzzling moment occurred?

Examine

What is the question I want to answer through this reflection?
Does it involve a single incident—a puzzling moment—or does my question involve multiple incidents or the intervention generally?

Were my interventions helpful to the participants? In what ways?
In what ways were any interventions not effective? Were there clues indicating they weren't helpful?
Was I curious and open to novelty? In what ways?
Did the process and my approach follow a prescribed and customary system? If so, what was my reasoning for this approach?
What was it that I found surprising or perplexing? Not just the incident, but why did I find this specific moment uniquely notable?
What was my initial explanation for the incident? What meaning did I ascribe to the parties' actions?
Was the puzzling moment similar to situations I previously experienced. If so, in what ways?
Or was my reaction or the event itself unfamiliar and new?

Reflect

What were my assumptions about the parties, the conflict, their behavior, or my beliefs about my role?
How did those assumptions influence my behavior?
Prior to the session, had I developed a working hypothesis, and was that hypothesis relevant and helpful in making sense of and responding to the puzzling moment?
Did I test out my hypothesis? In what ways and with what results?
Were there instances when my understanding of the parties' goals and needs shifted?
If so, in what ways, and what precipitated the change?
Through this reflection, am I aware of any bias that could have affected my work with the parties?

Synthesize

Was I able to achieve my goals for this reflection?
What have I learned about my practice generally or about my experience of the puzzling moment? In particular, was I able to reflect on my assumptions, biases, and expectations?
What insights have I gained regarding the puzzling moment?
What is the answer to my reflective question regarding the puzzling moment?
In what ways will these insights and lessons influence or change the nature of my practice in general or how I respond to a similar situation?

Act

Thinking of the spiral of professional growth and evolution, how will I integrate what I have learned through this reflection? In what ways has this reflection affected the nature of my practice and the quality and effectiveness of my work?
What lessons can I draw from these reflections that I might apply in other, similar contexts or in future sessions with the same participants?
Through this reflective process, am I able to understand how I might have acted differently, and why I would have done so?

APPENDIX B

Sample of Structured Reflective Instrument Questions

To provide an example of the Structured Reflective Instrument (SRI), the following is the Process section, one of the four sections of the SRI provided as an example. Each section is dedicated to a dimension: substantive, process, identity, and relational.

Instructions

Provide your evaluation from each of the four questions in each dimension (substantive, process, identity, and relational).

1	2	3	4	5	6	7	NA
Not at all			Moderately			Highly	

Process

1. Are you satisfied with supporting the parties' positive interaction? (Circle 1–7)
2. Are you satisfied with assisting the parties to explore and consider each other's concerns?[1] (Circle 1–7)
3. Are you satisfied with encouraging each party to voice their concerns? (Circle 1–7)
4. Are you satisfied with promoting a fair and equitable process? (Circle 1–7)

Note

1. Concerns: needs, wishes, interests, opinions, and goals.

APPENDIX C

Learning Journals

Basics of a Learning Journal

1. Use a notebook (or computer file) specifically for this purpose. The method should be convenient, accessible, and familiar. There is no one-size-fits-all; the method should suit you.
2. When reflecting on a puzzling moment, I suggest you keep to the six-stage Cycle of Reflection. It provides a useful structure for recording your observations, reflections, insights, and lessons learned.
3. Note the date and briefly identify the practice situation, learning event, or other circumstance.
4. Be honest. Be thoughtful. Challenge yourself. The learning journal is a personal, private, confidential means of examining your experiences, reactions, reflections, and perceptions.
5. Be yourself. For some, accurate grammar and spelling matter. For others, an informal series of notes may work well.

What Goes into a Learning Journal?

1. New ideas, comments, "aha" moments from your practice; people, behaviors, or situations that you find interesting, surprising, difficult, or inspiring.
2. Thoughts about a personal or professional conflict. What happened and why, what worked for you and what did not, and what have you learned?
3. Insights about your conflict style, values, preferences, assumptions, and theories.
4. Thoughts, questions, and reactions prompted by presentation or workshop or by an article, blog post, or book.
5. Reflections on a public conflict, your analysis of the conflict, and how it was addressed.
6. Notes, observations, and insights from any reflection-before-action or reflection-on-action.
7. Anything else that sparks your interest.

APPENDIX D

Some Guidelines for Reflective Debrief®

Trust the person presenting the puzzling practice situation (the *presenter*) to describe the situation and the question they want to discuss.

Be clear about your values in the process and work from those values.

Never make a statement when a question will do.

The focus of the debrief is determined by the presenter.

It is your job to support the presenter's reflection and not to substitute your own ideas about the problem situation.

It is the presenter's task to engage in sincere and candid reflection.

It is never your job to "get" the presenter to do or understand anything.

Sometimes, a neutral and objective observation can be helpful.

The presenter determines what they want to deal with. They may decline to answer a question. They may decline to follow the debriefer's proposed area of inquiry.

Any "telling" we want to do will be of far less value than the reflective process.

Attend to inner urges you may experience—such as to offer advice or to redefine the presenter's question. You can learn about yourself by paying attention to those urges.

There is no need to reassure the presenter. It is not helpful to offer comments such as "You were really effective," "You demonstrated great insight," or "Those were really difficult people." Instead, remain focused on your task, which is to help the presenter discover the answer to their question.

Use the experience of being a debriefer as an opportunity for your own reflective process.

The presenter decides when to end the debrief. We do not continue once the presenter asks us to stop. When the debrief is done, it is finished. If at the end of the debrief the presenter asks for tips or suggestions, you may respond.

APPENDIX E

Case Presentation Instructions for Reflective Debrief®

We know that deeper and long-lasting learning occurs when the learner identifies a surprising or unsettling practice situation, reflects on and explores the problem, and discovers a solution that is responsive to the learner's question. Lessons gained from the process of reflective debrief are relevant, practical, and durable.

Before the reflective practice group meeting, prepare a case description of no more than one page according to the guidelines below. This document is for your own use.

Description

Identify a practice situation (Puzzling Moment) you find surprising or confusing. The dilemma may involve either something from the past or an ongoing practice matter. The experience might involve a success, something that went well, or a situation that was frustrating or confusing or possibly something you aren't sure how to handle. The Puzzling Moment you choose doesn't need to be a horrible experience—just something you find perplexing. Prepare a summary (possibly in your learning journal) that includes the following:

- Explain the context—type of intervention (mediation, coaching, and so on) and type of dispute; identify the participants (including attorneys or other representatives) and their roles.
- Describe the incident or experience you found puzzling or surprising.
- Indicate whether a similar situation occurred in any other conflict work or whether this is the first time you've been unsettled or surprised by such an experience.

You don't need to explain why you found the situation unsettling.

Reactions

Identify what you were seeing observing/noticing/experiencing.
Describe your internal processes—emotional, cognitive, strategic.
What was I thinking at the time?
Did I experience an emotional reaction—what was I feeling?
What was I intending to achieve?

Analysis

Most important, set out your question—what puzzles you. What do you want to learn? This will be the basis for the reflective debrief.

Look at your proposed question—does it focus on what you should have done or what you should do in the future? If yes, then consider the following questions:

How could I explain what I was seeing at the time?
Why did the puzzling incident occur?
Which explanation seems to be the most significant?

Now, what is the question that describes what you want to learn in this debrief?

APPENDIX F

Reflective Practice Group Basics

1. Our objective is to improve the quality and effectiveness of our mediator choices by learning from and through our experiences.

    To do this, we value *self-exploration* that leads to *self-discovery*. The most pertinent, individually relevant, and long-lasting solutions are those we discover for ourselves.
2. We respect the privacy and risk-taking that self-exploration requires. We understand that the presenter will offer information about the dispute and the participants that would otherwise be private and confidential. Therefore, we promise to maintain confidentiality.
3. We seek to make evident the often-unacknowledged connection between theory and practice—the idea that the choices we make are shaped by what we think and believe.
4. To encourage individual and group exploration, we do the following:

    We ask questions rather than make statements. We use questions that invite reflection and self-examination and refrain from interrogating types of questions.

    We do not judge, criticize, or second-guess one another, overtly or subtly.

    We do not offer opinions, advice, or recommendations unless specifically requested by the person presenting a practice dilemma (see also appendix G).

    We focus on and attend to the problem as presented to the group. Our charge, as group members, is to help the presenter clarify the dilemma, understand the source of that puzzlement, and find relevant and useful solutions.

    We respect each other's airtime, remembering that participation is a license not to prove one's knowledge or insights but rather to learn together and hopefully even have fun in the process.

APPENDIX G

Reflective Debrief®—What Not to Ask or Say/What to Ask or Say

Participants in reflective practice groups contribute through questions, observations, and (occasionally) comments in a process called Reflective Debrief®. Reflective Debrief® is a focused conversation to help the practitioner discover insights into or solutions for a surprising or unsettling practice situation. Reflective Debrief® is based on the principles that

> with guidance and encouragement, practitioners can make sense of and discover their own answers to puzzling situations, and self-discovery results in learning that is both practical and enduring.

In Reflective Debrief®, group members are guides; they do not offer advice, direction, or recommendations. With questions and observations, they encourage exploration and self-reflection.

Frequently, in their well-intended effort to assist the practitioner solve their dilemma, participants offer advice, opinions, and recommendations. Instead, group members are encouraged to use questions rather than statements to encourage critical self-reflection.

The following, *in italics*, are statements of opinion or advice followed by alternative, elicitive questions that address the same idea or issue.

What *not* to say:

Here's what I've done in a similar circumstance.

How to be helpful:
    Have there been similar situations where you were puzzled?
        If so, what happened?
        How did you respond?
        Was that response helpful?

Did you consider . . . ?

- When that situation occurred, were there other choices you considered?
- What were those options? How did you come to your decision?

What would have happened if you had . . . ?

- When you did "X," what were you expecting or hoping?
- What were your thoughts when that didn't occur?

What a really unpleasant person to deal with.

- What was it like for you to deal with this individual?
- Was there something you found difficult in working with this person?
- If so, what was the challenge for you?

The timing of your intervention was really appropriate.

- How did the timing of your intervention affect the parties and the mediation?
- What influenced your decision to do something at that time?

Anyone would have been confused by . . . (only if the presenter indicates confusion)

- What likely caused the confusion?

Why did you decide to . . . ?

- When you chose to act, what influenced your decision?
- At that moment, what thoughts occurred to you?

Why didn't you . . . ?

- Were there other approaches you considered?
- If so, what were they?

Couldn't you have just . . . ?

- Among the options you considered, what influenced your choice?
- What persuaded you to decide that option would be helpful?
- What persuaded you that the other options weren't likely to be helpful?

What you did well was . . .

- Reflecting on the experience, were there moments when your actions had the result you intended?
- Thinking of the parties' responses, were there moments when you sensed that your actions were welcome and valued?

You should have tried . . .

- When you look back at the situation, do you see opportunities to try other interventions?
- If so,
    What are they?
    Why might you have chosen them?
    What impact would you expect?

Note: There are *no reasonable alternatives* to the following four statements, which are never helpful because the underlying assumptions are (1) that the person presenting the practice dilemma made a mistake or was otherwise inept or (2) that the person offering the statement is more knowledgeable, competent, and effective.

I didn't like how you . . .
>[Why does your opinion matter?]

I liked it when you . . .
>[Why does your opinion matter?]

I would have tried . . .
>[If you weren't there, how could you possibly know what might have worked well?]

Let me tell you about a similar situation I had . . .
>[Even if there appear to be some similarities, there will always be far more differences. Here are two examples: (1) the person presenting the dilemma doesn't share the same values and beliefs about mediation and conflict as you or practice in the same manner, and (2) the parties are unique and will not experience conflict in the same way.]

APPENDIX H

Asking Elicitive Questions

In Reflective Debrief,® questions are used to stimulate reflection, elicit a candid and meticulous self-assessment, and nurture exploration, leading to self-discovery. Reflective Debrief® is not formulaic; it does not follow a prescribed pattern, as the questions are not predetermined. The process is, however, systematic and purposeful, guided in the first instance by the presenter's question about a puzzling moment, then spirals outward and upward, continuing nurturing reflection. Each element or stage has a distinct and crucial function. Yet they are not independent; instead, they are mutually reinforcing. The unfolding of the debrief is organic, responding moment to moment to the call and response of the debriefer's questions and the presenter's answers. Learning to ask elicitive questions effectively and usefully begins, like everything associated with reflective practice with the mindset. It is a mindset grounded in a commitment to learning from experience, in the principle of self-determination (self-exploration and self-discovery) and is energized by a sense of curiosity that is an attribute of a reflective practitioner. If you adopt this mindset, then the act of eliciting questions will become natural, unforced, and elegant.

The following are examples of elicitive questions; use them as a general guide, not a template. Your own questions will necessarily reflect your style and temperament, and, as always, be responsive to the presenter's dilemma and the individual circumstances of each reflective conversation:

Describe the puzzling moment—and, if necessary, provide context for the incident.
What did you experience as surprising, puzzling, or unsettling about this incident?
What did you expect to see/hear, and what did you actually observe?
What did you consider doing, and what made you choose the intervention you chose?
How did you know what to do?
What was your explanation (hypothesis) that led to your decision to act in a certain way?
    How did your explanation (hypothesis) shape your intervention?
Did you find a particular theory or assumption helpful in deciding how to respond?
Why was that theory relevant and useful in this situation?
Did you consider other theories that you decided not to use?
When you decided to intervene as you describe, what were your assumptions about how the
    party would react?
Is this what occurred?

- If you could have turned to someone for advice about how to deal with this situation, what would you have asked? In what way would this advice have been helpful?
- Has your approach been influenced by any particular style or model? If so, what has proved useful to you in the past about this style or model? In what ways were they helpful in deciding how to respond in this situation?
- In your initial or advanced training courses, had you learned how to respond to this type of incident?

APPENDIX I

Guidelines for Your Debriefing

1. Everything is about what you can learn. This debrief is solely for your benefit, for the lessons you can pull out of the conversation.
2. You determine the question to be addressed—the surprising or puzzling moment.
3. Think about your goal for the debrief, the question you want to address, and what you want to learn. The clearer you define your question, the more likely you will find a useful answer.
4. Don't try to kid yourself or take the easy way out. This is a gift—use it well.
5. Give yourself time to reflect before responding to a comment or question.
6. You are the only person who knows what it was like to be in your place, to have observed, listened to, wondered about, and responded to the parties.
7. You are unique. Your perspective, your way of making sense of the puzzling moment, is distinct and individual. No one else would have the same way of looking at and responding to the practice situation.
8. You aren't making a movie here—you only need to provide the context for your question along with key facts to set the stage.
9. You aren't obligated to answer any question. If you feel doubtful about a topic or line of inquiry, say so. If you aren't being understood, say so.
10. Treat yourself with kindness.
11. It's okay to laugh.
12. You may also use a debrief to explore why something worked well and what you can learn from that experience.
13. Be willing for the answer to come tomorrow, next week, or next month.
14. If you need a follow-up conversation/debrief, seek it out.
15. Do your work and walk away. Appreciate the effort of the debrief no matter the outcome. You will always learn something of value.
16. Resist efforts of a group to prolong a debrief once you feel finished. Just because someone may still have a question doesn't mean it will be helpful for you to continue the debrief.

APPENDIX J

Comparison of Roles—Mediator/Debriefer

Attitude

Mediator/Coach/Facilitator	Reflective Debriefer
Belief in parties	Belief in presenter
Self-determination is the guiding principle	Self-determination is the guiding principle
Parties determine outcome	Presenter determines outcome
Do not give the answer	Do not give the answer
Maintain curiosity	Maintain curiosity
How can I help you?	How can I help you?
They are the experts	They are the experts
Build trust	Build trust
Encourage careful analysis	Encourage careful analysis
Not your problem to solve	Not your problem to solve
Never work harder than the parties	Never work harder than presenter

Actions

Mediator/Coach/Facilitator	Reflective Debriefer
Use of elicitive questions	Use of elicitive questions
Define the issues	Define the issues
Invite self-reflection	Invite self-reflection
May share information	May share information
Encourage exploration	Encourage exploration
Reality test—without judgment	Reality test—without judgment
Reduce defensiveness and increase openness	Reduce defensiveness and increase openness
Open the door to options	Open the door to options
Nurture self-discovery	Nurture self-discovery
Support self-examination	Support self-examination

These charts are based on the work of Susanne Terry.

APPENDIX K

Potential Roles of a Reflective Practice Group Leader/Facilitator

Organizer   Describe the process and goals; get folks to the groups; sustain interest
Facilitator   Keep the group moving; manage the overall process
Debriefer   Focus on learning through experience; address puzzling practice situations
Supervisor   Provide clinical guidance on administrative and clinical matters
    Note and respond to participant failure to grasp and follow requirements
Educator   Identify gaps in knowledge and skill
    Offer information in the moment or as part of in-service or other trainings
    Fill in gaps in knowledge and techniques
Evaluator   Assess and assure competence according to professional and/or organizational standards
    Systematically and regularly apply tools/standards/criteria
    Don't rescue—there are appropriate moments for comfort or encouragement

Goals of Clinical Supervision

Restorative/Supportive

Develop a supportive relationship with supervisor
Help mediators deal with challenges of practice (clinical, personal, emotional)

Normative/Managerial

Adhere to professional and organizational standards
Need for competency and accountability
Help mediators meet clinical governance and deal with clinical challenges

Formative/Educative

Experiential learning
Professional and skill development
Use of reflection to understand one's abilities, needs, assumptions, and blind spots

This guide was developed in collaboration with Susanne Terry.

APPENDIX L

Guidelines for Starting a Reflective Practice Group

There is no "one size fits all" when it comes to organizing and managing reflective practice groups (RPGs). The following are some guidelines for creating an RPG. Once a group has formed, the participants will determine what works in terms of format, structure, and other elements.

Two guiding principles apply to all RPGs:

1. Participants are committed to learning from their experiences through candid and rigorous self-examination.
2. Helpful and relevant learning comes through a process of self-exploration (not from prescriptive advice or recommendations) and self-discovery.

Why Should Conflict Resolution Professionals Get Involved in an RPG?

We work in a bubble; observed only by the participants and their representatives.

We seldom solicit (and they almost never offer) their feedback. Therefore, apart from whether the dispute was resolved, we have little if any basis for understanding whether our efforts were useful, effective, and responsive and why.

As our profession has evolved, we have been slow to create opportunities for supervision or peer mentoring. There are very few situations in which we can engage with other practitioners to discuss difficult or unusual situations and to seek advice. Where mentoring or supervision exists, the methods are generally prescriptive and directive—essentially offering advice.

Professional development programs almost universally emphasize the acquisition of skills and strategies or the application of these techniques to novel conflict situations. However, filling one's toolbox is not the same as being adept at knowing when, how, and why those tools can be most effectively used. Capably applying mediator tools is important. Learning to use them purposefully and with clear intention is essential.

Within this context, certain questions naturally arise for practitioners seeking to improve the quality and effectiveness of their practices:

- How do I know that I am doing the best I can?
- What interventions were helpful that were off the mark, and why?
- Apart from settlement rates, how can I understand whether my efforts are as effective and resourceful as possible?
- How do I learn from difficult and frustrating experiences or from surprising successes?

Participation in a reflective practice/case consultation group offers practitioners an opportunity, with like-minded colleagues, to address such questions and learn from puzzling practice situations. Consider the following questions as you design, promote, organize, and manage an RPG.

Format

Are likely participants able and willing to meet face-to-face? Do they live/work within a reasonable distance, or are they widely dispersed? Even if participants could attend meetings, is this an ideal or essential format for the group?

Comment: Even though geography may be a significant factor, it's important to think through the benefits and challenges for each option.

Face-to-face: In in-person meetings, collegial relationships develop more quickly, thereby building trust and encouraging candor. It's easier for members to figure out how to avoid interruptions and to know when it's okay to offer comments. Complicating factors include finding a suitable and mutually convenient location, ensuring privacy, and members' ability and willingness to travel.

What setting is best suited to the group? Would you gather in a courthouse, community mediation center, or public library, or will you meet at your facility or the office of one of the participants?

Comment: Factors to consider are availability for the date and time your group wants to meet; adequate size, seating arrangements, and resources (whiteboard etc.); accessibility for anyone with physical limitations; convenient location; and suitability with respect to confidentiality (e.g., is the room reasonably soundproof).

Videoconference: This method has many of the advantages of face-to-face meetings. In addition, you won't need to find a convenient and suitable location. It's important to ensure that all members have access to a reliable internet connection with video. No turning off cameras!

Comment: For those unwilling or unable to meet in person, the convenience of videoconferencing may encourage or permit them to participate. In the past few years, we have learned how to manage the technology and to appreciate the ease and effectiveness of video meetings.

Scheduling

When, How Long, and with What Frequency?

Time of day, day of the week, length of the gathering, and the frequency. Finding a mutually workable date and time for meetings in consultation with the members; this is never a simple process.

Comment: One factor that helps determine the length of the meeting is the number of participants. With fewer people (six to eight), it's possible to meet for only an hour. As the number of participants increases and in order to ensure that everyone who wishes to do so can participate in the discussion, it may be a good idea to extend the meeting time to ninety minutes or even two hours. Another factor is the frequency of meetings; a longer meeting is a good idea if you meet less often than monthly. Most groups follow a monthly schedule, but that choice is one made by group members.

Participation

Fixed Membership or Drop-In?

Will members be asked to commit to regular attendance, providing a consistent cadre of members? Or will this be a drop-in group with participants where attendance may change from meeting to meeting?

Fixed Membership

Participants commit to attending the meetings on a regular basis and place a priority on their availability.

Comment: When participants make a commitment to show up regularly, they tend to form durable and helpful professional relationships, build trust in one another, more readily share puzzling or unsettling practice experiences, and are less self-conscious and more candid in their self-reflections. At the outset, participants should make a commitment to attend for at least six months, possibly twelve.

Drop-In Group

Some groups—though few in number—operate on a drop-in basis, with attendance shifting from meeting to meeting.

Comment: Managing a drop-in group requires considerable skill. You won't know in advance how many people (and who they are) will attend. Some will be familiar with the group's reflective process; for others, it may be the first time. Shifting membership means that participants may not know one another and may not have the benefit of common experiences. As a result, some may be reluctant to speak candidly or at all. The challenges of a drop-in group are also the reasons for its distinct advantage. Having an open membership allows for a larger group of practitioners with a wide range of practice experiences.

Participants

Homogeneous or Mixed Group?

It can be helpful to have a homogeneous group with members whose area of practice is relatively similar. There is, however, a benefit in opening group membership to those with different practice arenas and different content areas.

Comment: Diversity can enrich the discussion. Conversely, it can become more difficult for those who practice in different arenas to understand and relate to colleagues who do not share the same experiences. Another benefit of a diverse membership is that participants learn about and gain insights into other areas of practice.

When membership is limited to practitioners in a single area of practice, discussion of case situations can be more fluid. All members can, to some degree, relate to the problem being discussed; they use a common language to describe their work, and it's likely that they have had similar experiences.

Should Members Have a Minimum Degree of Practice Experience?

Participation is generally limited to active practitioners with a certain amount of practice experience—for two reasons. To have a rich and dynamic group, participants need to be active practitioners with some degree of experience who have developed practice routines and gained insights about the nature of practice. Novices may view the group meetings as an extension of their training course, a purpose for which these groups are not intended, and may therefore be more interested in practical advice about beginning their practices.

Comment: A minimum level of experience should be required. That said, there is an advantage to a group with varied levels of experience (provided that each member has some degree of practice experience). For example, novices tend to ask questions that at first seem so obvious that they needn't be asked but that, on reflection, are profound and helpful. There are at least a couple risks of having a mixed group. More experienced practitioners may begrudge simplistic comments and questions about establishing their practice. In addition, less experienced members may be intimidated and participate less actively.

Is There an Ideal Group Size?

Comment: Assuming one to two hours for presentation and discussion, a maximum membership of twelve is ideal. If there are more members, there is a chance that several could become conversational wallflowers, observing without participating. Also, while the choice to present a case at any meeting should be voluntary, it's essential for group trust and cohesion that each member take a turn. Groups can function quite well with a minimum membership of eight or fewer.

Comment: A facilitator for groups larger than eight is invaluable. Leading the reflective debrief as well as managing the participation of group members requires special skills.

Group Process

Will There Be a Leader/Facilitator, or Will the Group Be Self-Managed?

Comment: Most groups benefit from having a leader or a facilitator, someone to coordinate the conversation, encourage participation, keep the focus on the practice dilemma presented, maintain the guiding principles of reflective practice, and, on a more mundane level, manage time. These advantages hold whether leadership rotates among the members or one person acts as the leader.

Self-managed groups work well only when group members are familiar with and experienced at the process of reflective practice and when there is a reliably consistent membership.

Another question to consider: If the group elects to have a facilitator, will that person be a group member or an outside individual with skills and knowledge?

Trust and Confidentiality

Candid conversations require trust. Consequently, it is essential to ensure that confidentiality is strictly maintained. Before discussing any practice situations, participants should talk about and reach an understanding on the meaning of confidentiality within the group. Within the agreed framework, individuals will decide how much client-related detail to share.

Other Ground Rules or Guidelines Essential for the Group

Perhaps the most important guideline is also the most obvious—do not judge, criticize, or second-guess one another, either overtly or subtly. Participation is not a license to spout off, to prove oneself, or to show up a colleague. Reference the guiding principles noted at the beginning (see appendix G).

Would It Be Helpful to Provide/Share Articles about Reflective Practice or Other Similar Resources to the Participants?

Comment: Ask a dozen people to describe reflective practice, and you're likely to get that many responses, with some overlap and substantial divergence of opinion. As a result, it's helpful if everyone is singing from the same song sheet. Among those you might share is "Why Case Consultation/Reflective Practice Groups Matter for Mediators" (Lang and Arms Almengor 2017) and "Excellence: Using Reflective Debrief to Build Competence" (Lang and Terry 2013). Both can be found at https://www.thereflectivepractitioner.com/resources.

APPENDIX M

Initial Handout—Reflective Practice Group

I was first drawn to the principles and methods of reflective practice in 1986, when I read Donald Schön's (1983) *The Reflective Practitioner*. No book has shaped my professional work more than this one. I have been a member of case consultation/reflective practice groups since the late 1980s and have organized and facilitated many such groups. In the early 1990s, I introduced the concept and methods of reflective practice to the mediators through conference presentations, seminars, and workshops. I published an article on reflective practice in the journal *Consensus* in 1997 (also at https://www.mediate.com). In 2000, I coauthored *The Making of a Mediator: Developing Artistry in Practice*, applying reflective practice methods to improving the quality of mediation practice, and in 2019, I published *The Guide to Reflective Practice in Conflict Resolution*.

The goal of a reflective practice group is to discuss interesting, frustrating, unusual, and successful mediations, and though our discussions, we will learn how to become more responsive, resourceful, and effective.

What Are Some of the Problems Our Group and the Reflective Practice Approach Is Intended to Address?

1. As mediators, we work in a bubble. Our actions are observed only by the parties and their representatives to protect confidentiality. There are no outside observers who might comment on our work or provide feedback. Moreover, with notable exceptions, mediators seldom solicit feedback from the parties or their attorneys. As a result, we have little if any basis for understanding whether our efforts were effective and responsive. Settlement rates are of limited benefit. Whether a dispute is resolved has as much or more to do with the attitude of the parties and their counsel as with the mediator's abilities.
2. Limited by our commitment to protect confidentiality of the mediation and because mediations are most often conducted by a single mediator, we operate in a vacuum. There are limited opportunities for collegial support and input. We are solitary beasts, prowling the savannas of conflict, not part of a herd (or practice group).
3. Professional development takes the form of seminars, webinars, conference presentations, and workshops. These are communal learning experiences where the objective is either gaining knowledge about theory or research, hearing about new skills and strategies to address common problems, or learning about the novel use of conflict resolution skills in new types of disputes. There are limited opportunities to practice and gain feedback on the use of new techniques. We build larger and larger tool chests without any way to assess whether we are applying the new skills thoughtfully and effectively.

How a Reflective Practice Group Functions

A reflective practice group is a unique learning environment that uses a process drawing on the participants' knowledge and experience and focusing on individualized rather than communal learning. This process involves self-exploration leading to self-discovery.

We know from adult learning principles and from those who have studied reflective practice methods that a unique type of learning occurs when the learner identifies a surprising or unsettling practice situation, struggles with the problem, and discovers a solution that is particular to the learner. Lessons gained from the reflective process fit the learner and in that way are relevant, responsive, practical, and durable.

The learning process (the Reflective Debrief®) begins when a participant (the presenting mediator) identifies a moment in a mediation that was surprising and unsettling. As the group facilitator, I will use questions to encourage the presenting mediator to describe what occurred and, most important, why he or she finds the situation remarkable—surprising, awkward, or confusing. Becoming aware of the reasons for one's discomfort is an essential (and first) step in discovering a solution. The questions then move to helping the presenting mediator search for the lessons from the experience.

Group members can help the presenting mediator resist the tendency to shrug off the importance of finding the underlying cause for his or her uneasiness and uncertainty. Searching for our own answers can be discomforting; we may want others to provide the solution to our dilemma. We do not benefit from merely telling stories without reflection on their meaning and the lessons they provide.

Questions by the facilitator as well as group members are never intended to second-guess the presenting mediator, offer judgments about the situation or the mediator's decisions, or propose solutions. Instead, questions help the presenting mediator engage in self-discovery. The objective is to achieve learning that is personal, relevant, and lasting.

We restrain our impulse to express an opinion or offer solutions. Just as we can never fully understand why the situation was troubling or surprising, we can never think of a solution that will necessarily work for the presenting mediator. Resisting the impulse to give advice encourages the mediator to discover the answers him- or herself. In the same way that we as mediators believe in self-determination—that parties to a conflict are capable of and best suited to making choices for themselves—the success of Reflective Debrief® relies on the presenting mediator gaining insight into and learning from the disquieting situation.

Reference

Lang, Michael D., and Susanne Terry. 2013. "Excellence: Using Reflective Debrief to Build Competence." *ACResolution*, Spring, 21–25.

Bibliography

Abramowitz, Ava J. 2018. "Toward a Definition of Success in Mediation." *Dispute Resolution Magazine*, Summer 2018: 23–28.

American Arbitration Association, American Bar Association, and Association for Conflict Resolution. 2005, September. "Model Standards of Conduct for Mediators." https://www.adr.org/sites/default/files/document_repository/AAA-Mediators-Model-Standards-of-Conduct-10-14-2010.pdf.

American Bar Association, Section of Dispute Resolution. 2017, June 12. "ABA Section of Dispute Resolution Report of the Task Force on Research on Mediator Techniques." https://www.aboutrsi.org/library/aba-section-of-dispute-resolution-report-of-the-task-force-on-research-on-mediator-techniques.

Amulya, Joy. 2011, May. "What Is Reflective Practice?" Community Science. https://communityscience.com/wp-content/uploads/2021/05/What-is-Reflective-Practice.pdf.

Argyris, Chris. 1990. *Overcoming Organizational Defenses: Facilitating Organizational Learning*. Upper Saddle River, NJ: Prentice Hall.

Argyris, Christopher, and Donald A. Schön. 1974. *Theory in Practice: Increasing Professional Effectiveness*. San Francisco: Jossey-Bass.

Arms Almengor, Rochelle. 2017. "Reflecting through Conflict: Action Research on the Utility of Reflective Practice Groups for Mediator Learning." PhD diss., George Mason University.

———. 2018. "Reflective Practice and Mediator Learning: A Current Review." *Conflict Resolution Quarterly* 36, no. 1: 21–38. https://doi.org/10.1002/crq.21219.

———. 2022. "A Veteran Mediator's Guide to Becoming a Reflective Practitioner: A Review of *The Guide to Reflective Practice in Conflict Resolution*." *New York Peace and Conflict: Journal of Peace Psychology* 28, no. 4: 567–68. https://doi.org/10.1037/pac0000630.

Avon Maitland District School Board. 2012. "Video 4 Reflective Practice." https://www.youtube.com/watch?v=x8D37JJrIfc.

Balsam, Jodi S., Susan L. Brooks, and Margaret Reuter. 2017. "Assessing Law Students as Reflective Practitioners." *New York Law School Law Review* 64 (December): 45–67. Brooklyn Law School Legal Studies Research Papers, Accepted Paper Series, Research Paper No. 545. http://ssrn.com/abstract=3059777.

Bargh, J. A., and T. L. Chartrand. 1999. "The Unbearable Automaticity of Being." *American Psychologist* 54, no. 7: 462.

Bassot, Barbara. 2016. *The Reflective Journal.*, 2nd edition. London: Macmillan Education UK.

———. 2023. *The Reflective Practice Guide: An Interdisciplinary Approach to Critical Reflection*. 2nd ed. London: Routledge.

Battaglio, R. P., P. Belardinelli, N. Bellé, and P. Cantarelli. 2019. "Behavioral Public Administration *ad fontes*: A Synthesis of Research on Bounded Rationality, Cognitive Biases, and Nudging in Public Organizations." *Public Administration Review* 79, no. 3: 304–20.

Benjamin, Robert D. 1990. "The Physics of Mediation: Reflections of Scientific Theory in Professional Practice." *Mediation Quarterly* 8, no. 2: 91–113.

Birkhoff, Juliana E., and Wallace Warfield. 1996. "The Development of Pedagogy and Practicum." *Mediation Quarterly* 14, no. 2: 93–110.

Bodenhausen, G. V., and A. R. Todd. 2010. "Automatic Aspects of Judgment and Decision Making." In *Handbook of Implicit Social Cognition*. New York: Guilford Press.

Bolton, Gillie. 2010. *Reflective Practice: Writing and Professional Development*. 3rd ed. Thousand Oaks, CA: Sage Publications.

Bouchier, Margaret. 2014. "A Study of the Role of External Mediation in Enhancing Workplace Productivity." *MII Ezine.* http://kiwmrg.ie/wp-content/uploads/2016/11/A-study-of-the-role-of-external-mediation-in-enhancing-workplace-productivity.pdf.

Boud, David, Rosemary Keogh, and David Walker, eds. 1985. *Reflection: Turning Experience into Learning.* New York: Kogan Page.

Boulding, Kenneth E. 1978. *Stable Peace.* Austin: University of Texas Press.

Bronson, Sue. 2000. "Improving Mediator Competence through Self-Assessment." *Mediation Quarterly* 18, no. 2: 171–79.

Bronson, Sue, et al. 1998. *Self-Assessment Tool for Mediators.* Madison: Wisconsin Association of Mediators.

Bruce, Linda. 2013. *Reflective Practice for Social Workers: A Handbook for Developing Professional Confidence.* Maidenhead: Open University Press.

Buchanan, Ruth Margaret. 1994. "Context, Continuity, and Difference in Poverty Law Scholarship." *University of Miami Law Review* 48: 999–1062.

Bunker, Barbara B., Jeffrey Z. Rubin, and Associates, eds. 1995. *Conflict, Cooperation and Justice.* San Francisco: Jossey-Bass.

Bush, Robert A. Baruch, and Joseph P. Folger. 1994. *The Promise of Mediation: Responding to Conflict through Empowerment and Recognition.* San Francisco: Jossey-Bass.

Cameron, Julia. 1997. *The Artist's Way Morning Pages Journal: A Companion Volume to the Artist's Way.* New York: TarcherPerigee.

Chamorro-Premuzic, Tomas. 2014, August 27. "Curiosity Is as Important as Intelligence." *Harvard Business Review.* https://hbr.org/2014/08/curiosity-is-as-important-as-intelligence.

Charkoudian, Lorig. 2014a, April. "Impact of Alternative Dispute Resolution on Responsibility, Empowerment, Resolution, and Satisfaction with the Judiciary: Comparison of Self-Reported Outcomes in District Court Civil Cases." Maryland Administrative Office of the Courts.

———. 2014b, September. "What Works in Child Access Mediation: Effectiveness of Various Mediation Strategies on Custody Cases and Parents' Ability to Work Together." Maryland Administrative Office of the Courts.

Charkoudian, L., C. D. Ritis, R. Buck, and C. L. Wilson. 2009. "Mediation by Any Other Name Would Smell as Sweet—Or Would It? The Struggle to Define Mediation and Its Various Approaches." *Conflict Resolution Quarterly* 26, no. 3: 293–316.

Çimer, Atilla, Sabiha Odabaşi Çimer, and Gülşah Sezen Vekli. 2013. "How Does Reflection Help Teachers to Become Effective Teachers?" *International Journal of Educational Research* 1, no. 4: 133–49.

CIPD. 2017. "Introduction to Reflective Practice." https://www.youtube.com/watch?v=M9hyWVEG2x0.

Clarke, Jenny, and Sabne Dembkowski. 2006. "The Art of Asking Great Questions." *International Journal of Mentoring and Coaching* 4, no. 2: 1–6.

Clutterbuck, David, and Sheila Hirst. 2003. *Talking Business: Making Communication Work.* London: Butterworth-Heinemann.

Cohen, Judith. 2003. "Reflective Practice: How Veterans Can Benefit from Rookie Training." http://www.mediate.com/articles/cohen5.cfm#.

Coleman, Peter T., Morton Deutsch, and Eric C. Marcus, eds. 2014. *The Handbook of Conflict Resolution: Theory and Practice.* 3rd ed. San Francisco: Jossey-Bass.

Collin, Simon, Thierry Karsenti, and Vassilis Komis. 2013. "Reflective Practice in Initial Teacher Training: Critiques and Perspectives." *Reflective Practice* 14, no. 1: 104–17. http://dx.doi.org/10.1080/14623943.2012.732935.

Corry, Geoffrey, and Pat Hynes. 2015. "Creating Political Oxygen to Break the Cycle of Violence 1981–1994: Lessons from the Northern Ireland Peace Process." *Journal of Mediation and Applied Conflict Analysis* 2, no. 2: 259–75.

Coser, Lewis A. 1956. *The Functions of Social Conflict.* New York: Free Press.

Cropley, Brendan, Andy Miles, and John Peel. 2012, March. "Reflective Practice: Value of, Issues, and Developments within Sports Coaching." Cardiff Metropolitan University.

Csikszentmihalyi, Mihaly. 1996. *Creativity: Flow and the Psychology of Discovery and Invention.* New York: HarperCollins.

Curhan, J. R., H. A. Elfenbein, and N. Eisenkraft, 2010. "The Objective Value of Subjective Value: A Multi-Round Negotiation Study." *Journal of Applied Social Psychology* 40, no. 3: 690–709.

Curhan, J. R., H. A. Elfenbein, and H. Xu. 2006. "What Do People Value When They Negotiate? Mapping the Domain of Subjective Value in Negotiation." *Journal of Personality and Social Psychology* 91, no. 3: 493.

Curran, Deirdre, et al. 2016a, September. "Shaping the Agenda, Part 1: Exploring the Competencies, Skills and Behaviours of Effective Workplace Mediators." Kennedy Institute Workplace Mediation Research Group, NUI Maynooth.

———. 2016b, September. "Shaping the Agenda, Part 2: Implications for Workplace Mediation Training, Standards and Practice in Ireland." Kennedy Institute Workplace Mediation Research Group, NUI Maynooth.

Dawson, Phillip. 2012. "Reflective Practice." https://www.youtube.com/watch?v=r1aYWbLj0U8.

Deason, Ellen E., et al. 2016, April. "Debriefing the Debrief." Public Law and Legal Theory Working Paper Series No. 202. Ohio State University Moritz College of Law, 301–32. http://ssrn.com/abstract=2251940.

Department of Education and Training, Victoria, Australia. 2016. "VEYLDF Practice Principles—Reflective Practice." https://www.youtube.com/watch?v=OJXvTW0C-iA.

Destination Social Work. 2013. "Study Guide 16: Reflective Practice." https://www.youtube.com/watch?v=HedCG30WqSI.

Deutsch, R., and Strack, F. 2010. "Building Blocks of Social Behavior: Reflective and Impulsive Processes." In *Handbook of Implicit Social Cognition.* New York: Guilford Press.

Duncan, David T. 2009. "The Executive Coach and Clients in Reflective Practice: Levelising as a Special Case." PhD diss., University of Tennessee. http://trace.tennessee.edu/utk_graddiss/35.

Early Childhood Australia. 2012. "Self-Assessment, Reflective Practice and Quality Improvement Processes." https://www.youtube.com/watch?v=lU65AjcHVJg.

Edwards, Allan. 1999. "Reflective Practice in Sport Management." *Sport Management Review* 2, no. 1: 67–81.

Farrell, Thomas, S. C. 2004. *Reflective Practice in Action: 80 Reflection Breaks for Busy Teachers.* Thousand Oaks, CA: Corwin Press.

Farres, Laura G. 2004. "Becoming a Better Coach through Reflective Practice." *BC Coach's Perspective* 6 (Fall): 10–11.

Finlay, Linda. 2008, January. "Reflecting on 'Reflective Practice.'" Practice-Based Professional Learning Centre, Open University. https://www.open.ac.uk/pbpl.

Freire, Paolo. 1993. *Pedagogy of the Oppressed.* New York: Continuum.

Gates, Bill, and Warren Buffett. Interview with Charlie Rose, January 28, 2017. http://www.youtube.com/watch?v=lNRWxN7jKlI&t=6m35s.

Gatti, Shelley Neilsen, Christopher L. Watson, and Carol F. Siegel. 2011. "Step Back and Consider: Learning from Reflective Practice in Infant Mental Health." *Young Exceptional Children* 14, no. 2: 32–45.

Gibbs, Graham. 1988. *Learning by Doing: A Guide to Teaching and Learning Methods.* Oxford: Further Educational Unit, Oxford Polytechnic.

Gladwell, Malcolm. 2005. *Blink: The Power of Thinking without Thinking.* Boston: Little, Brown.

———. 2008. *Outliers: The Story of Success.* Boston: Little, Brown.

Griffiths, Liz. 2004. "Time for Reflection." *Occupational Health* 56, no. 5: 20–21.

Hardy, Samantha. 2009. "Teaching Mediation as Reflective Practice." *Negotiation Journal* 25, no. 3: 385–400. https://doi.org/10.1111/j.1571-9979.2009.00232.x.

Harrell, Susan W., and Richard E. Doelker Jr. 1994. "Mentorship in Family Mediation." *Mediation Quarterly* 12, no. 2: 151–63.

Hartog, Mary. 2002. "Becoming a Reflective Practitioner: A Continuing Professional Development Strategy through Humanistic Action Research." *Business Ethics: A European Review* 11, no. 3: 233–43.

Harvey, Jerry B. 1988. *The Abilene Paradox and Other Meditations on Management*. Hoboken, NJ: Jossey-Bass.

Hatton, Neville, and David Smith. 1995. "Reflection in Teacher Education: Towards Definition and Implementation." *Teaching and Teacher Education* 11, no. 1: 33–49. https://doi.org/10.1016/0742-051X(94)00012-U.

Hawkins, Peter, and Robin Shohet. 2000. *Supervision in the Helping Professions*. 2nd ed. Buckingham: Open University Press.

———. 2006. *Supervision in the Helping Professions*. 3rd ed. London: YHT Ltd.

Hedeen, T., S. S. Raines, and A. B. Barton. 2010. "Foundations of Mediation Training: A Literature Review of Adult Education and Training Design." *Conflict Resolution Quarterly* 28, no. 2: 157–82.

Herman, Howard, and Jeannette P. Twomey. 2005. "Training outside the Classroom: Peer Consultation Groups." *Dispute Resolution Magazine*, Fall, 15–16.

Herrman, Margaret S., Nancy Hollett, Jerry Gale, and Mark Foster. 2001. "Defining Mediator Knowledge and Skills." *Negotiation Journal* 17, no. 2: 139–53.

Hewson, Daphne, and Michael Carroll. 2016a. *Reflective Practice in Supervision*. Hazelwood: MoshPit Publishing.

———. 2016b. *Reflective Practice in Supervision: Companion Volume to the Reflective Supervision Toolkit*. Hazelwood: MoshPit Publishing.

Hickson, Helen. 2011. "Critical Reflection: Reflecting on Learning to Be Reflective." *Reflective Practice* 12, no. 6: 829–39. https://doi.org/10.1080/14623943.2011.616687.

Inskipp, Francesca, and Bridgid Proctor. 2001. *The Art, Craft and Tasks of Counselling Supervision: Part 1. Making the Most of Supervision*. Twickenham: Cascade Publications.

Jackson, Peter. 2004. "Understanding the Experience of Experience: A Practical Model of Reflective Practice for Coaching." *International Journal of Evidence Based Coaching and Mentoring* 2, no. 1: 60.

Johns, Christopher. 2000. *Becoming a Reflective Practitioner*. Oxford: Blackwell Science.

———. 2004. "Becoming a transformational leader through reflection." *Reflections on Nursing Leadership*, Sigma Theta Tau International, Honor Society of Nursing, 30(2): 24–26.

———, ed. 2010. *Guided Reflection: A Narrative Approach to Advancing Professional Practice*. Oxford: Blackwell.

Judicial Council of Virginia. 2011, April 5. "Mentorship Guidelines for the Certification of Court-Referred Mediators."

Kadushin, Alfred, and Daniel Harkness. 1976. *Supervision in Social Work*. New York: Columbia University Press.

Kahn, Peter. 2006, October. "The Role and Effectiveness of Reflective Practices in Programmes for New Academic Staff: A Grounded Practitioner Review of the Research Literature." Higher Education Academy, University of Manchester. https://www.heacademy.ac.uk/system/files/reflective_practice_full_report.pdf.

Kahneman, D. 2011. *Thinking, Fast and Slow*. New York: Farrar, Straus and Giroux.

Kahneman, D., and G. Klein. 2009. "Conditions for Intuitive Expertise: A Failure to Disagree." *American Psychologist* 64, no. 6: 515.

Kinsella, Elizabeth Anne. 2001. "Reflections on Reflective Practice." *Canadian Journal of Occupational Therapy* 68: 195–98. https://doi.org/10.1177/000841740106800308.

Kolb, David A. 1984. *Experiential Learning: Experience as the Source of Learning and Development*. Upper Saddle River, NJ: Prentice Hall.

Kressel, K., T. Henderson, W. Reich, and C. Cohen. 2012. "Multidimensional Analysis of Conflict Mediator Style." *Conflict Resolution Quarterly* 30, no. 2: 135–71.

Kressel, Kenneth, Dean G. Pruitt, and Associates. 1989. *Mediation Research*. San Francisco: Jossey-Bass.

Kurtz, Arabella. 2020. *How to Run Reflective Practice Groups: A Guide for Healthcare Professionals*. London: Routledge.

Lang, Michael D. 2000, July. "Becoming a Reflective Practitioner." https://www.mediate.com//articles/reflect.cfm.

———. 2003, June. "Out of the Rut and into the Groove: Developing Excellence in Practice." Keynote address delivered at the Mediators Institute of Ireland Annual Conference, Dublin, November 15, 2002. https://www.mediate.com//articles/langM1.cfm.
———. 2009. "Interview with Michael Lang by Robert Benjamin." https://www.mediate.com//articles/langfull.cfm.
———. 2016, June 16. "Interview with Michael Lang by Tammy Lenski." https://tammylenski.com/michael-lang.
———. 2018, February 9. "Questions." *Academy of Professional Family Mediators Newsletter.* https://apfmnet.org/questions.
———. 2019. *The Guide to Reflective Practice in Conflict Resolution.* Lanham, MD: Rowman & Littlefield.
Lang, Michael D., and Rochelle Arms Almengor. 2017, August. "Why Case Consultation/Reflective Practice Groups Matter for Mediators." https://www.mediate.com//articles/langarmsreflective.cfm.
Lang, Michael D., and Alison Taylor. 2000. *The Making of a Mediator: Developing Artistry in Practice.* San Francisco: Jossey-Bass.
Lang, Michael D., and Susanne Terry. 2013. "Excellence: Using Reflective Debrief to Build Competence." *ACResolution*, Spring, 21–25.
———. 2017, September 26. "Why Do We Do the Things We Do? Reflective Practice—The Artful Mastery of Mediation." Webinar. Association for Conflict Resolution.
Langer, Ellen J. 1989. *Mindfulness.* Reading, MA: Addison-Wesley.
———. 1992. "Matters of Mind: Mindfulness/Mindlessness in Perspective." *Consciousness and Cognition* 1, no. 3: 289–305. https://doi.org/10.1016/1053-8100(92)90066-J.
———. 1997. *The Power of Mindful Learning.* Reading, MA: Addison-Wesley.
———. 2015, September 10. "Science of Mindlessness and Mindfulness." Interview by Krista Tippett. On Being. https://onbeing.org/programs/ellen-langer-science-of-mindlessness-and-mindfulness.
Langer, Ellen J., and Mihnea Moldoveanu. 2000. "Mindfulness Research and the Future." *Journal of Social Issues* 56, no. 1: 129–39. https://doi.org/10.1111/0022-4537.00155.
Larrivee, Barbara. 2000. "Transforming Teaching Practice: Becoming the Critically Reflective Teacher." *Reflective Practice* 1–3: 293–307. https://doi.org/10.1080/14623940020025561.
Lashley, Conrad. 1999. "On Making Silk Purses: Developing Reflective Practitioners in Hospitality Management Education." *International Journal of Contemporary Hospital Management* 11, no. 4: 180–85.
The Learning Centre, University of New South Wales. 2010. "Reflective Writing." http://www.lc.unsw.edu.au.
Lederach, John Paul. 1995. *Preparing for Peace: Conflict Transformation across Cultures.* Syracuse, NY: Syracuse University Press.
Leering, Michele. 2017. "Integrated Reflective Practice: A Critical Imperative for Enhancing Legal Education and Professionalism." *Canadian Bar Review* 95, no. 1: 47–89.
Lenski, Tammy. 2014. *The Conflict Pivot: Turning Conflict into Peace of Mind.* Peterborough: MyriaccordMedia.
Leti, Therese. 2016. "Reflective Journal Writing." https://www.youtube.com/watch?v=lGTSct2Z-GY.
Lucas, Michelle. 2023. *Creating the Reflective Habit: A Practical Guide for Coaches, Mentors and Leaders.* London: Routledge.
Macfarlane, Julie, and Bernie Mayer. 2005. "What Theory? How Collaborative Problem-Solving Trainers Use Theory and Research in Training and Teaching." *Conflict Resolution Quarterly* 23, no. 2: 259–76. https://doi.org/10.1002/crq.136.
Malthouse, Richard, Mike Watts, and Jodi Roffey-Barentsen. 2015. "Reflective Questions, Self-Questioning and Managing Professionally Situated Practice." *Research in Education* 94, no. 1: 71–87. https://doi.org/10.7227/RIE.0024.
Mamede, S., and H. G. Schmidt. 2023. "Deliberate Reflection and Clinical Reasoning: Founding Ideas and Empirical Findings." *Medical Education* 57, no. 1: 76–85.

Maughan, Carolyn. 1996. "Learning How to Learn: The Skills Developer's Guide to Experiential Learning." In *Teaching Lawyers' Skills*, ed. Julian Webb and Caroline Maughan. London: Butterworths.

Mayer, Bernard. 2000. *The Dynamics of Conflict Resolution: A Practitioner's Guide*. San Francisco: Jossey-Bass.

McEwen, Craig A., and Richard J. Maiman. 1981. "Mediation in Small Claims Court: An Empirical Assessment." *Maine Law Review* 33: 237–68.

———. 1989. "Mediation in Small Claims Court: Consensual Processes and Outcomes." In *Mediation Research*, ed. Kenneth Kressell and Dean G. Pruitt, 53–67. San Francisco: Jossey-Bass.

McIntosh, Paul. 2010. *Action Research and Reflective Practice: Creative and Visual Methods to Facilitate Reflection and Learning*. London: Routledge.

McMahon, Joseph P., Jr. 2008. "Moving Mediation Back toward Its Historic Roots—Suggested Changes." *Colorado Lawyer* 37, no. 6: 23–36.

Meierdirk, Charlotte. 2017. "Schon's Reflective Practice." https://www.youtube.com/watch?v=Tzjz-l8L1lc.

Merryfield, Merry M. 1993. "Reflective Practice in Global Education: Strategies for Teacher Educators." *Theory Into Practice* 32, no. 1: 180–85.

Milne, Derek. 2009. *Evidence-Based Clinical Supervision: Principles and Practice*. Oxford: Blackwell.

Minkle, Beryl, Anthony S. Bashir, and Claudia Sutulov. 2008. "Peer Consultation for Mediators: The Use of a Holding Environment to Support Mediator Reflection, Inquiry, and Self-Knowing. *Negotiation Journal*, July, 303–23.

Mohrman, S. A., and E. E. Lawler III. 2011. "Research for Theory and Practice: Framing the Challenge." In *Useful Research: Advancing Theory and Practice*, ed. Susan Albers Mohrman, Edward E. Lawler III, and Associates. San Francisco: Berrett-Koehler.

Moon, Jennifer A. 1999. *Reflection in Learning and Professional Development: Theory and Practice*. London: Kogan Page.

Moore, Christopher W. 1996. *The Mediation Process: Practical Strategies for Resolving Conflict*. 2nd ed. San Francisco: Jossey-Bass.

Morris, Michael, et al. 2002. "Schmooze or Lose: Social Friction and Lubrication in E-Mail Negotiations." *Group Dynamics: Theory, Research, and Practice* 6, no. 1: 89–100. https://doi.org/10.1037//1089-2699.6.1.89.

Moston, Forrest S. 2006. "The Path of the Peacemaker: A Mediator's Guide to Peacemaking." *ACResolution* 5, no. 1: 8–11.

Munby, Hugh. 1989. "Reflection-in-Action and Reflection-on-Action." *Current Issues in Education* 9, no. 1: 31–42. https://muse.jhu.edu/article/592219.

Noble, Cinnie. 2014. *Conflict Mastery: Questions to Guide You*. Toronto: CINERGY Coaching.

O'Donnell, Michael. 1997. *A Sceptic's Medical Dictionary*. Oxford: Blackwell BMJ Books.

Oduro, Isaac Kwame and Azare Bertha Akuta. 2022. *Tutors' Use of Reflective Practice to Promote Teaching and Learning*. Creative Education 13(7): 2308–20.

Ogilvy, J. P. 1996. "The Use of Journals in Legal Education: A Tool for Reflection." *Clinical Law Review* 3: 55–107.

Paterson, Colin, and Judith Chapman. 2013. "Enhancing Skills of Critical Reflection to Evidence Learning in Professional Practice." *Physical Therapy in Sport*, April, 1–6. http://dx.doi.org/10.1016/j.ptsp.2013.03.004.

Pearce, W. Barnett, and Stephen W. Littlejohn. 1997. *Moral Conflict: When Social Worlds Collide*. Thousand Oaks, CA: Sage Publications.

Peleg-Baker, Tzofnat. 2012a. "Beyond the Dichotomy of Styles—The Cognitive Characteristics of Mediators' Decision Making: The Devil Is in the Details." Paper presented at the Conflict Studies Conference—Ninth Biennial Graduate Student Conference, University of Massachusetts Boston, October 20, 2012.

———. 2012b. "The Cognitive Characteristics of Mediator's Decision Making." Paper presented at the Conflict Studies and Global Governance Conference, University of Massachusetts, Amherst.

———. 2014, December 1. "Improving Mediators' Decision-Making by Becoming Conscious of the Unconscious Cognitive Considerations for Reflection to Attain Social-Psychological Goals." http://dx.doi.org/10.2139/ssrn.2443930.

Peleg-Baker, T., and M. Lang. 2022. "A Structured Reflection for Improving Third Party Interventions and Mediation Practice: Reconsidering Debrief." *Conflict Resolution Quarterly* 40, no. 2: 213–29. https://doi.org/10.1002/crq.21361.

Picard, Cheryl A. 2002. "Learning about Learning: The Value of Insight." *Conflict Resolution Quarterly* 20: 477.

———. 2016. *Practising Insight Mediation*. Toronto: University of Toronto Press.

Picard, Cheryl A., and Kenneth R. Melchen. 2007. "Insight Mediation: A Learning-Centered Mediation Model." *Negotiation Journal*, January, 35–53. https://doi.org/10.1111/j.1571-9979.2006.00126.x.

Proctor, B. 1997. "Contracting in Supervision." In *Contracts in Counselling*, ed. Charlotte Sills, 190–206. Thousand Oaks, CA: Sage Publications.

———. 2008. *Group Supervision: A Guide to Creative Practice*. 2nd ed. Thousand Oaks, CA: Sage Publications.

Quilty, Terry and Lyn Murphy. 2022. "Time to review reflective practice?" *International Journal for Quality in Health Care* 34(2): 1–2. doi: 10.1093/intqhc/mzac052.

Rackham, Neil. 1988. *SPIN Selling*. New York: McGraw-Hill.

Rackham, Neil, Peter Honey, and Michael J. Colbert. 1971. *Developing Interactive Skills*. London: Wellens Publishing.

Rackham, Neil, and John Carlisle. 1978. "The Effective Negotiator—Part I: The Behaviour of Successful Negotiators." *Journal for European Industrial Training* 2, no. 6: 6–11.

Raelin, Joseph A. 2002. "'Don't Have Time to Think!' versus the Art of Reflective Practice." *Reflections: The Sol Journal* 4, no. 1: 66–79. doi:10.1162/152417302320467571.

Rayford, Celes Raenee. 2010. "Reflective Practice: The Teacher in the Mirror." *UNLV Theses, Dissertations, Professional Papers, and Capstones*. Paper 5. University of Nevada, Las Vegas.

Riskin, Leonard L. 2002. "The Contemplative Lawyer: On the Contributions of Mindfulness Meditation to Students, Lawyers and Their Clients." *Harvard Negotiation Law Review* 7, no. 1. http://scholarship.law.ufl.edu/facultypub/420.

Riskin, Leonard, and Rachel Wohl. 2015. "Mindfulness in the Heat of Conflict: Taking STOCK." *Harvard Negotiation Law Review* 20 (Spring): 121.

Rochette, Annie, and Wesley W. Pue. 2001. "Back to Basics? University Legal Education and 21st Century Professionalism." *Windsor Year Book of Access to Justice* 20: 167–90.

Rogers, Carl. 1951. *Client-Centered Therapy: Its Current Practice, Implications and Theory*. London: Constable.

Ross, W. H. 2000. "Measuring success in mediation." *The Mediation Journal*, 1(1): 1–16.

Sanderson, John. 2015. "Introduction to Reflective Practice." https://www.youtube.com/watch?v=nXhCFGb9Pb4.

Schau, Jan Frankel. 2013. *View from the Middle of the Road: A Mediator's Perspective on Life, Conflict, and Human Interaction*. Bloomington, IN: AuthorHouse.

Schellenberg, James. 1996. *Conflict Resolution: Theory, Research, Practice*. Albany: State University of New York Press.

Schön, Donald A. 1983. *The Reflective Practitioner*. New York: Basic Books.

———. 1987. *Educating the Reflective Practitioner: How Professionals Think in Action*. San Francisco: Jossey-Bass.

Schweinsberg, M., S. Thau, and M. M. Pillutla. 2022. "Negotiation Impasses: Types, Causes, and Resolutions." *Journal of Management* 48, no. 1: 49–76. https://doi.org/10.1177/01492063211021657.

Senge, Peter M. 1990. *The Fifth Discipline: The Art & Practice of the Learning Organization*. New York: Doubleday/Currency.

Shakespeare, Pam. 2005. "Mentoring and the Value of Observation." *Nursing Management* 11, no. 10: 32–35.

State Government of Victoria, Australia, Department of Education and Training. 2007. "Maternal and Child Health Reflective Practice." Printed from *Reflective Practice*. CD-ROM. https://www.education.vic.gove.auDocuments/childhood/professionals/support/all.pdf.

Sterling, Belladonna. 2022a. *The Reflective Journal: Gibbs Reflective Cycle Model*. Orlando, FL: Author.

———. 2022b. *Reflective Practice Journal Borton's & Schon's (1983) Models of Reflection*. Orlando, FL: Author.

Stevens, Dannelle D., Serap Emil, and Miki Yamashita. 2010. "Mentoring through Reflective Journal Writing: A Qualitative Study by a Mentor/Professor and Two International Graduate Students." *Reflective Practice* 11, no. 3: 347–67. http://dx.doi.org.1080/14623943.2010.490069.

Stivers, Camilla. 2000. "The Reflective Practitioner." *Public Administration Review* 60, no. 5: 456.

Supreme Court of Virginia. 2022. "Mediation Program." https://www.courts.state.va.us/courtadmin/aoc/djs/programs/drs/mediation/home.html.

Surgenor, Paul. 2011, May. "Reflective Practice: A Practical Guide." UCD Dublin. http://www.ucd.ie/t4cms/Reflective%20Practice.pdf.

Suzuki, Shunryu. 1970. *Zen Mind, Beginner's Mind: Informal Talks on Zen Meditation and Practice*. 50th Anniversary ed. Boulder, CO: Shambhala Publications.

Sweeney, D. 2010. "The Map Is Not the Territory: An Application of Gestalt Psychotherapy Theory to Mediation." Paper presented to the Masters in Mediation and Conflict Intervention at National University Ireland, Maynooth.

Thompson, S. and Neil Thompson. 2023. *The Critically Reflective Practitioner*, 3ed edition. London: Bloomsbury Academic.

Thompson, Neil, and Jan Pascal. 2012. "Developing Critically Reflective Practice." *Reflective Practice* 13, no. 2: 311–25. http://dx.doi.org/10.1080/14623943.2012.657795.

Twomey, Jeannette P., Elizabeth Bissell, and Regina Olchowski. 2004. *Mediation Peer Consultation Project: Facilitator Guidebook*. Richmond: Virginia Mediation Network and Virginia Association for Community Conflict Resolution.

University of Worcester. 2016. "Learning Journals." *Study Skills Advice Sheet*. https://www.worc.ac.uk/studyskills/documents/Learning_Journals_2016.pdf.

Uswahzulhasanah, Uswahzulhasanah and Fitri Arofiati. 2021. "The effect of reflective listening in nursing and health students: a literature review." *Bali Medical Journal* 10(3): 1235–38. doi:10.15562/bmj.v10i3.2857

Velayutham, Sivakumar, and Hector Perera. 1993. "The Reflective Accountant: Towards a New Model for Professional Development." *Accounting Education* 2–4 (August): 287–301.

Vella, Jane. 1995. *Training through Dialogue: Promoting Effective Learning and Change with Adults*. San Francisco: Jossey-Bass.

Webb, Sam. 2016. "Gibbs' Reflective Cycle." https://www.youtube.com/watch?v=5WfnHGq6ztg.

Wellington, Bud. 1991. "The Promise of Reflective Practice." *Educational Leadership*, March, 4–5.

Wentworth Institute of Technology. 2015. "Kolb Learning Cycle." https://www.youtube.com/watch?v=DqoHn7xAlLQ.

Werner, Kenny. 1998. *Effortless Mastery: Liberating the Master Musician Within*. Louisville, CO: Alfred Music.

Wheately, Margaret J. 1994. *Leadership and the New Science: Learning about Organization from an Orderly Universe*. San Francisco: Barrett-Koehler.

Wilson, Barbara. 2012. "Mediator Expertise Live Interviews." http://dx.doi.org/10.2139/ssrn.2179587.

Wilson, T. 2011. *Redirect: The Surprising New Science of Psychological Change*. London: Penguin.

Wilson, T. D., S. Lindsey, and T. Y. Schooler. 2000. "A Model of Dual Attitudes." *Psychological Review* 107, no. 1: 101.

Winslade, John, and Gerald Monk. 2000. *Narrative Mediation: A New Approach to Conflict Resolution*. San Francisco: Jossey-Bass.

Zalipour, Arezou. 2015. "Reflective Practice." University of Waikato, Hamilton, New Zealand, June, 1–16.

Index

Abrahamson, Rebecca, 37. *See also Sarasota Herald Tribune*
Abramowitz, Ava, 12, 147, 149, 182–187, 189, 190, 193, 194, 197, 198; ABA, 147; ANM, 149; reflective practice in law school education, 182–187; relationship or outcome, 185–186; student log, 186–187
Academy of Family Mediators (AFM), 3
Academy of Professional Family Mediators (APFM), 148
Action research—reflective practice groups, 104. *See also* Almengor, Rochelle Arms
Akuta, Azare Bertha, 96
American Arbitration Association, 101,150
American Bar Association (ABA), 94, 101, 145, 147, 187, 190
Amulya, Joy, 13
Anderson, Kare, 82
Argyris, Chris, 29, 38, 58, 73, 75, 82, 83–90; espoused theory v. theory-in-use, 83–87; ladder of inference, 58; and Donald Schon, 29, 38, 73, 75, 82, 87–90; single-loop and double loop learning, 87–90
Arotiati, Fitri, 96
Arms Almengor, Rochelle, 95, 104, 136, 138, 229
Association for Conflict Resolution (ACR) 101, 148
Association of Northern Mediators (ANM), 149
attributes of a reflective practitioner, 42–66; curiosity, 43–46; be resilient, 46–48; nurture simplicity, 48–51; value ambiguity, 51–53; pay attention to detail, 53–55; listen ceaselessly, 55–57; resist certainty, 57–60; balance commitment and flexibility, 61–62; embrace failure as your mentor, 62–64; practice humility, 64–66

Bargh, J.A., 125
Barry, Ellen, 77
Barton, A.B., 126
Bassot, Barbara, 112, 117, 120, 130. *See also* learning journal
Battaglio, R.P., 125
Beckett, Samuel, 14, 64
Bodenhausen, G.V., 125, 128
Bouchier, Margaret, 105–106. *See also* Kennedy Institute Workplace Mediation Research Group
Boud, David, 37
Breathnach, Sara Ban, 15
Bronowski, Jacob, 163
Bronson, Sue, 194
Brooks, David, 73
Buchanan, Ruth Margaret, 26, 37
Bush, Robert A. Baruch, 125

Carroll, Lewis, 8, 77
Carroll, Michael, 167
Charkoudian, Lorig, 101, 102, 125. *See also* research
Chartrand, T.L., 125
Clutterbuck, David, 23
Colbert, M.J., 185
constellation of theories, 11, 73–82, 160; core values, 74; applied theories; models of practice, personal styles and norms of professional behavior, 74–75; contextual factors, 75
Contact, 48. *See also* Occam's razor, William of Occam
Contributions from members of reflective practice groups: Laurie Amaya, 147; Leon Bamforth, 8; Lewellyn Blanchard, 150; Colin Bourne, 135; Phillipa Brown, 140; Julia Burns, 135; Kristyn Carmichael, 7; Karen Carroll, 136; Georgia Daniels, 66; Dolores Geary, 35; Tim Hicks, 138; David Hubbard, 12; David Kendrew, 145; Jen Knauer, 144; Fritz Langrock, 134; Mandy Maleveti, 10; Phyllida Middlemiss, 134; Catherine O'Connell, 139; Hansa Patel, 18; Andi Paus, 144; Nancy Radford, 141; Kim Reisch, 158; Jonathan Rodrigues, 143; Tom Rothschild, 29; Frances Stephenson, 79; Ellen Waldorf, 10; Tracey-Leigh Wessels, 82; Tim Willis, 135

Corry, Geoffrey, 102–104
Court Annexed Mediation Pilot Project, 99–100
Covey, Stephen, M. R., 192
Covey, Stephen R., 78, 173
Curhan, J.R., 125
Curran, Diedre, 105, 106–108. *See also* Kennedy Institute Workplace Mediation Research Group

Deutsch, R., 125
Dillard, Annie, 133

Eliot, T.S., 171
espoused theory v. theory-in-use, 38, 83–87. *See also* Argyris, Chris; Schön, Donald A.
exercises, 39–40, 66–68, 90–91, 110, 131, 150, 190
experimental research, 108–09. *See also* Morris, Michael

Farres, Laura, 13, 32, 154
Fermi, Enrico, 55
Finlay, Linda, 11, 30, 78, 167
Folger, Joseph, P., 125
Frost, Robert, 134, 191–192

Galileo, 195
Gatti, Shelly Neilsen, 34, 53
Gibbs, Graham, 152
Gilbert, Elizabeth, 60
Gladwell, Malcolm, 33, 35, 76
Grant, Jodie, 12, 137, 152, 161, 165, 166–171, 198. *See also* supervision
Griffiths, Liz, 34
guides for reflection, 122–124, 199–202. *See also* Reflective Debrief®

Hagaman, Jody, 18, 20
Harkness, Daniel, 167
Hatton, Neville, 38
Hawking, Stephen, 60
Hawkins, Peter, 167
Hedeen, T., 126
Herman, Howard, 146, 147, 195
Hesse, Hermann, 41
Hewson, Daphne, 167
Hirst, Sheila, 23
Honey, P., 185
Hurston, Zora Neale, 94
Hynes, Pat, 102–104

Inskipp, Francesca, 167

Johns, Christopher, 11, 34, 119, 152
Jordan, Michael, 35, 63
Joyce, James, 63

Kadushin, Alfred, 167
Kahneman, D., 125, 127, 128
Kalantri, Amit, 64
Kant Immanuel, 90
Kanter, Rosabeth Moss, 151
Kennedy Institute, Workplace Mediation Research Group (KIWMRG), 104–108. *See also* Margaret Bouchier; Deirdre Curran
Keogh, Rosemary, 37
Klein, G., 125, 127, 128
Kolb, David A., 152, 166
Kressel, Kenneth, 83, 98, 100, 125
Kurtz, Arabella, 152, 165
Kwa-Zulu Natal Society of Mediators, 149

Lang, Jacob, 64
Lang, Michael: Almengor, Rochelle Arms, 136, 138, 229; constellation of theories, 181; *Guide to Reflective Practice in Conflict Resolution*, 126, 167; Peleg-Baker, Tzofnat, 33, 76, 83, 126, 127, 129, 136, 194; Taylor, Alison (*The Making of a Mediator*), 73, 112, 154, 166, 195; Terry, Susanne, 148, 157, 176, 229
Langer, Ellen J., 25, 36, 39, 53, 60
Lawler, E.E., III, 98
League of Mediators of Ukraine, 149–150
learning journal, 129–131, 205–206; reasons to make use of, 130–131
Lederach, John Paul, 196
Lehane, Niamh, 113–122; reflection-before-action, 113–115; reflection-in-action, 115–117; reflection-on-action, 119–122
Levitt, Joseph Gordon, 1
Lewin, Kurt, 97

Macklemore and Ryan Lewis, 35
Maiman, Richard J., 100–101: small claims mediation study,
The Making of a Mediator, 7, 37, 73, 152, 195, 231. *See also* Lang, Michael; reflective practice; Taylor, Alison
Mamede, S., 127
Maughan, Carolyn, 19, 36
McEwen, Craig A., 100–101: small claims mediation study
Measuring the effectiveness and efficiency of mediator approaches, 102. *See also* Charkoudian, Lorig

Mediator Experience Live Interview (MELI), 187–190; as teaching method, 188–189; process, 189–190. *See also* reflective practice; Wilson, Barbara

Mediator Peer Consultation Project, 195

Mediators Institute of Ireland, 149

Mentoring: Cohen, Judith, 193; Exercise 7.1, 150; lack of opportunities for, 136–37, 174; need for, 196–198; supervision and, 167; Supreme Court of Virginia requirement, 194; Virginia Mediation Peer consultation Project, 195. *See also* reflective practice groups

Michaels, Jullian, 36

Miller, Henry, 163

Mingus, Charles, 51

Mohrman, S.A., 97

Monk, Gerald, 125

Moon, Jennifer, A., 120, 129

Moore, Christopher W., 80–81

Morris, Michael, 94, 108; rapport building (schmoozing), 108

Naskar, Abhijit, 174

The New York Times: Barry, Ellen; Brooks, David; Onie, Rebecca.

Nebraska Mediators Association, 149

Nin, Anais, 61

The Northern Ireland peace process—a case study, 102–104. *See also* Corry, Geoffrey; Hynes, Pat

Occam's razor, 48–49. *See also* William of Occam

Oduro, Isaac Kwame, 96

Onie, Rebecca, 88. *See New York Times*

origin stories, 3–7

Parkinson, Robert, 54. *See Sarasota Herald Tribune*

Peleg-Baker, Tzofnat, 33, 38, 76, 83, 102, 111, 118, 124–129

Perera, Hector, 13, 97

Picard, Cheryl, 125

Picasso, Pablo, 20

Pound, Ezra, ix

practice tips, 68–69

Proctor, Brigid, 167

professional growth and evolution, 9–10; spiral metaphor, 1–3. *See also* Reflective Debrief®

Pruitt, Dean G., 98, 100

Rackham, Neil, 95, 98, 185. *See also* SPIN Selling

Raines, S. S., 126

reflection-before-action, 112–115, 199–202; *See also* Appendix A; Niamh Lehane

reflection-in-action, 115–119. *See also* Barbara Bassot; Farres, Linda; Niamh Lehane; Reflective Debrief®; Schön, Donald A.; spiral of professional growth and development

reflection-on-action, 119–122, 199–202. *See also* Appendix A; Niamh Lehane; Reflective Debrief®; Schön, Donald A.; spiral of professional growth and development; Zalipour, Arezou

Reflective Debrief®, 26, 28, 30, 31, 123, 134, 138, 139, 144, 146, 149, 151–171, 177, 178, 181, 189, 195–197, 207–210, 213–224; Lang/Terry model of reflection, 152–154; applying, 154–157; guided, 157–160; guiding principles, 161–165; Jodie Grant, 165–171; in mediator supervision, 166–171. *See also* Appendix D, E, G, H, I, J, K; figure 8.2; role-play; spiral of professional growth and development; Terry, Susanne

reflective practice, 15–39; commitment to lifelong learning 37–38; connection between theory and practice, 38, 76–78, 144, 189, 192, 211; definition, 29–33; distinction from reflection, 22–27, 30; in training and education, 173–190, 193–194; learn from experience, 35–37; making a difference, 111–112; methods, 111–131; professional organizations, 194–196; research, 95–97; tic-tac-toe story, 16–20; why, 11–14, 33–38; willingness to learn from experience, 35–37. *See also* Abramowitz, Ava; Argyris, Chris; attributes of a reflective practitioner; Grant, Jodie; *The Making of a Mediator*; Peleg-Baker, Tzofnat; reflection-before-action; reflection-in-action; reflection-on-action; Reflective Debrief®; reflective practice groups; spiral of professional growth and development; Schön, Donald A; Terry, Susanne

reflective practice groups (RPGs), 133–150, 193, 211–212, 223–232; benefit from, 142–144; description, 139–140; differences between RPGs and other groups, 140–142; examples of, 146–150; guidelines for, 144; organizing, 144–146; Reflective Debrief®, 138–139; research, 95–97; why practitioners need, 136–13; why practitioners participate, 134–136. *See also* ABA; ACR; Almengor, Rochelle Arms; APFM; Appendix F, K, L, M; Association of Northern Mediators; contributions from members of reflective practice groups; Kwa-Zulu Natal Society of Mediators; League of Ukrainian Mediators; *The Making of a Mediator*; Nebraska Mediation Association; spiral of professional growth and development

The Reflective Practitioner, ix, 4, 6, 7, 10, 29, 33, 112, 123, 142, 151, 191, 192, 231. *See also* Schön, Donald A.

reflective practitioner, 10, 11, 13, 14, 18, 21, 23, 25, 26, 34, 35, 37, 38, 42, 60, 65, 111, 171, 182, 217. *See also* attributes of a reflective practitioner; *The Making of a Mediator*; Schön, Donald A.

research, 93–111; benefits for practitioners, 98–99; importance to practitioners, 99–110; interaction of theory, research, practice, 97–98; reflective practice and reflective practice groups 95–98. *See also* Almengor, Rochelle Arms; Buchier, Margaret; Charkoudian, Lorig; Corry, Geoffrey; Curran, Deirdre; Hynes, Pat; Maiman, Richard J.; McEwen, Craig A.; Morris, Michael; Rackham, Neil

Rilke, Rainer Maria, x

Riskin, Leonard, 26

role-play coaching and reflective practice: application of reflective practice, 176, 178; Exercise 7.1, 150; Exercise 7.2, 150; limited opportunities, 136; prescriptive feedback, 174–176; Reflective Debrief® and, 176–177; use of reflective practice for beginning mediators, 179–182; Terry, Susanne, 177–182

Ross, W. H., 187

Rowling, J.K., 131

Rudd, Lauren, 79. *See Sarasota Herald Tribune*

Rumi, 192

Sarasota Herald Tribune: Abrahamson, Rebecca; Hagaman, Jody; Parkinson, Robert; Rudd, Lauren; Stahlmann, Jenni

Schau, Jan Frankel, 24

Schmidt, H.G., 127

Schön, Donald A.: Argyris, Chris, 29, 38, 73, 75, 82, 83, 85, 87, 89, 90; children's experiment, 31–32; cycle of reflection, 151–154; danger of specialization in practice, 58–64; *Educating the Reflective Practitioner*, 29, 137, 151; espoused theory v. theory-in-use, 83–86; journaling, 130; methods of reflection, 115–119; reflective practice and learning, 15, 16, 19, 22, 24, 29, 58, 151, 154, 166–167; *The Reflective Practitioner*, 4, 7, 29, 122, 133, 142, 151, 191, 192; single-loop and double loop learning, 87–90; theory and practice, 38, 44, 73, 75, 82

Schulz, Charles M., 62

Schweinsberg, R., 125

Self-Assessment Tool for Mediators, 194–195. *See also* Bronson, Sue; Wisconsin Association of Mediators (WAM)

Segal, William, 191

Shaikh, Ismat Ahmet, 165

Shohet, Robin, 167

Siegel, Carol, F., 34, 53

single-loop and double-loop learning, 87–90

Small Claims Study, 100–101. *See also* Maiman, Richard J., McEwen, Craig A.

Smith, David, 38

SPIN selling, 95, 98. *See also* Rackham, Neil

spiral of professional growth and evolution, 2, 7–12, 14, 15, 17, 19, 21, 28, 29, 31, 36, 55, 86, 93, 94, 97, 107, 109, 110, 131, 138, 152, 153, 163, 165, 182, 192, 194, 198

Stahlmann, Jenni, 18, 20; *See Sarasota Herald Tribune*

Strack, R., 125

Structured Reflective Instrument (SRI), 12, 111, 124–129, 149, 203. *See also* Appendix B; Peleg-Baker, Tzofnat

supervision, 166–171; context, 166; example of supervisee and supervisor, 168–170; goals, 166–167; lack of, 136–139; models, 167–168; use of reflective practice in, 168. *See also* Grant, Jodie; Reflective Debrief®; reflective practice

Supreme Court of Virginia, 136

Suzuki, Shunryu, 26

Sweeney, Delma, 121

system 1 and system 2, 128. *See also* Peleg-Baker, Tzofnat; Structured Reflective Instrument

Szasz, Thomas, 21

Szent-Györgyi, Albert, 109

Taylor, Alison, 73, 112, 154, 166, 195. *See also The Making of a Mediator*

Terry, Susanne, 7, 24, 141, 152: ACR, 148; Case Presentation Instructions, 141; Lang, Michael, 148, 157, 176; League of Mediators of Ukraine, 149–150; Reflective Debrief®, 151–165; reflective practice for beginning mediator training, 177–182

theory, 71–90. defining, 73–74; in everyday life, 75–77; in practice, 76–78, 144, 189; lens metaphor, 78–79; purposes, 82–83; role, 79–82; shaping action, 78–79. *See also* Argyris, Chris; constellation of theories; espoused theory v. theory-in-use; single-loop and double-loop learning; Schön, Donald A.

Thompson, S. and Thompson, N., 112

Todd, A.R., 125, 128

Twomey, Jeannette, P., 195. *See also* Virginia Mediation Peer Consultation Project

Uswahzulhasanah, Uswahzulhasanah, 96

Velayutham, Sivakumar, 13, 97
Virginia Mediator Peer Consultation Project, 195
Voltaire, 57
von Och, Roger, 56

Walker, David, 37
Watson, T., 34, 53
What is the effect of alternate dispute resolution on participants?, 101–102. *See also* Charkoudian, Lorig
Willard, Frances, E., 177
William of Occam; Occam's Razor, 48–49
Wilson, Barbara, 147, 177; Mediator Experience Live Interview (MELI), 187–189
Wilson, T.D., 125
Winslade, John, 125
Wisconsin Association of Mediators (WAM), 194. *See also Self-Assessment Tool for Mediators*; Sue Bronson
Workplace mediation research, 104–108. *See also* Bouchier, Margaret; Curran, Deirdre; Kennedy Institute Workplace Mediation Research Group

Zalipour, Arezou, 13, 25, 30, 33, 34, 85

About the Author and Contributors

Primary Author

Michael D. Lang

For more than forty years, Michael has mediated family, workplace, and organizational disputes.

He has designed and presented introductory and advanced mediation and conflict management courses, workshops, and webinars in the United States and internationally.

Michael created one of the first graduate programs in conflict resolution in the United States at Antioch University in 1992 and served in a similar role at Royal Roads University in Victoria, British Columbia.

In addition to numerous published articles, Michael authored *The Guide to Reflective Practice in Conflict Resolution* (2019, 2024), and coauthored *The Making of a Mediator: Developing Artistry in Practice* (2000). As part of his longtime commitment to mediator excellence, Michael currently facilitates seven monthly online reflective practice groups for mediators with participants from around the world. With Susanne Terry, he founded and is codirector of the Reflective Practice Institute International.

Michael received the John Haynes Distinguished Mediator Award from the Association for Conflict Resolution (ACR) in 2012 and was named Outstanding Professional Family Mediator for 2020 by the Academy of Professional Family Mediators.

Principal Contributors

Ava J. Abramowitz

A former assistant U.S. attorney for the District of Columbia, Ava J. Abramowitz taught negotiations at the George Washington University Law School for twenty years. In 2016, she organized a reflective practice group sponsored by the ABA Dispute Resolution Section that is still ongoing today. She is the author of *The Architect's Essentials of Negotiation* (2nd ed.). She has written many an article on negotiation and mediation issues facing lawyers and clients, including "Modern Consultative Sales Theory," published in *Negotiation Essentials for Lawyers*. She has been serving as a mediator for the federal courts for the District of Columbia since the late 1980s, mediating civil cases including corporate cases, class actions, and disputes involving civil liberties, intellectual property, and employment discrimination.

Jodie Grant

Jodie Grant is a highly skilled, experienced mediator with more than twenty years' practice. She has ten years' practice as a restorative engagement facilitator. Since commencing work in the family law field, she has concurrently held clinical practice and training roles, leading and supporting professional best practice. Jodie also provides clinical supervision and reflective practice. She is registered and accredited as a family dispute resolution practitioner under the Attorney General's Department and a nationally accredited mediator under the Mediator Standards Board.

Dr. Tzofnat Peleg-Baker

Dr. Tzofnat Peleg-Baker is an applied social psychologist merging theory with practice to enhance the quality of decision making in conflictual situations and third-party interventions. Her teaching, research, and publications center on transforming human relations, conflict, and leadership. Through consulting, publishing, and applying reflective practice, she helps dismantle implicit social-psychological drivers of destructive conflict, nurtures productive connections, and helps build capabilities to address differences and conflicts effectively. With teaching experience at all academic levels, she guides diverse cohorts and advises stakeholders ranging from politicians to peace organizations worldwide.

Susanne Terry

Susanne Terry is cofounder and codirector of the Reflective Practice Institute International. She is a contributor to and editor of *More Justice, More Peace: When Peacemakers Are Advocates*. She is coeditor of the ACR/Rowman & Littlefield joint publishing venture. As the creator and director of the Woodbury College Mediation and Applied Conflict Studies Program, she created a curriculum and teaching methodologies based on reflective practice principles. She is the Vermont Judiciary Parent Coordination Program statewide case supervisor.

"Greek Chorus" Contributors

Laurie Amaya—Pasadena, California
Leon Bamforth—Leeds, United Kingdom
Lewellyn Blanchard—Utica, New York
Colin Bourne—Leeds, United Kingdom

Philippa Brown—Hove, United Kingdom
Julia Burns—Ilkley, United Kingdom
Kristyn Carmichael—Phoenix, Arizona
Karen Carroll—Grand Island, New York
Georgia Daniels—Claremont, California
Dolores Geary—Bandon, Ireland
Tim Hicks—Eugene, Oregon
David Hubbard—Omaha, Nebraska
David Kendrew—Penrith Cumbria, United Kingdom
Jen Knauer—Jericho, Vermont
Fritz Langrock—Ferrisburgh, Vermont
Adamandia Maleviti—Zachynthos, Greece
Phyllida Middlemiss—Oxford, United Kingdom
Catherine O'Connell—Dublin, Ireland
Hansa Patel—Ross, California
Andi Paus—Phoenix, Arizona
Nancy Radford—Durham, United Kingdom
Kim Reisch—Geneva, New York
Jonathan Rodrigues—Goa, India
Tom Rothschild—El Cerrito, California
Frances Stephenson—County Wicklow, Ireland
Ellen Waldorf—Newton Upper Falls, Massachusetts
Tracey-Leigh Wessels—Durban North, South Africa
Tim Willis—Lincs, United Kingdom

www.ingramcontent.com/pod-product-compliance
Lightning Source LLC
Chambersburg PA
CBHW082033300426
44117CB00015B/2470